Germany in the Loud Twentieth Century

GERMANY IN THE LOUD TWENTIETH CENTURY

An Introduction

Edited by Florence Feiereisen

and

Alexandra Merley Hill

OXFORD
UNIVERSITY PRESS

OXFORD
UNIVERSITY PRESS

Oxford University Press, Inc., publishes works that further
Oxford University's objective of excellence
in research, scholarship, and education.

Oxford New York
Auckland   Cape Town   Dar es Salaam   Hong Kong   Karachi
Kuala Lumpur   Madrid   Melbourne   Mexico City   Nairobi
New Delhi   Shanghai   Taipei   Toronto

With offices in
Argentina   Austria   Brazil   Chile   Czech Republic   France   Greece
Guatemala   Hungary   Italy   Japan   Poland   Portugal   Singapore
South Korea   Switzerland   Thailand   Turkey   Ukraine   Vietnam

Copyright © 2012 by Oxford University Press

Published by Oxford University Press, Inc.
198 Madison Avenue, New York, New York 10016
www.oup.com

Oxford is a registered trademark of Oxford University Press

Library of Congress Cataloging-in-Publication Data
Germany in the loud twentieth century : an introduction / edited by Florence Feiereisen
and Alexandra Merley Hill.
    p. cm.
    Includes bibliographical references and index.
    ISBN 978-0-19-975938-5 (alk. paper) — ISBN 978-0-19-975939-2 (alk. paper)
1. Germany—Civilization—20th century. 2. Sound—Social aspects—Germany—History—20th century.
3. Loudness—Social aspects—Germany—History—20th century. 4. Space—Social
aspects—Germany—History—20th century. 5. Music—Germany—20th century—History and criticism.
6. German literature—20th century—History and criticism. 7. Sound in literature. 8. Germany—Intellectual
life—20th century. 9. National characteristics, German—History—20th century.
I. Feiereisen, Florence. II. Hill, Alexandra Merley.
    DD61.8.G465   2012
    943.087—dc22   2011008720

1 3 5 7 9 8 6 4 2
Printed in the United States of America

To my father, a terrific listener
A.M.H.

To Leo, my little noisemaker
F.F.

CONTENTS

Bonus track online at www.oup.com/us/GermanyintheLoud20thCentury

ACKNOWLEDGMENTS

The publication of any book necessarily involves the efforts of many people, and we would like to take the opportunity to single out some of those people.

First and foremost, we would like to thank our contributors for their thought-provoking research and for their enthusiasm, which fueled their and our work on this book over the course of several years. A special thank you goes to our editor at Oxford University Press, Norman Hirschy, for championing the project throughout the revision process and for holding our work to his exacting standards. Our anonymous readers provided insightful feedback that changed the way this book took shape.

Thanks also to our home institutions of Middlebury College and the University of Portland. An Arthur Butine Faculty Development Grant from the University of Portland in the summer of 2010 made uninterrupted editing possible at a critical phase. Our colleagues at both institutions (as well as at Williams College and University of Massachusetts Amherst) supported us throughout the various stages of this project.

Finally, thanks to both our families.

CONTRIBUTORS

Nicole Dietrich studied History and Anthropology at the University of Vienna, with a focus on Cultural Studies, Fin-de-Siècle Vienna, and modernity. She has authored many radio documentaries for ORF/Ö1, Austria's Public Radio. Supported by the European Journalist Fellowship at Freie Universität Berlin, Dietrich researched "Soundmemories between East and West" for an exhibition on nostalgia in Berlin. Other published works include articles on the visualization of the radio in the 1920s, Zeppelin and early broadcasting, and pop charts in 1960s Vienna. Her current project is editing the autobiography of Jewish Fin-de-Siècle writer Emma Adler.

Florence Feiereisen studied German Cultural Studies and Literature at the University of Massachusetts Amherst, where she received a Ph.D. with a dissertation on Thomas Meinecke. As Assistant Professor of German at Middlebury College, she teaches classes on German literature, pop culture, national identity, gender, and sound. Her areas of research include investigating the relationship of selected German contemporary literary texts with other media such as photography and sound. Feiereisen has just published a monograph on the concept of literary sampling and remixing in contemporary German literature.

Sabine von Fischer is an architect, writer, Ph.D. student in architectural history and theory at ETH Zurich (see www.alltagsakustik.ch), and a 2010 collection research grant recipient at the Canadian Center for Architecture, Montréal (see www.cca.qc.ca/en/study-centre/1029-noise-versus-noise-geoff-manaugh). Her research focuses on technological and aesthetic changes at the intersection of architecture and sound in the twentieth century. Von Fischer is also the founder of diaphanarch, a studio for architecture as concept, construction, and criticism in the form of drawings and texts. She has taught and lectured in Switzerland, the United States, and India.

John Goodyear is a Ph.D. candidate in the German Department at Queen Mary, University of London and the co-director of English Conversation and Culture Oldenburg (ECCO), an English-language center for adult learners. In his doctoral research project he examines musical images in German literature as a part of the wider urban soundscape. Goodyear has given lectures on Theodor Lessing's *Antilärmverein* in Germany, the United States, and the United Kingdom; a further publication on Lessing's society in its wider international context is forthcoming in a *Theodor Lessing Symposiums-Band*.

Alexandra Merley Hill is Assistant Professor of German at the University of Portland, where she teaches all levels of German language, literature, and culture. She received her Ph.D. in 2009 from the University of Massachusetts Amherst, after defending her dissertation on German writer Julia Franck. She has published and presented on diverse topics, including Soviet and post-Soviet art, contemporary German painting, propaganda, feminism, contemporary literature and film, motherhood, and teaching contemporary German culture. Hill is currently at work on a book manuscript on motherhood and domesticity in the works of Julia Franck.

Yaron Jean is a post-doctoral research fellow at the Simon Dubnow Institute for Jewish History and Culture in Leipzig. He studied at the universities of Tel Aviv, Munich, Cologne, and Jerusalem and received his Ph.D. from Hebrew University, Jerusalem in 2006 with a dissertation titled "Hearing Maps: Noise, Technology and Auditory Perception in Germany 1914–1945." His current work is on the cultural history of passports and travel documents and their influence on the establishment of a Jewish sense of belonging in Europe during the nineteenth and the twentieth centuries.

Christiane Lenk is a Ph.D. student in English at the University of Massachusetts Amherst. She completed her undergraduate work at Georg-August-Universität Göttingen in Germany and at the University of California at Santa Barbara. In her current research she focuses on aspects of transnational theory in modernist literature. One of her recent papers analyzes a former meeting place for German exiles during World War II, the mansion "Villa Aurora" in Los Angeles, in that context. She currently lectures on her dissertation topic at the University of Stuttgart in Germany.

Jean-Paul Perrotte is Lecturer of Music Theory and Composition at the University of Nevada, Reno. He is currently completing his Ph.D. in Music Composition at the University of Iowa. His electro-acoustic works have been performed in the United States and in Europe. Recent commissions include the musical score for the ballet, *Shanghaied*, sponsored by the School of the Arts at UNR, which debuted in November 2010. In 2008, he received the honor of Meritorious Achievement in Composition from the Kennedy Center American College Theater Festival for his musical score (cello, percussion, and computer) for the theatrical production, *The Burial at Thebes* (*Antigone*).

Robert Ryder studied Music and Comparative Literature in Canada and the United States. In 2009, he completed his dissertation titled "Hearing Otherwise: Towards a Genealogy of the Acoustical Unconscious from Walter Benjamin to Alexander Kluge" at Northwestern University. In his research, Ryder introduces a new way of thinking about German radio and sound film in relation to theories of modernity and trends in psychology in the early twentieth century. He currently teaches courses on German literature and media at the University of Chicago.

Maria Stehle received her Ph.D. in German Studies with a Certificate in Advanced Feminist Studies from the University of Massachusetts Amherst in 2005. After teaching in the German Studies Department at Connecticut College, she joined the Department of Modern Foreign

Languages and Literatures at the University of Tennessee Knoxville in the fall of 2007. She has published various articles in the fields of Feminist German Studies, Cultural Studies, and Media and Communication Studies. Her book manuscript, *Ghetto Voices in Contemporary German Culture: Textscapes, Filmscapes, Soundscapes*, is currently under review.

Curtis Swope holds a Ph.D. in Germanic Languages and Literatures from the University of Pennsylvania and teaches at Trinity University. His research focuses on representations of architecture, cities, and space in twentieth-century German literature with a focus on social-ist theater and novels. Swope's most recent scholarly contribution is a forthcoming article on architecture and texts of childhood in the GDR. He is currently working on a book project, tentatively titled *Building Socialism: Architecture and Literature in the GDR*, about dramatists' and novelists' critiques of modernist architecture in East Germany from the 1950s to the 1970s.

David Tompkins holds a Ph.D. in History from Columbia University and is Assistant Professor of History at Carleton College, where he teaches courses on modern Central Europe. He is completing a book manuscript on music and politics in Stalinist East Germany and Poland. Tompkins has presented and published internationally on the "sound of the Stalinist era"; his most recent project looks at the formation and propagation of images of friends and enemies and their reception by the populations of the Soviet bloc.

Brett M. Van Hoesen is Assistant Professor of Modern and Contemporary Art History at the University of Nevada, Reno. She holds a Ph.D. in Art History from the University of Iowa. She is currently finishing a book manuscript on the legacy of Germany's colonial history in the visual culture of the Weimar Republic. Topics of her recent publications include the tactics of Weimar photomontage and documentary photography as well as postcolonial readings of the Weimar New Woman. Van Hoesen's current research project involves chart-ing the role that new media plays in the construction and reauthorship of art museums in the digital age.

Introduction

Tuning in to the Aural Ether: An Introduction to the Study of German Sounds

FLORENCE FEIEREISEN
AND ALEXANDRA MERLEY HILL

Like American children, Germans learn the lyrics of their national anthem in elementary school, but, unlike their American counterparts, not every grown-up remembers each line. A famous incident occurred in 2005 when German singer Sarah Connor was hired for the official opening of the Allianz Arena in Munich to sing the national anthem. When Connor sang "Brüh im Lichte dieses Glückes" ("be scalded in the light of this fortune") instead of the correct "Blüh im Glanze dieses Glückes" ("bloom in the blessing of this fortune"), sixty-six thousand people in the stadium and eight million people glued to their televisions became ear-witnesses to her memory lapse—but not everyone noticed immediately. For Americans who grow up singing their anthem on a regular basis, this story might seem anomalous, but it reveals an important difference between American and German sound cultures. Germans rarely sing their national anthem, and, when they do so, it is largely at international sporting events, especially the Germans' favorite pastime *Fußball*, or soccer. More important, singing the German national anthem is not imbued with the same kind of national pride as in other countries; in fact, for people of some generations, knowing the exact lyrics and singing along loudly is considered overly nationalistic. Without going into detail about German national identity after World War II, as numerous scholars have already done,[1] it remains interesting that the singing of the national anthem—or, rather, the *not* singing of the anthem—can grant insight into the importance of sound and its connection with national identity.[2]

The significance of the national anthem can be heard when one reflects on recent FIFA World Cups. In 1990, cameras recorded the West German players singing the national anthem,[3] but the microphones revealed that the vast majority of the soccer players were not in fact singing along but only moving their lips in sync to the music. In 1994, 1998, and 2002, the microphones, again, picked up only a general mumbling; distinct words could not be deciphered. By contrast, when Germany hosted the 2006 FIFA World Cup under the slogan "Die Welt zu Gast bei Freunden" ("A Time to Make Friends"), and even more so during the EURO 2008 in Austria and Switzerland, one could not only see almost all of the national players moving their lips, but now also hear their enunciated sing-along. This signified a newly reclaimed national pride: sound—or silence—can indicate national identity. The same holds true for Lukas Podolski, a German national player with dual German-Polish citizenship, who refused to sing along to the German anthem at the World Cup in 2006. His silence indicated a different allegiance, and he later described having to play against Poland— and score for Germany—as symptomatic of his personal national-identity crisis.

During the World Cup in South Africa in 2010, the discussion of who sang and who did not became a public debate, because more players with dual citizenship and/or a non-German background formed the tournament's team than ever before. Simply reading the names Piotr Trochowski, Mesut Özil, Cacau, and Sami Khedira off the roster indicates the mixed national heritage represented by the German team, and the majority of the players opted not to sing along. When former coach "Kaiser" Franz Beckenbauer took over in 1984, he demanded that all players sing the anthem, yet not all did. The current coach, Joachim Löw, sings along himself, but according to an interview with him in the German tabloid *Bild*, he leaves it up to his players to follow his lead. In a *Bild* poll, 79 percent of over fifty thousand participating readers, and therefore the overwhelming majority, declared that all national players on the German team should sing along regardless of their families' backgrounds.[4] This *Hymnen-Streit* (conflict over the national anthem) shows that by singing (or by not singing) people intentionally act to declare their national identity (and other identities, as this volume shows). It is not simply singing, however, that can demonstrate one's relationship to a country. Sonic acts as diverse as playing the drums, cheering, or falling silent indicate one's national allegiance. Sound, therefore, is another manner of expressing national identity— just like wearing a team's colors—and thus begs to be studied.

SOUND: LEAVING A MARK

Sound and humankind are closely interconnected. In ancient times, the Latin word *persona* referred to a mask, usually worn by actors, through which speech was disseminated.[5] People, whether speaking, singing, or sneezing (i.e., consciously producing sound or not), are by definition sounding entities. All sounds that people make—dropping a book on the floor, closing the car door, the hum of the hair dryer, the construction site in front of our window—contribute to our sonic environment, which can be studied to tell us more about our world.

In addition to creating nationally distinct identities, sound can create a sense of community, even when functioning in a very practical capacity. "The general acoustic environment of a society," Canadian composer and founder of the World Soundscape Project R. Murray Schafer wrote, "can be read as an indicator of social conditions which produce it and may tell us much about the trending and evolution of that society."[6] For example, sirens (i.e., their emergence) have been studied due to their embeddedness in cultural, political, and physical contexts. In Mozart's Vienna, for instance, the sonic environment was quiet enough that firemen could simply (though quite loudly) call their team to the firehouse in case of an emergency; a guard stood on top of St. Stephan's Cathedral to warn citizens of danger.[7] When life became louder, a fire bell was used, which was then later replaced by a two-tone horn. What changed the sonic environment of Vienna? The answer lies in the increased noise level due to the industrial revolution, which ushered in a new era in Vienna and cities around the world. While steamship navigation on the Danube and railway lines to the city already existed, the urban infrastructure received a facelift. New sounds to be heard might have included diesel-electric generator houses (96 decibels), sawmill chippers (105 decibels), and engines of all kinds.[8] It is easy to see that a man's shouting or a fire bell was not loud enough to compete with these new sounds, hence sirens emerged.

In the shape of bells, alarm clocks, and even roosters, sound can also act as a marker of time. Bells are an interesting example to consider, because their chiming was considered an "acoustic calendar, announcing festivals, births, deaths, marriages, fires and revolts."[9] Furthermore, "bells warned of imminent danger from nature, called men to arms in defense of the community, honored the loss of great leaders, signaled the beginning of public ceremonies, and celebrated victory over battle."[10] Friedrich Schiller's "Das Lied der Glocke" ("The Song of the Bell") not only describes the technical details of bell-founding around the time of the poem's publication in 1798, but uses the bell as a framework to comment on human life, both its ups and downs. The poem opens with the Latin lines: "Vivos voco. Mortuos plango. Fulgura frango." In the English translation, the bell, or sound, proclaims: "I call the living. I mourn the dead. I repel lightning." The same bells, rung in a different order or placed in different contexts, have the power to structure an individual's life. In a time when no one wore personal wristwatches or carried a cell phone as a timekeeper, Schiller's poem describes the bell's call for men to come in from the fields to rest in the shade and eat their lunches. Again, sound is the driving force, the trigger of rituals that brought the village together. Schafer noticed that most other clocks at the time (water clocks, sand clocks, and sundials) were silent and thus did not unite the community as the bells did through sound.[11]

The sound of the ringing bells is not only a marker of time, but also a marker of space. Scholars studying England's bells as far back as the seventh century read bells as sounds of belonging: "When they heard [the bell in the tower] ringing, villagers, townsfolk, and those 'in trades' in the centres of ancient towns experienced a sense of being rooted in space that the nascent urban proletariat lacked."[12] The bell tower is not only a visual marker of the town or city, but it claims space through sound. In other words, it is both landmark and soundmark for the community. Functioning similarly by calling from a mosque's minaret, muezzins claim the space around them and sonically enter spaces where they can be heard, although not necessarily seen. Moreover, the muezzins' calling effectively creates community: those who understand the sound and respond to it affirm their participation and membership in the group. This holds true for muezzins in Istanbul and also, for example, at the Şehitlik mosque in Berlin's Neukölln (see Figure I.1).[13] In this case, the space claimed by sound is not dependent on national boundaries.

THE GUTENBERG BIAS

In their introduction to *Sound Matters*, Nora Alter and Lutz Koepnick describe sound as a "medium through which the boundaries of shared meanings, ethnic differences, political

Figure I.1
Şehitlik mosque in Berlin Neukölln.
Photograph by Frank Swenton, 2010.

representation, codes of gender identity, and the organization of private and public spaces are constituted."[14] If sound is such an interesting topic that tells us so much about the cultural history of a city or country, about its sentiments, concepts, and beliefs, why hasn't sound been studied more? There are numerous answers to this question. One place to start with is an investigation of the emergence of the visual as the "first sense."

"Speech before the age of Plato," according to Marshall McLuhan in his *The Gutenberg Galaxy: The Making of Typographic Man*, "was the glorious depository of memory."[15]

Information was conveyed orally and retained through repeated telling, creating a rich story-telling tradition. The development of the alphabet as a translation from sound into visual code set the wheels in motion; later, in the fifteenth century, the emergence of print culture as a result of Gutenberg's movable type promoted the cultural dominance of the visual over the aural. The increasing focus on the printed word and the visual in general resulted in a reconceptualization—indeed, a reorganization—of the world. "Ever since the collapse of the oral tradition in early Greece, before the age of Parmenides, Western civilization has been mesmerized by a picture of the universe as a limited container in which all things are organized according to the vanishing point, in a geometrical order."[16] According to McLuhan, this concept of "visual space" that pushed out the oral tradition resulted above all in the human tendency to approach the world in a linear manner. Approaches that advantage the eye over the other senses, such as a book, a document on a computer, or a film, suggest that everything in a visual plane has a beginning, a middle, and an end and can be read like words on paper—one after another. As a result, people in visually oriented cultures try to understand the world by understanding one thing after another, and this presupposes that these things are made up of concrete parts—distinct units that can be assembled and reassembled. Conversely, to understand the whole and all the connections of its parts, one first must dissect the parts. This introduced the concept of objectivity to the world, forcing subjectivity to find refuge in the realm of art. The intensity of this conception and therefore the dominance of the visual, McLuhan argues, have resulted in the "desensitization" of many people to touch and hearing.

Oral cultures existed in acoustic space, because speech was the primary mode of communicating. McLuhan describes the "acoustic space" as engaging multiple senses at the same time. Instead of focusing on one part only, auditory culture demands the simultaneous perception of many factors and components. This is very hard for those trained over many centuries to think within the linear concept of "visual space." The visual has taken over as the primary sense in understanding one's surroundings, yielding to hearing only when vision is obstructed. One only has to think of stethoscopes, which use sound to explore that which is hidden to the eye, or the sonogram, which produces pictures of the womb when cameras do not have access.

Despite sound's importance in the medical field, the visual still serves as a synonym for the objective. Police and paparazzi believe what they see—eye-witnesses are much more common and accepted, for example, than ear-witnesses. Interestingly enough, there are "hearings" in court, but one statement can stand against another, whereas one image—such as a photograph or film footage—can suffice as factual evidence. Photography, however, can be quite removed from objectivity; simply imagine all the different subjective factors that come into play when taking a picture: the photographer's choice of subject; choice or manipulation of lighting, posing, embedding in a background; choice of frame or cropping—not to mention Photoshop-ing. Even a casual "snapshot" is necessarily informed by the photographer's perspective and is in no way a reliable means of factual documentation. Everyone experiences the world differently and therefore can only document that world based on his or her own perspective.

The dominance of visual evidence is also a testimony to the state of recording technology. Whereas the translation of sound into visual code is many centuries old, only relatively recently have there been recording and broadcasting technologies widely available to the public. An eye-witness can now record a crime on his or her cell phone, or the jury can listen to a voicemail. Yet oral testimony of witnesses, formerly the realm of the acoustic sphere, only becomes evidential when transcribed by a court official or a journalist. Therefore, it becomes a fixed part of the "visual space" again. The desire to record and document through the visual is related to the belief that what can be written down, captured in words or images, is fixed, static, "exists"; it enters public, permanent space. Who is to say, however, that sound can not function in a similarly documentative manner?

Perhaps the point of contention rests in the impossibility of capturing both the objective and subjective dimensions of a sound: i.e., both the noise that occurred and can be measured, and the personal associations or memories that are evoked by it. At a sound performance in Buffalo, NY, electro-acoustic engineer Jean-Paul Perrotte presented one of his compositions, a multidimensional sound collage, on which he had recorded the sounds he encountered during his daily travels through Berlin on the S-Bahn. The chairs in the performance room formed a circle, and four speakers, one in each corner of the room, evoked the feeling that all members of the audience were sitting inside the train. His piece, "Berlin Pankow-Schönhauser Allee," was as long as his daily train ride from the Pankow to the Schönhauser Allee stops in Berlin. The audience ear-witnessed the rattling of the train between stops, people getting in and out, music playing in the stations, people talking, loud and quiet moments. Each stop had its own unique sound profile. Each perception of the piece by the audience members was different, too. The piece reminded them, as they later shared with the audience, of their Berlin stays, or their trips on other subway systems, for example in New York City. Due to the quadraphonic experience, a geographic space was evoked, but nobody was limited to it. Rather, it added layers of tactility, emotion, and memory. It was a heard and felt trip to Berlin that everyone perceived in a unique and unforgettable way.[17]

It is time to change the paradigm of our perception of the world: according to Bruce Smith, "knowing the world through sound is fundamentally different from knowing the world through vision,"[18] so it behooves us to extend our understanding into the aural realm, as well. To be clear, the authors of this book are by no means advocating giving up the visual in favor of regaining the acoustic. Nor do they advocate abandoning "visual space" or linear thinking. This book argues that it is in combination with the other senses that the visual makes more "sense." Only by experiencing the world through all senses with their emotional overtones and memories, does one come closer to understanding it—and claiming back the "close second" of hearing is a good avenue to begin regaining all senses. Like Bull and Back, this book argues that one should experience the world through more senses and attach greater value to them: "Thinking with our ears," a translation from Theodor W. Adorno's famous phrase "mit den Ohren denken," "offers an opportunity to augment our critical imagination, to comprehend our world and our encounters with it according to multiple registers of feeling."[19]

AN INTRODUCTION TO SOUNDSCAPES

How does one conceptualize sound? McLuhan's concept of "acoustic space" as a metaphor serves as training wheels for this experience. Space is traditionally associated with geography and topography, with borders and shapes, and therefore belongs to the visual realm. McLuhan introduces the concept of "acoustic space" as a space that cannot be limited, a space with many centers and no boundaries. It is important to note that McLuhan does not define the acoustic space as something that can only be perceived acoustically, but with all senses, even vision. At the same time, his metaphor emphasizes moving away from the "Augengläubigkeit" (the old adage "seeing is believing") and the linearity of print society, and moving toward conceiving of various dynamic relationships with all senses.

This concept is well suited to our postmodern society that is defined through its dynamic, vanishing borders and that is always in flux. Our society is no longer a container but a network, within which new relationships emerge daily. The technology of our times—the World Wide Web—encapsulates the tension between the visual and the acoustic: at first glace, the Internet is a primarily visual medium and one dependent on space (chat rooms, MySpace, Facebook, inboxes, and the German Facebook equivalent StudiVZ—literally, student directory), but its language is conceptually more affiliated with orality than with literacy (voicemail, chatting or instant messaging). The Internet promotes interdependent relationships and constant exchanges between people and institutions; it is ever-changing and opens into all directions. Therefore, though a visual medium, it is part of the "acoustic space."

In this book, and in scholarship on sound studies as a whole, the term "soundscape" is frequently used as a tool to conceptualize sound and, more particularly, how it interacts with space. The term was coined by R. Murray Schafer in *The Soundscape* as "our sonic environment, the ever-present array of noises with which we all live."[20] He studies soundscapes as "a field of interactions, even when particularized into its component sound events."[21] Yet, how does one study a soundscape? In his definition, Schafer mentions both the "component sound events" and the broader "field of interactions," and there is a tension between these two perspectives. The challenge for those who wish to analyze a soundscape is to dissect it into its components without losing sight of the whole. Soundscapes can be studied like any other -scape. Just as a landscape consists of individual components (e.g., a tree, a stone wall, clouds), a soundscape consists of distinct "sound events" (i.e., individual sounds, such as a bird singing and wind shaking the leaves of a tree) that should be studied as parts of their environment. When these sound events are taken out of context, such as when recorded and analyzed in a laboratory, Schafer calls them "sound objects."[22] Their physical characteristics can be examined, and one can document how the sound waves of sound objects work together, how they are perceived and when. Less tangible and less easy to study, however, are the function and meaning of sound events, the emotional response they inspire in the listener, and the effect they have on memory.

To put the problem differently: sounds, as every physics book will state, are periodic waves of air molecules that travel through space. They hit the eardrum, setting up vibrations inside resonance cavities within space (the human body has many cavities, so sound can be felt throughout the body). Without geographical space, there would be no sound. McLuhan's conception of acoustic space and Schafer's definition of soundscapes, however, move beyond this scientific analysis of sound. Adding to the dimensions of space and time, already accounted for in physics, these theories factor in more senses, emotions, and memories, in order to consider how the listener connects to his world.

This kind of meaning or significance lies in the context in which the sound objects appear. Wind can be ominous in the context of a wild landscape and darkening skies, or it can be soothing on a hot day under the sun. Like a mosaic, sound objects can be studied by themselves, but they reveal more information when considered within a larger context. Depending on this context, sound has both utopian and dystopian qualities: "it enables individuals to create intimate, manageable and aestheticized spaces to inhabit but it can also become an unwanted and deafening roar threatening the body politic of the subject."[23] For example, depending on one's self-identification, the roar of helicopters over Northern Ireland can trigger feelings of protection or of threat. Protestants understand them as signs of security, whereas Catholics read them as danger.[24] While bird songs are fascinating to ornithologists, they could mean the abrupt termination of a student's good night's sleep at the same day and time. Pianist Glen Gould perceived the sound of his vacuum cleaner as something utterly soothing, although this opinion is far from the norm. Furthermore, the difference in meaning or perception of sound can also depend purely on the context in which it is heard, regardless of one's relationship to the sound. R. Murray Schafer considers the example of car horns: the acoustic qualities of two horns might be identical (frequency of 512 hertz, volume of 90 decibels) but can mean either "Get out of my way!" or "I've just been married!"[25] Conversely, the music of a street musician in Berlin can be understood as beautiful art or as an assault on the senses. Thus, all components of a soundscape must be considered in their larger context including the context of their reception.

CAN YOU HEAR THE CONTEXT?

In his "Ethnography of Listening" Canadian sound artist S. Arden Hill defined hearing as an involuntary act that happens—if there is sound, the vibrations will be picked up by ears and/or felt in the body.[26] Listening, however, does not just "happen," but is "noticing and directing attention and interpreting what is heard." This is a complex endeavor, a "social act, one that invokes the materiality of the human body as well as the cultural and political environment."[27] In other words, just as one sees through a "filter" of one's experience, so, too, does one listen through a similar filter. Bull and Back argue for more "agile listening and this involves tuning our ears to listen again to the multiple layers of meaning potentially embedded in the same sound."[28]

During the FIFA World Cup 2010 in South Africa, soccer fans worldwide were introduced to an instrument called a "vuvuzela," a horn about two feet long, made of plastic or aluminum, and used to create noise during soccer matches. Its sound has been described as a herd of elephants or a swarm of bees. Although part of the game for South African soccer fans, not everyone approved of the sounds the vuvuzelas made. International television stations complained that the constant noise would drown out their commentators' voices; at a large public-viewing event in front of Berlin's Olympic Stadium, all vuvuzelas were confiscated; and FIFA president Joseph "Sepp" Blatter was even asked to officially forbid vuvuzelas during international events. This was a plea that he rejected for cultural reasons: for him, the sound of vuvuzelas presented the sonic business card of a country, in this case the host country South Africa, and he did not want to impose cultural sound laws on any of his association's members. In other words, when considered within the cultural context of South African sporting events, vuvuzelas should not be viewed as an annoyance but as an important part of witnessing and participating in the game.[29]

Just as understanding sound depends on its context, so, too, does understanding our environment depend on hearing sound. In the epic work *The Odyssey*, Odysseus put beeswax into his ears to escape the Sirens' lure, or to prevent hearing sound. As a result, this sound environment was a confined sound space around him. What he heard (his breath, his heartbeat, the blood pulsing in his veins) belonged only to him, and thus scholars speak of this experience as "the first description of the privatization of experience through sound."[30] A modern-day parallel can be found in the listener of the iPod. By putting on headphones, the listener only listens to (that is, hears intentionally) the music and other sounds in his newly restricted sound space. Depending on the volume of the music, the listener may be completely prevented from experiencing his sonic environment (such as the ambulance approaching or the other people on the bus). The listener of the iPod has limited auditory spatial awareness, for he does not fully experience the space around him and is not conscious of the surrounding soundscapes.

What comprises this sonic environment? Blesser and Salter call "aural architecture" all those objects and surfaces from which sound waves are reflected and bounce back.[31] This is best illustrated if one thinks of what one's singing sounds like in a church, the shower, a small study, or on a hike. The same song, sung at the same volume, sounds different in each space because of the manner in which it interacts with the aural architecture of the space. The "aural architect," then, is someone who designs a church, a college lecture hall, or a concert hall, i.e., a space created with aural perception in mind. Blesser and Salter argue that the sonic manipulation of space can trigger feelings of "anxiety, tranquility, socialization, isolation, frustration, fear, boredom, [and] aesthetic pleasure."[32] Yet, the aural architect is often not a human being but a force of nature, chance, or mistake. Although few call themselves aural architects, everyone is unconsciously acknowledging aural architecture by making choices each day: where to sit in a loud restaurant, to go out of one's way to drive to a movie theater that has THX, or where and when to use a cell phone in public and at what volume to speak on the phone. Everyone experiences and interacts with aural architecture, although not everyone is aware of it. This auditory spatial awareness is the "emotional and behavioral experience of space."[33]

Even if one has auditory spatial awareness and has learned how to listen, it is difficult to put sound into words.[34] We lack the vocabulary to adequately describe the aural experience. During the EURO 2008, the European soccer championships, Germany played Turkey in the semifinal—a significant game considering the many thousands of Turkish-Germans in Germany. Millions of people watched the game on television at home or gathered at public-viewing spots to cheer for their team.[35] Many people even moved their television sets outside onto the streets, so that the event—the traveling sounds of the game and locals' cheers— flooded the soundscape. All of a sudden, the screen turned dark—a blackout had cut the lines to the visual coverage of the event while the audio channels were still working. The German newspaper *Der Spiegel* remarked in their article "Seher im Stadion" ("Seer in the Arena"): "With a clap of thunder, Germany became blind—and only heard him: TV sports caster Béla Réthy."[36] Trained only in television broadcasting, Réthy was forced to switch gears in order to moderate the event like a radio commentator. Since he could no longer assume that people saw the events on the field, he had to see for them and narrate everything that was happening. The public viewing places thus became public listening places.

This event, although reminiscent of Herbert Zimmermann's coverage of the 1954 World Cup in Switzerland, is different in important ways.[37] The 1954 game resulted in Germany's victory over Hungary and made Germany world champions, restoring their confidence and national pride in the aftermath of World War II. The game was played at a time when few Germans had access to television, and millions of people gathered in front of their radios to become ear-witnesses to Helmut Rahn's historic goal. Unlike Réthy, Zimmermann was trained as a radio commentator. Compare the two commentaries of the crucial goals. Réthy: "Yessss, well done by Lahm. Hitzelsberger. Lahm. Onto Lahm's right foot. Goal! Goal by Philip Lahm! Goal in the ninetieth minute!" And now consider Zimmermann's commentary: "Another six minutes to go at the Wankdorf stadium in Berne, nobody falters, the patter of rain beating down relentlessly . . . Schäfer puts in the cross . . . header . . . Cleared. Rahn should shoot from deep . . . Rahn shoots! Goal! Goal! Goal! Goal!" He continues to summarize even after the goal: "Goal for Germany, left-footed shot by Rahn, Schäfer put in the cross . . . Germany leads three to two, five minutes before the end of the game."[38] Which conveys more information?

By contrast, Réthy's six-minute stint as commentator for the listening audience infuriated the fans, as one journalist witnessed. Reinhard Mohr declared in *Der Spiegel*: "The advanced age of television has developed its very own visual language."[39] In other words, the practiced and careful manner of describing events to a nonseeing audience has become a thing of the past. When the image suddenly disappeared, it became clear how much the audience relies on the visual and how little sports fans are used to listening. Since the widespread availability of television, soccer has become a spectacle and is no longer an "audicle" as it was in 1954.[40]

LEARNING TO AURALIZE

Through the centuries-long bias in favor of sight, all but the seeing-impaired have become more proficient with their eyes than with their ears. Blesser and Salter argue that one can gain back the skill of auralizing[41]—yet it requires some rethinking of our relationship to sound. A part of having been socialized within "visual space" is the desire to preserve things in the aforementioned linear container. The study of soundscapes demands a different path. One of the main qualities of all -scapes, including soundscapes, is their fluid character. Soundscapes are always changing, every second is different: a car is passing, the bird is changing its song, the humming of the ceiling fan in brutally hot July is different from the banging and hissing of the radiator in January. In their introduction to *Sound*, Patricia Kruth and Henry Stobart argue that the study of sound is so tricky, because once sounds are perceived, the sound waves have already departed.[42] A natural problem exists for the reconstruction of a sound environment.

Since the industrial revolution, two technological developments have changed how people deal with and think of sound: "the discovery of packaging and storing techniques for sound and the splitting of sounds from their original context," which Schafer calls "schizophonia."[43] Think about the three most important technological achievements of the electric age: the telephone, the phonograph, and the radio.[44] All of these are sound devices, but they have also contributed to both the wide dissemination and the isolation or compartmentalization of sound. Divorcing sound from its context means that recordings of some sounds are available, yet with little sense of their meaning; there is technology at hand to measure sound waves, for example, but nothing that can record or even measure the emotional impact that this experience has on those who perceive sounds. Only to biometrically measure skin resistance would not do justice to this multisensory experience. Furthermore, recordings of *some* sounds exist, but scholars such as Leigh Eric Schmidt claim that the sounds of the past have been (largely) lost. One cannot eavesdrop in retrospect if nothing has been recorded, and, consequently, everything is left to the individual's acoustic imagination. "Almost all of history is eerily silent and so, to evoke those stilled and faded voices, the historian must act as a kind of necromancer."[45]

If the sounds of the past haven't been recorded, historical research can help with auralizing. By posing questions to create a sound profile of a city, for example, one can piece the mosaic of the past together. How many people lived in the city and in the countryside? Did the countryside consist of forests or farms? Was there hunting? What were the hunting weapons of the time? How big was the city? What was the building material for the houses? What was the layout of the city? Was there a marketplace? Were there street criers? Schafer, for example, found out what street criers in Elizabethan England must have advertized: "13 different kinds of fish, 18 different kinds of fruit, 6 kinds of liquors and herbs, 11 vegetables, 14 kinds of food, 14 kinds of household stuff, 13 articles of clothing." Yet who were these criers—or, who cried? Schafer notes "9 tradesmen's cries, 19 tradesmen's songs, 4 begging songs for prisoners, 5 watchman's songs, 1 town crier."[46] Imagine the sound level!

But even this gives an insufficient sense of the soundscape. It is important to consider the context of sound, and the more one knows of the context, the more sounds one can extrapolate from that knowledge. Some questions to ask about the sound environment include: how often did the market take place? What jobs did people work? Was there a river close by with mills? What was the demography of the population in terms of class, gender, and ethnicity? What sounds would be specific to occupations based on gender or class? What about religion and the sound qualities of their corresponding practices? Was there a monarch and was his presence announced by fanfare? Were there wars? Epidemics? What kind of climate was typical? What sort of animals or pets were kept? What sort of wild animals were native? Was there a prison? A hospital? What festivals or celebrations took place? Were there theaters? Opera houses? Fairs? What instruments were dominant? Was there a curfew? How did people get from A to B? By sled through the snow? By carriage over cobblestone streets? If so, did they have iron-girt wheels? By asking questions in more and more detail, one has begun to auralize. The authors of the following chapters use a similar technique to uncover Germany's sonic history. This line of inquiry is an invitation to rethink noise, silence, language, identity, power, and—considering the history of recording technologies—the nature of knowledge itself.

TRANSDISCIPLINARY SOUNDSCAPE STUDIES

Although the visual has long been the dominant sense and schematic for organizing the manner in which one thinks of the world, scholars are demanding a renewed consideration of the impact of other senses, such as sound. Jim Drobnick, in *Aural Cultures*, wrote:

> Although an aural equivalent to "visual studies" has yet to become firmly established in the academy, there is nevertheless a distinct and vibrant "sonic turn" that can be discerned in the recent upsurge in sound-based scholarship and artistic work. A phrase such as "sonic turn"— referring to the increasing significance of the acoustic as simultaneously a site for analysis, a medium for aesthetic engagement, and a model for theorization—self-consciously echoes

W.J.T. Mitchell's articulation of a "pictorial turn" a decade ago. Making a claim for a sonic turn, like its pictorial predecessor, would depend upon several factors, not the least of which is the emergence of a critical mass of sound-inflected theory and art.[47]

Due to the novelty of sound studies as a field, it is no surprise that it has not been institutionalized yet. This is, among other things, a matter of the wide range of discipline-distinct approaches: Schafer explains, one could analyze sounds "according to their physical characteristics (acoustics) or the manner in which they are perceived (psychoacoustics); according to their functions and meanings (semiotics and semantics); or according to their emotional or affective qualities (aesthetics)."[48] Schools and universities teach acoustics, the science of sound, as a part of physics instruction, but not many educational institutions offer the latter two approaches teaching "[a]ural aesthetics, or sensual sociology."[49] Since the millennium, there has been an increase in scholarship and art in the field of sound that attests to the "sonic turn." A number of scholars have done important research contributing to the newly emerging field of sound studies, from their "home" disciplines of media studies (especially "mass media" and film studies), urban studies, music and (music) history. By combining the scholarship from many fields, one can only gain a better understanding of the complexity of sound studies. To this end, this book draws on the expertise of German area studies scholars from a variety of disciplines, literature, cultural studies, history, art history, music, architecture, and journalism—often found on diametrically opposed ends of a campus—seeking to create a transdisciplinary dialogue. By collecting work from scholars in a variety of fields, this book pushes the discussion of sound further by connecting it to a national context, in effect asking: what does Germany *sound like*?

The section organization of the book concentrates on topics that the various chapters have in common rather than focusing on too strict a chronology. The authors gladly acknowledge the important research that has been done on sound, noise, music, and voice in the context of nineteenth-century Germany. Yet the focus of this book is placed on the "loud twentieth century"—a playful rewriting of Hobsbawm's "long nineteenth century" (1789–1914)—that continues into the present. The first section, "New Sounds in the Twentieth Century: Sounds, Noise, Silence," centers on new wanted and unwanted sounds in both private and public spaces. The author of each chapter argues that listeners can create their own private or collective sound spaces. Section II, "Defining Space through Sound: Battlefields and Concert Halls," views space with the ears both outside (on the ground, in the air, and in the sea) and inside (in specially constructed environments such as concert halls) and investigates how the experience of space influences the experience of sound. Section III, "East and West: Sounds in the Shadow of the Wall," explores whether East and West really did sound different by analyzing a work of fiction and by conducting journalistic interviews with people from both East and West Berlin. Both authors ask how the perception of sound is linked to identity formation in the context of a divided Germany. Section IV, "The Politics of Sound: Walls with Ears," deals with the sonic manipulation of citizens by GDR authorities both by regulations of the music scene and acoustic surveillance. The final section, "Soundscapers of the Millennium: Sound Art and Music Sounds," looks at art production (German sound art and hip-hop) to position the sound artists as pioneers of a new era. McLuhan has already suggested that the beginning of electric culture might signal a renewed interest in the acoustic. This book is an invitation to tune in to the aural ether and to actively engage with the sonic

Figure I.2
Inside a train of the Deutsche Bahn.
Photograph by Frank Swenton, 2010.

environment. Embracing John Cage's philosophy of music as any and all sounds (and even silence), Schafer invitingly says, "The universal concert is always in progress, and seats in the auditorium are free."[50]

NOTES

1. See for example Mary Fulbrook, *German National Identity after the Holocaust* (Cambridge, MA: Polity Press, 1999).
2. For more on the history of German national anthem(s) (especially the controversy surrounding the first verse of the "Deutschlandlied") as a part of German heritage and current politics,

see Michael E. Geisler, "Germany's National Symbols and Public Memory after 1989," in *National Symbols, Fractured Identities*, ed. Michel E. Geisler (Middlebury, VT: Middlebury College Press, 2005), 63–100.

3. Though the World Cup took place after the fall of the Berlin Wall, the team was composed of only West German athletes. The 1992 UEFA EURO would be the first international soccer tournament with a unified team.

4. For more details about the coach's attitude toward this issue see "Löw gegen Beckenbauer. Der Hymnen-Streit," *Bild online*, June 2, 2010, http://www.bild.de/BILD/sport/fussball-wm-2010-suedafrika/2010/06/02/hymnen-streit-mit-franz-beckenbauer/jogi-loew-ich-zwinge-keinen-zum-singen.html (accessed June 30, 2010).

5. It is a common misconception that the term "person" derives from the Latin *per* (through) and *son* (from *sonare* = sound) and describes (a being) "through sound" (i.e., "through language").

6. R. Murray Schafer, *The Soundscape: Our Sonic Environment and the Tuning of the World.* (Rochester, VT: Destiny Books, 1994), 7.

7. Ibid., 166.

8. Ibid., 177.

9. Ibid., 55.

10. Barry Blesser and Linda-Ruth Salter, *Spaces Speak, Are You Listening?* (Cambridge, MA: MIT Press, 2007), 29.

11. Schafer, *The Soundscape: Our Sonic Environment and the Tuning of the World*, 55.

12. Alain Corbin, "The Auditory Markers of the Village," in *The Auditory Culture Reader*, eds. Michael Bull and Les Back (Oxford: Berg Publishers, 2003), 117–125, 117.

13. Recently, many mosques have added loudspeakers to their minarets. The increased volume of the muezzin's voice means an increased radius of space reached.

14. Nora Alter and Lutz Koepnick, *Sound Matters: Essays on the Acoustics of Modern German Culture* (New York: Berghahn Books, 2004), 4.

15. Marshall McLuhan, "Visual and Acoustic Space," in *Audio Culture. Readings in Modern Music*, eds. Christoph Cox and Daniel Warner (New York: Continuum International, 2004), 67–72, 68.

16. Ibid., 68.

17. Compare this to Marcel Proust's encounter with a Madeleine cookie in *In Search of Lost Time* (*À la recherche du temps perdu*, 1913–27): the smell, taste, and texture of the cookie combined with a sip of tea triggered important personal memories for the narrator. For a comprehensive overview of sensory studies from a historical point of view see Mark M. Smith, *Sensing the Past: Seeing, Hearing, Smelling, Tasting, and Touching in History* (Berkeley, Los Angeles: University of California Press, 2007).

18. Bruce Smith, "Tuning into London c.1600," in *Auditory Culture Reader*, eds. Bull and Back, 127–136, 129.

19. Bull and Back, eds., *Auditory Culture Reader*, 2.

20. As seen on the back of the book.

21. Schafer, *The Soundscape: Our Sonic Environment and the Tuning of the World*, 131. Arjun Appadurai borrows from terminology traditionally associated with topography and the visual by examining -scapes. He uses the suffix borrowed from "landscape" in order to describe ethnoscapes, mediascapes, technoscapes, finanscapes, and ideoscapes, exploring all dimensions of the global cultural flow. We see soundscapes as an equally telling kind of -scape. For more, see Arjun Appadurai, *Modernity at Large. Cultural Dimensions of Globalization* (Minneapolis: University of Minnesota Press, 1996).

22. Schafer, *The Soundscape: Our Sonic Environment and the Tuning of the World*, 131.

23. Bull and Back, eds., *Auditory Culture Reader*, 1.

24. For a more detailed discussion on the different soundscapes in Northern Ireland, the Catholic versus the Protestant, the Irish versus the English, and the rural versus the industrialized, see

Paul Moore, "Sectarian Sound and Cultural Identity in Northern Ireland," in *Auditory Culture Reader*, eds. Bull and Back, 265–79.

25. Schafer, *The Soundscape: Our Sonic Environment and the Tuning of the World*, 149.

26. S. Arden Hill, "Listening to Myself Listen. The Performance of Listening in Actual and Constructed Sonic Environments—An Ethnography of Listening," http://www.phonography.org/listening.htm (accessed June 16, 2011).

27. Jim Drobnick, ed., *Aural Cultures* (Toronto: YYZ Books, 2004), 11.

28. Bull and Back, eds., *Auditory Culture Reader*, 3.

29. The end of the FIFA World Cup brought new developments concerning the use of vuvuzelas, when the European soccer association UEFA banned the horns from stadiums during UEFA events such as the EURO, qualification tournaments, and Champions League games. The reasons given included that these loud sounds were not part of the European "soccer culture and tradition" and would considerably change the familiar atmosphere in the stadiums, culminating in the statement: "At the Cape of Good Hope, this is a tradition and local peculiarity, yet it could not be translated to European soccer as this permanent background noise is not appropriate." See "UEFA verbannt Vuvuzelas, HSV verleiht Rozenahl." *Spiegel Online*. September 1, 2010, http://www.spiegel.de/sport/fussball/0,1518,714075,00.html (accessed September 16, 2010). In chapter 1, John Goodyear discusses noise as a class disease. In the context of the UEFA's statement, one must wonder about sonic racism: the European soccer association equates South Africa with peculiar loud noise, whereas Europe's quiet, civilized tradition should be preserved.

30. Ibid., 8.

31. Blesser and Salter, *Spaces Speak, Are You Listening?* 2.

32. Ibid., 11.

33. Ibid., 11.

34. Besides the concept of a "hearing" before a judge, another interesting case is the term "audit" after filing an income tax return. This only means that more written (visual) evidence, such as receipts and other printouts, have to be submitted. Usually, however, the vocabulary at our fingertips is connected to the visual: consider "enlightenment" and "observation"—the first refers to something being illuminated, thus brought into the area of inspection by light, i.e., a visual image. The latter stems from Latin and the verb *servare* (to watch).

35. The English term *public viewing* as used in Germany might sound like a wake at a funeral parlor that involves an open casket, but it only means the showing of a soccer game on a big screen, an event at which many people gather.

36. "Mit einem Donnerschlag war Deutschland blind—und hörte nur noch ihn: Fernsehkommentator Béla Réthy." Reinhard Mohr, "Seher im Stadion." *Spiegel Online*. June 26, 2008. http://www.spiegel.de/kultur/gesellschaft/0,1518,562213,00.html (accessed July 10, 2008).

37. Zimmermann's broadcast can be viewed and listened to on YouTube http://www.youtube.com/watch?v=R6EaOiIQ7Xs. A fictional account that feeds off this is Sönke Wortmann's 2003 film *Das Wunder von Bern* (*The Miracle of Berne*).

38. 2008: "Jaaaa, gut gemacht von Lahm. Hitzelsberger. Lahm. Lahm auf dem rechten Fuß. Tor! Tor durch Philip Lahm! Tor in der 90. Minute!" 1954: "Sechs Minuten noch im Wankdorf-Stadion in Bern, keiner wankt, der Regen prasselt unaufhörlich hernieder . . . Schäfer nach innen geflankt . . . Kopfball . . . Abgewehrt. Aus dem Hintergrund müsste Rahn schießen . . . Rahn schießt! Tor! Tor!" And after eight seconds of silence he screams enthusiastically: "Tor für Deutschland, Linksschuss von Rahn, Schäfer hat die Flanke nach innen geschlagen . . . Drei zu zwei für Deutschland fünf Minuten vor dem Spielende."

39. "Das fortgeschrittene Fernsehzeitalter hat eine ganz eigene Bildsprache entwickelt." Mohr, "Seher im Stadion."

40. The experience is different for blind people. Les Back examines the experience of blind soccer fans in England who go to the stadium every other Saturday to absorb the acoustic

atmosphere. The local soccer club provides them with headphones, so that they can hear the local commentator. Yet, not only do they hear through the headphones, they also hear the other fans' reactions, the chants, and the drums. One not only hears through the ear, after all, but rather with the entire body. Les Back, "Sounds in the Crowd," in *Auditory Culture Reader*, eds. Bull and Back, 311–27.

41. Blesser and Salter coined this term to mean "aurally visualize," 70.

42. "Sound moves through time and space and it both literally and metaphorically moves us." Patricia Kruth and Henry Stobart, eds., *Sound* (Cambridge, UK: Cambridge University Press, 2000), 3.

43. Schafer, *The Soundscape: Our Sonic Environment and the Tuning of the World*, 88.

44. Other technological achievements connected to sound include the gramophone, sound film, tape, CD, DVD recorders, and players. The latest sound applications can be found online, for example, calling a friend via Skype and sending each other MP3 files via e-mail.

45. Leigh Eric Schmidt, "Hearing Loss," in *Auditory Culture Reader*, eds. Bull and Back, 41–59, 41. For more discussions on sounds that have emerged since the invention of recording devices, see Alter and Koepnick's *Sound Matters*.

46. Schafer, *The Soundscape: Our Sonic Environment and the Tuning of the World*, 65. Over time, street criers were considered noise pollution and were phased out. Just an example of how Turkey differs from Europe in terms of sound: "By 1960, the only European city in which street cries could still regularly be heard was Istanbul," 66. Why were the sounds phased out of Europe and why did they stay in Turkey? What are the regulations for street musicians in Germany today?

47. Drobnick, *Aural Cultures*, 10.

48. Schafer, *The Soundscape: Our Sonic Environment and the Tuning of the World*, 133.

49. Blesser and Salter, *Spaces Speak, Are You Listening?* 6.

50. Schafer, *The Soundscape: Our Sonic Environment and the Tuning of the World*, 206. For more on John Cage's take on sounds and silence as music see John Cage, *Silence* (Middletown, CT: Wesleyan University Press, 1961); and Richard Kostelanetz, ed. *Conversing with Cage* (New York: Limelight, 1984).

SECTION ONE
New Sounds in the Twentieth Century
Sounds, Noise, Silence

In the introduction, several examples showed that a soundscape consists of distinct sound events that must be considered in their larger context including the context of their reception. What about silence? In *Spaces Speak, Are You Listening?* Barry Blesser and Ruth-Linda Salter explain:

> [Silence] can signal: a cessation of both social and natural activity, a state of psychological tranquility, a powerful emotion that transcends speech, a cooperative agreement to respect the public soundscape, a silent prayer communicating with a deity, a preoccupation with an inner thought, a punitive response to social and political transgressions, or an acceptance of the right to be left in peace.[1]

Because silence has the ability to signify so many diverse things, one would expect silence to be more prevalent than it is; yet, it is increasingly difficult to find silence. The world becomes noisier each day. Referring to both the amplitude and the frequency of sound waves, "noise" has become a negative term. The concept of noise as "unwanted sounds" has led to the emergence of new technologies such as mass-produced earplugs, soundproof walls, and white-noise generators.[2] These developments, however, are not as new as one might think.

The first chapter of this book is concerned with Germany at the beginning of the twentieth century, a time of increased noise levels on the streets due to the advancement of industry and technology. John Goodyear examines the quest for quiet as a counterphenomenon to this new noise by juxtaposing two concurrent approaches to the alleged noise pollution of the time: anti-noise movements and commercially available earplugs. He concentrates on Theodor Lessing's *Antilärmverein* (Anti-Noise Society), which sought to protect Hannover's citizens from the harsh sounds of modernity. By outlining the society's agenda and analyzing its publications—such as the wide distribution of a "blue list" of quiet hotels and the monthly publication *Das Recht auf Stille* (*The Right to Quiet*)—Goodyear explains the multiple avenues through which Lessing attempted to combat the noise of modernity. Around the same time, pharmacist Maximilian Negwer started to mass-produce earplugs made of wax, a man-made solution to our inability to close our "earlids." Goodyear presents a short history of the earplug, starting with Odysseus sticking his fingers into his ears to escape the Sirens' song and ending with the celebrations of the one-hundredth anniversary of the *Ohropax* earplug. By auralizing *Ohropax*'s commercial posters, Goodyear investigates the quest to escape the urban din, which also drove Lessing's actions. The chapter concludes with an analysis of why the earplug was ultimately successful, while Lessing's project was doomed to fail.

Not only did sounds become louder as the twentieth century progressed, but radio spread sound as it gained in popularity. From the 1920s on,[3] Germany was listening. Similar to church bells, radio also functions as a mediator between the individual and the outside world. It can provide material to hear as well as to actively listen to: one can use radio for background noise while cleaning the apartment (and hear without realizing it), or one can actively listen to the news, political talk shows, commercials, sports commentary, music, and quiz shows. Robert Ryder examines the genre of the radio play in German culture, more specifically Günter Eich's 1951 radio play *Dreams*, to uncover the potential of the acoustic medium of the radio. Ryder contends that, by tapping into his audience's "acoustical unconscious," Eich forces listeners to awaken to and contend with the collective history of which they are a part. Using the theories of Sigmund Freud, Walter Benjamin, and others to decipher Eich's radiophonic language, Ryder argues that this language calls attention to the disjunction between word and sound: the relationship between signifier and signified falls apart, and names begin to peel away from their meaning. The listener is not only a passive consumer, but often the speech is directed at him, engaging the listener and seemingly transporting him into the play's space. Ultimately, Ryder argues, when listening to Eich's radio play, the listener cannot remain a passive consumer but is forced via sound to experience the play's soundscape.

NOTES

1. Barry Blesser and Ruth-Linda Salter, *Spaces Speak, Are You Listening?* (Cambridge, MA: MIT Press, 2007), 32.
2. It should not be forgotten that noise can be used in productive ways as well; for example, noise bands turn noise into art through their excessive use of volume and distortion. They use cacophony and dissonance in and as their music. This questions the commonly accepted definition of noise as "unwanted" sounds.
3. For a detailed discussion on the history of the radio see Wolfgang Hagen, *Das Radio. Zur Geschichte und Theorie des Hörfunks—Deutschland/USA* (München: Wilhelm Fink, 2005). The 1930s *Volksempfänger* (the people's receiver) is also worth a mention: this affordable device commissioned by Joseph Goebbels for mass production made sure that the general public in Germany was able to hear National Socialist propaganda.

CHAPTER 1
Escaping the Urban Din

A Comparative Study of Theodor Lessing's Antilärmverein
(1908) and Maximilian Negwer's Ohropax *(1908)*

JOHN GOODYEAR

From the multilingualism of the ancient city of Babylon to the diverse soundscapes of modern-day Berlin, cities have always been synonymous with noise. Urban noise, one of a city's principal hallmarks, is a powerful, yet invisible force laden with contradictions: it has been a source of fascination and frustration, attraction and repulsion, inspiration and distraction. The turn of the twentieth century appears to showcase these contradictions in sonic terms, because the era was marked by rapid urban-population growth, unrelenting expansion of the urban rail and road networks, new machinery, and ground-breaking inventions of sonic devices, such as the gramophone and the telephone. In 1909, Otto Eisenschitz (1863–1942), theater director and actor at the Wiener Burgtheater (People's Theater of Vienna), passionately appreciated the then-modern urban sounds: "I love city noise. I love every kind of noise which is indicative of a care-free, bustling, lively, merry and cheerful life. I crave the noise of the urban hustle and bustle."[1] Here the noisy soundscapes of the city satisfy cravings, like an intoxicating drug, without which this particular city dweller could not live.

However, not all of Eisenschitz's contemporaries shared such a passion for urban noise, although the analogy of urban noise as a drug does resonate with the anti-noise discourse at the turn of the penultimate century. The German-Jewish philosopher, writer, and cultural critic Theodor Lessing (1872–1933) described urban noise as a *Reiz- und Rauschmittel* (a means of stimulation and intoxication) as well, but chose to abstain. For him, it was anything other than a source of fascination, attraction, or inspiration. In stark contrast to Eisenschitz, Lessing equated the affinity for urban noise with a disease, a plague that desperately needed treating. From *Lärmverseuchung* (noise contamination) to *Klavierpest* (plague of the piano) and *Gesangseuche* (the pestilence of singing), Lessing understood noise as *hygienische Delikte* (hygienic offenses) and set out on a mission to persuade the German public that it should be legally defined as such.

In March 1908, Lessing published the manifesto *Der Lärm* (*Noise*), in which he vented and philosophized about his long-held frustrations, dating back to his sleepless nights in Munich as a student. The book featured elaborations on the constant bombardment of noises, predominantly of then-modern-day urban life—ranging from *Teppichklopfen* (carpet beating) to the *Hupe des Automobils* (hooting of the car horn)—and their debilitating psychological and physiological effects on the human ear. Interrogating existing noise legislation enshrined in the *Strafgesetzbuch* (Criminal Code) as well as putting past judicial verdicts against noise complaints under the spotlight, Lessing's book also identified loopholes and limitations in the German legal framework that prevented the law from standing behind those searching for quiet. With these considerations and complaints in mind, Lessing's book, as his introduction concluded, was to be

> a signal for a universal fight against excessive noises in everyday life. . . . I am setting my hopes on the establishment of a universal and international association against noise, which will have influence on criminal and civil law, administrative and police legislation. The banner of the association should read: "non clamor sed amor."[2]

Soon thereafter, in mid-1908, Lessing founded the first nationwide German *Antilärmverein* (Anti-Noise Society) with its official headquarters in his native city of Hannover.[3] In the first of a series of monthly pamphlets initially titled *Der Anti-Rüpel* (*The Anti-Lout*), published a few months after the formation of the society, Lessing called for the creation of a *Kulturmacht* (cultural force) and a *Partei der anständigen Leute* (party of respectable people). The imposed membership fee of three *Reichsmark* to join the society supported the *Verein*'s editorial activities and the financing of two secretaries in its headquarters on Hannover's Stolzestraße.

In the same year as Lessing's foundation of his Anti-Noise Society, the pharmacist Maximilian Negwer (1872–1943) started to mass-produce a new range of earplugs in Berlin. Drawing on the German word for ear, *Ohr*, and the Latin word for peace, *pax*, the name Negwer gave to his new invention would become a generic trademark in Germany, synonymous with the earplug: *Ohropax*. Although there is no biographical evidence to suggest that Lessing and Negwer knew each other personally,[4] the striking parallels between their two projects suggest more than a mere historical coincidence. On the surface, they were, in their own ways, responding to the phenomenon of urban noise in early twentieth-century Germany. Also, there was a commercial element behind both of their projects, from Lessing's imposed membership fee to Negwer's charge of one *Reichsmark* for a pair of six earplugs. Last and by no means least: both Lessing and Negwer attempted, albeit in varying ways, to engineer not just a significant reduction in unwanted urban noise but quiet or total silence. The titles of both of their projects suggest as such: Lessing's monthly journal, later renamed *Das Recht auf Stille* (*The Right to Quiet*), and *pax* in Negwer's *Ohropax* both point to this quest.

But what can be deduced from studying both projects? What can be gained from investigations of soundscapes (or, as Lessing and Negwer would argue, noisescapes) of the time and their treatments? I am building the answers to these questions on Peter Bailey's essay "Breaking the Sound Barrier," in which he argues that

> historians habitually invoke the "sights and sounds" of an era as necessary objects of their enquiry, but the latter rarely receive more than lip service. Of course, if we are to listen as well

as look to any real effect we must learn how to listen more acutely as well as how to reconstruct the listener in history and identify its more reliable ear witnesses. We must attend not only to noise but to the whole range of sounds that enliven the past and contribute to its changing sensory orders.[5]

For Bailey, the "whole range of sounds"[6] includes silence: silence as the sound of authority (church and state), silence as a highly qualitative and rarely empty force, and silence as an act and not necessarily a total absence of sound.[7] Recognizing, just as Bailey did, that silence is as important as noise for historians of aurality, this project shall examine the quest for quiet as a counterphenomenon to the noise of the early twentieth-century German city. Given that Lessing's manifesto and establishment of his *Antilärmverein* (Anti-Noise Society) coincided with the debut of Negwer's *Ohropax* on the market in 1908, this particular year lends itself as the ideal keynote year to analyze these two specific, yet very different quests, and to compare their successes and failures in tackling urban noise.

HEARING SILENCE DOWN THE YEARS: A HISTORICAL TAKE ON THE EARPLUG

The earplug and its history, perhaps due to its mundane and matter-of-fact nature, have not been the focus of much sustained academic attention. Indeed, there is no *magnum opus* devoted to the history of the earplug; historical references seem to be brief and fleeting, mostly confined to scientific investigations of modern-day earplug performance; and no one inventor is singled out as having invented the earplug, commercial or otherwise. Though the history of the earplug may, on the surface, seem an unlikely and unimpressive subject of research in the field of sound studies, uncovering such a history can reveal an untold story of the soundscape: that of the individual's attempt, over the course of time, to block out the perceived din in a quest for quiet.

In her short but detailed study titled *Antique Hearing Devices* (1994), Elisabeth Bennion argues that it is "virtually impossible to go back far enough to discover the first use of a hearing device."[8] Though Bennion's study refers specifically to the hearing device as hearing aids, the same argument could easily apply to the earplug: a precise dating of the invention of the earplug would also prove a Herculean task for any researcher. The hearing aid, Bennion writes, is

> defined as a device that increases the degree of sound to the user and consequently includes the oldest of all forms and still the most frequently used: the hand cupping behind the ear. This elementary method additionally shields off disturbing background noises so that the masking effect is reduced, a point borne in mind in the devising of many later methods.[9]

As opposed to a hearing aid, the earplug, then, is a device that, at best, blocks out unwanted sound and, at worst, decreases the degree of sound. The best example is "the oldest of all forms and still the most frequently used": the human hand. For some, the palm of the hand, covering the entire ear, blocks out noise; for others the pushing-in of the tragus with one of the fingers to cover the entrance of the auditory canal is the preferred method to drown out the din. The hand, I suggest, is the oldest earplug.

In another striking parallel between the hearing aid and the earplug, Bennion identifies Homer's *Iliad* from 850 BC as containing one of the first known written references to "a speaking trumpet,"[10] a forerunner to the modern-day hearing aid. Homer's epic poem *The Odyssey* contains the scene of Odysseus instructing his crew to fill their ears with beeswax so that they are not lured away by the enchanting song of the Sirens. The Greek myth of the Sirens not only inspired works by Goethe, Rilke, and Kafka in German literature, but is said to have also inspired a group of early twentieth-century chemists, among them Negwer, to develop disposable, soft cotton-wool earplugs, soaked in skin-friendly paraffin waxes and Vaseline. A century later, *Ohropax* is one of the most recognizable trademarks in Germany.[11]

The *Ohropax* company recently celebrated its one-hundredth anniversary at its headquarters in the peace and tranquility of Wehrheim im Taunus, a sound world away from its previous headquarters in Berlin. The anniversary received much media attention: the *Frankfurter Rundschau*'s article "Die Ruhekugel" ("The Peace Ball"),[12] Bonn's *General Anzeiger*'s headline "Die Stöpsel, die für Ruhe sorgen" ("The Plugs Providing Peace and Quiet"),[13] and the *Berliner Morgenpost*'s article titled "100 Jahre Frieden im Ohr" ("100 Years of Peace in the Ears")[14] applauded *Ohropax*'s longevity. Though these newspaper articles loosely presented Negwer's *Ohropax* as a pioneer in earplug technology, German patent records from a century ago and earplug advertisements in Lessing's Anti-Noise Society journals reveal a more complex story: *Ohropax*, surprisingly not patented by Negwer at the time, belonged to an emerging trend of earplugs on the market at the turn of the century. These earplugs had names ranging from *Antiphon* to *Kopfbinde* and *Paraphon*. The latter product was advertised as "weiche, unsichtbare Ohrkugel" ("soft, invisible balls for the ears") in Lessing's *Das Recht auf Stille* (*The Right to Quiet*) in June 1909.[15]

In 1903, officials responsible for the following year's *Verzeichnis der Patente* (German Patent Register)[16] widened the scope of category 30d of patents to include, for the first time, *Ohrheilkunde* (ear medicine), *Ohrschutz* (hearing protection), and *Schalldämpfer* (sound absorbers),[17] reflecting a heightened sensitivity to noise at the start of the twentieth century and proving that concerted efforts were under way by scientists and medical experts to patent practical sound-reducing devices as early as 1903. One such invention, successfully patented in September 1906 and registered under category 30d, was Heinz Bothmer's *Kopfbinde* (Head Band). Its description found in the German Patent Register published in 1909 reads: "Head band against insomnia with adjustable cords and wads of cotton wool for insertion into the auditory canals."[18]

In the same 1909 volume, another invention, patented by Dr. Emil Sprenger in Stettin in July 1907, bears some resemblance to Negwer's *Ohropax* earplugs. Sprenger's *Antiphon* invention, patent number 205 305, was described as consisting of "a wad of cotton wool soaked in paraffin oil and hard paraffin."[19] Interestingly, the term *Antiphon* as a "device to seal the ears" had already been registered by the Stuttgart inventor and captain in the Royal Prussian Army, Maximilian Plessner, as early as May 30, 1884.[20] Unlike Bothmer, Sprenger, and Negwer, the inventor Plessner, the keen writer and author of *Die Zukunft des elektrischen Fernsehens* (*The Future of Electrical Television*, 1893), also published an extensive brochure titled "Das Antiphon: Ein Apparat zum Unhörbarmachen von Tönen und Geräuschen" ("The Antiphon: A Device for Making Sounds and Noises Inaudible"). Printed in 1885, one year after the patenting of his invention, Plessner's brochure is partly a programmatic philosophical pamphlet and partly an instruction manual outlining the appropriate method of inserting the spherical, metal *Antiphon* into the ear.

Addressed to "Allen Leidensgenossen" ("All Suffering Comrades"), to those individuals who were sensitive to the "betäubenden Lärm der Straßen" ("deafening noise of the streets"), Plessner's stated aim in inventing the *Antiphon* was to create peace and quiet in a sea of noise, especially for the intellectually minded:

> The inexpensive *Antiphon* will now grant relief, even for the most impecunious of brainworkers, living in the noisiest parts of the city, to conduct their business in uninterrupted peace. Millions of hours' worth of thinking will be gained and the most fruitful of thoughts will stem from researchers' minds.[21]

Here, Plessner differentiates between brainworkers who need quiet and those who work with their hands, assuming that the latter do not mind the roaring noises of the streets and factories. The quest for quiet is used to separate the middle and upper classes from the working class who did not have the luxury of—or supposedly even the desire for—silence in their lives.

In the early years of the new German Reich, Plessner characterizes the city, most probably Stuttgart where the *Antiphon* was patented, as a place of noise where millions of contemplative thought hours were lost to urban din. Intellectuals' search for silence was no new phenomenon in the nineteenth century: the Scottish essayist Thomas Carlyle had the attic at his London home converted into a soundproof study so that he could work without disruption from the street-level noises and street musicians. Richard Wagner was, as evident in his autobiography *Mein Leben* (*My Life*), often troubled by the amateurish playing of musical instruments by his next-door neighbors. German philosopher Friedrich Nietzsche berated the lack of quiet urban space for contemplation in his 280th aphorism in *Die fröhliche Wissenschaft* (*The Gay Science*), insisting that cities lacked "stille und weite, weitgedehnte Orte zum Nachdenken"[22] ("quiet and open, stretched-out places for contemplation"). Arthur Schopenhauer, too, said of noise that it is "the most impertinent of all forms of interruption. It is not only an interruption; it is, moreover, a disruption of thought."[23]

Theodor Lessing, finally, would not only draw on these aversions expressed by Carlyle, Wagner, Nietzsche, and Schopenhauer in his first anti-noise article, but also would document his own personal experience in trying out the *Antiphon*. Characteristically for Lessing's mindset, the *Antiphon* earplug was an object of praise and derision:

> A song of praise must be sung for the inventor of the Antiphon earplug, but only if these devices were actually of any use! After experiencing the most unpleasant effects of all kinds of antiphons, I now use small plugs made out of hard rubber which are the best sound absorbers and real human comforts.[24]

It is interesting to note that Lessing, in 1901, is unaware of the name of the inventor of the *Antiphon*. Plessner's name does not feature anywhere in this text or his second anti-noise essay, *Noch Einiges über den Lärm* (*Some More About Noise*) that was published a year later in the same journal. It is unclear from this first text whether Lessing is actually referring to the

Antiphon of a single company when he uses the plural form *Antiphone*; or whether he is referencing other *Antiphon* earplugs that may have come on the market since Plessner's patenting of the invention in 1884. On the other hand, Lessing may, when using the plural *Antiphone*, be referring to the different sizes of Plessner's *Antiphone*, which were available for purchase. As articulated in Plessner's brochure, the invention was, in fact, available in different sizes to suit the ear holes of each customer.

What does this brief historical contextualization of the earplug reveal? How does *Ohropax* fit into the wider picture of the history of the earplug? From the creation of the German Reich in 1871 until the invention of Negwer's *Ohropax* in 1907, there were at least three different earplugs or ear protectors registered for patents: Plessner's *Antiphon* (1884), Bothmer's *Kopfbinde* (1906), and Sprenger's *Antiphon* (1907). *Ohropax* should, in this respect, be seen as a consequential continuation of this trend and not really as the first earplug. Yet out of all of these inventions, *Ohropax* stood the test of time, and this formulation of the earplug was, according to the company's Web site, "so perfect that it has remained practically unchanged up to the present day!"[25] Besides the perfect formula of stable and skin-friendly paraffin waxes and types of Vaseline, what other factors can be attributed to Negwer's initial success, which would lay the foundations for the future? In addition to the fact that Negwer supplied earplugs to the German army toward the end of the loud First World War,[26] another possible answer to this question lies in Negwer's own marketing campaign: a set of posters encapsulating sounds and silence, displayed in German pharmacies from the 1930s, by which time *Ohropax* was fast becoming a household name.

LET THE NOISY NEIGHBORS' MUSIC PLAY ON: NO NEED TO TURN DOWN THE VOLUME WITH *OHROPAX*

Despite R. Murray Schafer's claim that all "visual projections of sounds are arbitrary and fictitious,"[27] some soundscape experts have started to argue for the importance of acoustic interpretations in visual imagery, especially given the absence of audio sound recordings prior to the invention of sound recording equipment in the late nineteenth century. In his wide-ranging music-historical publication *Music in Late Medieval Bruges* (1985), Reinhard Strohm argues convincingly that late medieval Bruges is known to us through the stillness of pictures. Motion and sound are contained in them, but in a frozen form: reduced to an infinitely small fraction of time. Given the added dimension of time, the pictures would start to move, and the music would be heard.[28]

Under the chapter title "Townscape-Soundscape," Strohm enters the realm of soundscape studies with his interdisciplinary method, combining visual analysis of artistic depictions of urban musical life with traditional methods of historical archival research. With his background firmly rooted in music, Strohm uses his eye to listen to sounds gone-by. This theme has not only been picked up by, among others, Steven Connor in his essay "Sound and the Self,"[29] but the detailed pictorial analysis of perceived *sound images* to discover past soundscapes has fed into Simon Schema's sensual investigation of Amsterdam in *Rembrandt's Eyes* (1999).[30] All of these examples have at least one thing in common: a space that is experienced through sound. Following this strand, how are sound, noise and even silence depicted in the posters that Negwer had commissioned for pharmacies in Berlin in the late

1920s and early 1930s? How is Negwer's *Ohropax* invention portrayed in these images? What kind of space is created to allow the wearer of *Ohropax* to temporarily escape the urban din?

Advertising *Geräuschschützer für Lärmnervöse* (Ear Protectors for People Nervous because of Noise), the designer of the poster commissioned by Negwer in the 1920s portrays the *Ohropax* earplug as the respite from a particular type of noise: the noise generated by a then-new blending of airplanes, trains, motors, and automobiles (see Figure 1.1). In an era of increased mobility, a significant rise in the decibel level around cities was documented, so much so that Negwer clearly saw a need to commission a poster subtitled *Gegen Maschinen & Motorenlärm auf Reisen über Land und Meer* (Against the Noise of Machines and Motors when Traveling over Land and Sea). Here, the *Ohropax* earplugs are targeted at certain customers: those who want to escape the din of traffic whilst on the move.

The effect of the earplugs is illustrated in this commercial poster (Figure 1.1) by the winged angel figure. More notably, *Ohropax* is embodied in the angel's palms that cover the ears of the *Lärmnervöse[n]* (person nervous because of noise). The obvious connection here is between the company, the earplugs, and the palms (the oldest and most frequently used earplug of them all), creating a private sound "bubble" in which noise has no place. This interpretation bears striking similarities to today's iPod-wearing urban commuter, attempting to create his or her own soundspace while moving through various soundscapes. It is noteworthy that the eyes of the angel and the *Ohropax*-wearing individual appear closed: the earplugs not only have the desired effect of bringing peace and quiet to the individual's ears, but they appear to make these modes of transport invisible. Moreover, the merging of these different modes of transportation at the bottom left-hand side of the poster reflects the merging of these sounds in the acoustic environment, from which the *Lärmnervöse[r]* is so desperately trying to escape. The black bar running down the center-left of the poster, reminiscent of a *Lärmschutzwand* (soundproof wall), creates a private soundspace inside of which the *Lärmnervöse[r]* escapes the noise of traffic and finds silence and tranquility.

Advertising a box of six pairs of *Ohropax* earplugs for two *Reichsmark*, the underlying message of this particular poster is the ability of the *Lärmnervöse[n]* to shut himself off from the noisy urban soundscape by wearing *Ohropax* earplugs. Yet these noises, depicted on the poster and pushed to its outer extremities, are, nevertheless, still present in the auditory environment. There seems to be a general acceptance by the poster's creator, whose signature appears at the top left-hand side of the poster, and, indirectly by the commissioner, Negwer, that noises cannot simply be eliminated from the auditory environment altogether. Earplugs can, nevertheless, engineer a significant reduction in unwanted noise without the *Lärmnervöse[r]* demanding an unrealistic and nonimplementable halt to *all* transport. The earplug, one might venture to suggest, is a solution that is tailor-made to the needs of the silence-searching individual in an increasingly noisy world.

It was not only the sounds and noises of the "lo-fi soundscape" or "sound congestion"[31] of the inventions from the industrial and electric revolutions, against which Negwer targeted his advertising; it was the scourge of neighbors' noise penetrating through the cavities in the walls (see Figure 1.2). In the second in a series of posters,[32] given the simple title *Geräuschschützer* (Ear Protectors), the scene differs slightly from the previous poster. Referring specifically to everyday life rather than special vacation or travel purposes, the

Figure 1.1
"Ear Protectors for People Nervous because of Noise" poster commissioned by Maximilian Negwer for chemists' shop windows, c. 1930.

Figure 1.2
"Ear Protectors" poster commissioned by Maximilian Negwer for chemists' shop windows, c. 1930.

poster depicts the well-deserved German *Feierabend* (evening after work) after a long hard day: on the left-hand side of the poster, the two young gentlemen are having fun playing musical instruments, and on the right-hand side of the poster, an elderly gentleman is relaxing in his armchair, smoking a cigar and reading his newspaper. The dress and activities of the figures point to the connection between noise and age, if not (very subtly) to noise and class; while the two younger gentlemen are of a somewhat indeterminate class, their older neighbor's more luxurious lifestyle is indicated by his three-piece suit (now without the jacket at the end of the day), bowtie, and cigar. What we see in the poster, however, is that there is no reason for tension to exist between neighbors or classes. Neither disturbed nor agitated by the music making of his neighbors, the elderly gentleman is in the company of the winged angel, who is once again covering his ears. The music can continue, but the man is not bothered by it. Though the earplug buyer does not hear the sounds and noises evoked in the posters per se, they would not only understand the auditory message contained in the frozen poster, but they may recall similar auditory experiences involving anything from noisy neighbors to the din of traffic. In this respect, the visual triggers an auditory recall of the previously heard.

One such purchaser of the *Ohropax* brand, who definitely would have sympathized with the central figure suffering from the scourge of noise in these posters, was Franz Kafka, the German-language author and playwright who suffered from a hypersensitivity to noise and noises. Kafka could not have seen the *Ohropax* posters, as they did not start appearing in chemist outlets until the 1930s, some six years after his death in 1924. Nevertheless, the solitary figure searching for peace and quiet in Negwer's posters could just as easily have been Kafka, who is known to have sent for *Ohropax* earplugs from Prague. In a letter to Felice Bauer, dated 1915, just one year after the start of the First World War, Kafka informs his female companion: "For the day-to-day noise I have had an aid sent in from Berlin . . . OHROPAX, a type of wax wrapped in cotton wool."[33] Unlike the impression gained from the poster, Kafka admits that the insertion of the earplugs into the auditory canal does not completely stop the noise, just simply reduces it: "[The *Ohropax* earplug] is a little greasy and tiresome blocking one's ears up whilst still alive. However, they don't stop the noise, just muffle it—but still."[34]

Kafka's concluding sentences on the earplug do make for interesting reading. Quoting the novel *Am offenen Meer* (*By the Open Sea*, 1890) by the Swedish author August Strindberg, Kafka equates himself with the main protagonist of this novel, presumably Axel Born: "the hero, suffering from a similar affliction as mine, had some so-called sleeping balls, which he bought in Germany—little steel balls that slide into one's ears. But, alas, I think they were just invented by Strindberg."[35] Given the fact that Strindberg had this book published in 1890, six years after the patenting of a prototype earplug, and given that Kafka's description of the earplug worn by the protagonist in Strindberg's novel resonates with Plessner's *Antiphon*, Strindberg may in fact have been referring to Plessner's invention, of which Kafka, in turn, may not have been aware, as Plessner's *Antiphon* had long since been replaced by very different, chemically based earplugs. Though feasible, because of the sheer lack of evidence this claim remains unsubstantiated. Herein lies the problem with the untold history of the earplug: the sound experience (or lack of it) whilst wearing earplugs is difficult, if not impossible, to record in audio. It has, therefore, gone largely unrecorded and undocumented at the expense of audible soundscapes, heard without earplugs and with two ears. Any future *magnum opus* of the earplug, yet to be written, will have to take this untold story into account.

LESSING'S ANTI-NOISE SOCIETY

As a keen collector of newspaper articles, Theodor Lessing kept weighty scrapbooks of cuttings from local, national, and international newspapers and magazines. One such scrapbook, today housed in the *Stadtarchiv Hannover* (Hannover City Archive), features a number of cuttings from 1908 on the urban noise problem blighting German cities, from full-spread newspaper articles on noisy neighbors and late-night gramophone playing to calls by health professionals for tighter laws against noise to halt the rapid rise of cases of the modern illness of neurasthenia. Lessing would have sensed, through this visual media, that he was not alone in his aural sensibilities toward the acoustic bombardment of urban noise on the ear. The scrapbook's existence proves that he would have been fully aware of the call of Richard Batka, music critic of the German *Kunstwart* magazine, for a society against the "Verlärmen unsres Lebens" ("noise pollution of our lives") in April 1908.

Lessing was acquainted, too, with a proposed law concerning the damage to health through noise by the Frankfurt neuropsychologist Siegmund Auerbach, who just five years prior had linked urban noise with neurasthenia. Lessing clearly followed scientific breakthroughs in acoustics as well, ones that would eventually lead to quantitative measurement of sound in the 1920s: he knew, for instance, of the invention of a so-called *Lärmmesser* (noise meter) by a Professor Rubner in Berlin in early 1908 that could determine the number of acoustic shockwaves that hit the ear at any one time.[36] It is in the context of heightened public sensitivities toward urban noise as expressed in numerous newspaper articles and journals at the time, of legal loopholes that did little to protect the sanctity of quiet, and of scientific endeavors to give numerical value to the subjective phenomenon of noise, that this earplug-wearing, noise-sensitive German philosopher and cultural critic established the *Antilärmverein* (Anti-Noise Society).

Lessing's endeavor was much more than the mere establishment of a noise-abatement movement to reduce the city's volume, either by public agitation or practical and legal measures. The publication of *Der Lärm* (*Noise*) months before the establishment of the Anti-Noise Society proved, beyond a shadow of a doubt, that a deeply complex, in part Nietzsche-inspired and in part Schopenhauer-inspired, cultural philosophical critique on noise informed his public call in mid-1908 to declare a war against the urban din. Though Lessing later toned down his theoretical language for newspaper articles and the society's monthly journal to cater to a wider, popular audience, anyone who referred back to his quasi-manifesto *Der Lärm* would have been greeted with theses on noise that were highly critical of modern-day culture and not just of noisy gramophones, telephones, automobile horns, piano playing, factory machines, church bells, chiming clocks, barking dogs, and carpet beating. Noise as an instinctual human "Urtrieb" (primal urge) that satisfies a drug-dependent-like consciousness or "Bewußtseinsnarkose"[37]; noisemaking as a will to power, more evident in working classes as opposed to upper classes; and the noise generated by elites in voicing their loud opinions in newspapers, magazines and journals—these theses would clearly speak to intellectuals and cultural critics, but did little to engage a wider audience. It is no wonder, then, that Lessing was dismissed as a nervous *Lärmprofessor* (noise professor) by some quarters of the press and newly created automobile associations, when he founded the society: his sociophilosophical thoughts, expressed in *Der Lärm* in a rather pseudo-academic manner, would have alienated popular opinion makers, offended working-class people, and baffled nonintellectual classes.

The personality, philosophy, and polemic nature of Theodor Lessing predetermined the fate of the Anti-Noise Society: it was one of a quick decline and then a retreat by its founder, who gave up the editorship of the journal in 1911. Members who joined the cause within the first year, such as the authors Hugo von Hofmannsthal, Alfred Kerr, Ludwig Fulda, and the cultural historian Max Dessoir, gave Lessing's Anti-Noise Society some of the cultural acceptance for which he yearned in the attempted establishment of a *Kulturmacht* (cultural force) and a "Partei der anständigen Leute" ("party of respectable people") to fight noise. But by November 1909, just over a year after the creation of the *Antilärmverein*, he reported, somewhat disheartened and disappointed, that he had fallen well short of the projected 6,000-member target despite prior reassurances of support and offers of help. Lessing's first end-of-year report in 1909 gave a sense of what he was up against: criticisms about the title of the journal (which was changed no fewer than three times), complaints about the too wide or too narrow approach of the society, as well as accusations of inaction and class warfare. Ironically for Lessing, a society established to combat noise was—to use his own thesis of noise in the written media—creating more noise than the founder bargained for. To add insult to injury, the press played on the German word *Termiten* (termites) and poked fun at the expense of the Anti-Noise Society members, who were ridiculed as *Antilärmiten* (Anti-Noise-ites) in caricatures and humor columns of newspapers. Lessing's sociophilosophical enterprise, then, perhaps owing to its inherent "anti-" nature and its scorn by the press, failed to capture the public's imagination in a way that Negwer's colorful depictions of noise and silence, together with his one- or two-line slogans, later would.

Despite its short life and a membership profile confined to the intellectual and professional classes, predominantly in the urban centers of Berlin, Munich, Hannover, and Frankfurt, the society did score some limited successes, most notably the publication of *Blaue Listen* (*Blue Lists*) of quiet hotels and resorts where one could escape the urban din. Lessing reported this idea to Julia Barnett-Rice, the chairwoman of the New York based Society for the Suppression of Unnecessary Noise, at the first ever international anti-noise conference held at the Ritz Hotel in London in August 1909, and it was soon adopted by Rice in the form of "houses of silence" in the United States.[38] However, these minor successes, some local, others international, did little to alter public perceptions that Lessing's society was an intellectual-class attack on the whole auditory environment. The *Antiphon*, the earplug that Lessing tried, is, semantically speaking, the single best word to describe his own writings on noise and his social fight against it: *antiphonic*. The word embodies an aversion to anything phonic and noisy, and stands in direct contrast to the sound- or noise-generating devices of the time: the gramophone and the telephone. Whilst Lessing berated such phonic devices in his writings, these were, for the vast majority of the population, objects of fascination and symbols of technological advancement and progress. For many Germans, living in a relatively new nation that was trying to project its technological prowess to the outside world, Lessing's written attacks on, for instance, the telephone and the gramophone were *viel Lärm um Nichts* (literally: lots of noise about nothing; the idiomatic equivalent: much ado about nothing).

PARALLEL PROJECTS FOR SILENCE

For urban noise to receive such sustained treatment by German cultural figures, scientists, doctors, and legal experts in the early twentieth century, sensitivities to noise were heightened to an extent whereby the search for antidotes to the city din was, by 1908, well under way. These antidotes were direct responses to a surge in complaints about urban noise, a sense by the medical community that noise was one of the causes of the modern-day illness of neurasthenia, and a fear that hearing loss was on the rise. As this study has shown, Theodor Lessing's Anti-Noise Society and Maximilian Negwer's *Ohropax* were two such antidotes in a number of quests to engineer a significant or total reduction of urban noise. Some similarities between the two particular projects existed: the chronological start, the emphasis of quiet in their proposed remedies, the employment of the print media to get their message or product across, and the commercial aspect to their endeavors. Behind these similarities, however, hide fundamental differences in their projects, ones that are bound up in the contrasting biographies of a controversial philosopher from Hannover and a fairly unknown chemist in Berlin; in differing theorizations between Lessing and Negwer of what noise, quiet, and silence were; and in distinct class interests to exert direct control on the loud, boisterous urban noisescape—or to leave one's neighbors in peace. Herein are the underlying reasons why Negwer's *Ohropax* can be regarded as achieving great success and Theodor Lessing cannot.

Negwer's antidote was disposable, easy-to-use, and tailor-made to externalize the individual's aural sensory sphere from the loud interior of the urban din without having to physically leave this noisy auditory environment. Through its marketing, *Ohropax* created the impression of private sound bubbles, where its users could find some sense of peace and quiet. But as Franz Kafka attests, *Ohropax* did not seal off all urban noise from the ears, but just partially absorbed it. The earplugs, therefore, offered temporary relief, not complete escape, until these irritable noises had died down. Lessing's antidote, on the other hand, was trying to call "time!" on many of these irritable noises through a philosophy on noise, public agitation, and tighter legislation prohibiting the playing of musical instruments during the day, legally pursuing persistent noisemakers, and classifying noisemaking as a hygienic offense. On attempting to end these noises, he alienated those individuals who were fascinated by, attracted to, or inspired by them.

Lessing's theorization of noise as a serious disease-ridden plague and menace to public health, as a hallmark of cultural degeneration and primitive behavior, informed his project to create a cultural force to exert social pressure on the wider society to change its noisy ways. This theorization of noise spoke predominately to the intellectual class, consisting of doctors, academics, philosophers, and historians: quiet was imperative for their work and for intellectual contemplation, in the absence of which they would not be able to concentrate on the tasks at hand. As both Plessner and Lessing observed, thousands of intellectual work hours were being lost to the urban din. But this theorization would not have spoken to the working classes, many of whom worked to and depended on the rhythm of the loud drone of machines in factories on a daily basis. Negwer's theorization of noise neither entertained this sort of intellectual elitism toward noise displayed by Lessing, nor could his colorful poster campaign be seen as an attack on the working classes. Indeed, Negwer's caricaturization of noisy situations satirized noise and skillfully employed symbolic visual imagery that spoke to a range of thoughts and emotions of his customers, irrespective of class: the winged angel suggests religious notions of peace and quiet; the palms indicate a deep human, even primitive, instinct to use one's hands to plug one's ears; and, to the technologically minded, manmade sound barriers speak to creating private silent sound spaces. Attuned to deep human and religious instincts as well as technological ideals, Negwer's theorization of noise did more to transcend class distinctions in the debate on urban noise while Lessing, perhaps subconsciously, did more to entrench them through his Anti-Noise Society.

NOTES

1. My translation of the following text: "Ich liebe den großstädtischen Lärm. Ich liebe jeden Lärm, der auf ein freies, reges, temperamentvolles, lustiges, heiteres Leben schließen läßt. Der Lärm des großstädtischen Betriebes ist mir Bedürfnis." Quoted in Theodor Lessing, *Recht auf Stille* (Munich: Verlag der Aerztlichen Rundschau, April 1909), 110.
2. My translation of the following text: "Mein Buch soll Signal werden zu einem allgemeinen Kampf gegen das Übermaß von Geräusch im gegenwärtigen Leben . . . [Ich] hoffe auf Verwirklichung eines allgemeinen, internationalen Bundes wider den Lärm, der Einfluß auf Strafgesetz, Zivilgesetz, Verwaltungs- und Polizeigesetzgebung erlangt. Auf seinem Banner soll stehen: 'non clamor sed amor.'" In Theodor Lessing, *Der Lärm* (Berlin: Mayer, 1999), 44.
3. Though the exact dating of the formation of the *Antilärmverein* is difficult, the first traceable reference of Lessing's *Antilärmverein*, which exists in a newspaper scrapbook in the Theodor Lessing *Nachlass* (Estate) in Hannover's City Archive, is a newspaper article dated April 3, 1908, one month after the publication of his work *Der Lärm*. This article places the *Antilärmverein* in Munich. Months later, on August 18, 1908, however, the *Bonner Zeitung* reports: "Ein Bund gegen den Lärm ist, wie schon berichtet nach amerikanischem Vorbild von Dr. Theodor Lessing in Hannover gegründet worden." Found in Theodor Lessing's estate at the Stadtarchiv Hannover, No. 2555, 18–20.
4. I refer to my correspondence with Michael Negwer, the grandson and current managing director of the *Ohropax* company, now based in Wehrheim im Taunus in the federal state of Hesse. After sifting through the company's archives in the run-up to the hundredth anniversary of the *Ohropax* invention, Michael Negwer informed me that there is no documentary evidence available to suggest that Negwer knew or was aware of Theodor Lessing's Anti-Noise Society and vice-versa. Writing on September 20, 2007, Michael Negwer informs that "wir haben keine Hinweise darauf, dass sich Theodor Lessing und mein Großvater Max Negwer kannten." Michael Negwer, e-mail messages to author, September 19, 2007 and September 20, 2007.
5. Peter Bailey, "Breaking the Sound Barrier," in *Hearing History. A Reader*, ed. Mark Smith (Athens: University of Georgia Press, 2004), 34. This article first appeared in 1996.
6. Ibid., 34.
7. Ibid., 26.
8. Elisabeth Bennion, *Antique Hearing Devices* (London: Vernier Press, 1994), 3.
9. Ibid., 1.
10. Ibid., 3.
11. This claim was made on the front page of Bonn's *General Anzeiger* newspaper with the headline: "Zum Weghören: Ohropax gehört zu den bekanntesten Markennamen in Deutschland" Bonn, October 22, 2007, 1.
12. Muriel-Larissa Frank, "Die Ruhekugel," *Frankfurter Rundschau*, September 13, 2007, 29.
13. Sabine Maurer, "Die Stöpsel, die für Ruhe sorgen," *General Anzeiger*, October 22, 2007, no page number.
14. Sabine Maurer, "100 Jahre Frieden im Ohr," *Berliner Morgenpost*, October 22, 2007, 1.

15. Theodor Lessing, *Recht auf Stille*, 156.

16. "German Patent Register" is my own anglicized abbreviated version of the "Register zu den Auszügen aus den Patentschriften Jahrgang 1903. Verzeichniss der von dem Kaiserlichen Patentamt im Jahre 1903 ertheilten Patente" (Berlin: Carl Heymanns Verlag, 1904). Herein referred to as "*German Patent Register*" in English and "*Verzeichnis der Patente*" in German.

17. *Verzeichnis der Patente* (Berlin, 1903), 132; and *Verzeichnis der Patente* (Berlin, 1904), 124.

18. My own translation of the following text from the *German Register of Patents*: "Kopfbinde gegen Schlaflosigkeit mit an verstellbaren Schnüren endenden Bauschen aus Watte udgl. zum Einführen in die Gehörgänge." *German Patent Register* (Berlin, 1909), 550.

19. My own translation of the following description of the *Antiphon* in the *German Patent Register*: "Wattebausch, mit Paraffinöl und Hartparaffin getränkt 205 305." Ibid., 550.

20. The full entry from the *German Patent Register* for 1884 (1885): "29 516—Plessner, M., Königl. Preuss. Hauptmann a. D. in Stuttgart, Kronprinzstr. 20b. Vorrichtung zum Verschliessen der Ohren, genannt Antiphon 30. Mai 1884." In *German Patent Register* (Berlin, 1885), 52.

21. My translation of the following text: "Mit Hilfe des billigen Antiphons wird nunmehr namentlich auch den unbemittelteren, die geräuschvolleren Stadtviertel bewohnenden Kopfarbeitern die langentbehrte Wohlthat gewährt werden, ihren Berufsgeschäften in ungestörter Ruhe nachgehen zu können. Millionen von Stunden werden solcher Weise der produktiven Gedankenarbeit gewonnen werden, und die fruchtbarsten Ideen dem ungestörten Denkorgan der Forscher entkeimen können." In Maximilian Plessner, *Die neueste Erfindung. Das Antiphon: Ein Apparat zum Unhörbarmachen von Tönen und Geräuschen* (Rathenow: Verlag von Schulze und Bartels, 1885), 16–17.

22. Friedrich Nietzsche, "Architektur der Erkennenden," in *Friedrich Nietzsche. Die fröhliche Wissenschaft. Gesammelte Werke. Zwölfter Band* (Munich: Musarion Verlag, 1924), 204–205.

23. My translation of the following text: "Der Lärm aber ist die impertinenteste aller Unterbrechungen, da er sogar unsere eigenen Gedanken unterbricht, ja zerbricht." In Arthur Schopenhauer, "Über Lärm und Geräusch," in *Parerega und Paralipomena. Kleine philosophische Schriften. Zweiter Band*, ed. R. von Koel (Berlin: Verlag von Moritz Boas, 1891), 647.

24. My translation of the following text: "Ein wahres Loblied müßten wir bei diesem Ueberfluß an Geräusch dem Erfinder der Antiphone singen, wenn diese Apparate nur brauchbarer wären. Ich verwende, nachdem ich von Antiphonen aller Art die unangenehmsten Wirkungen gesehen habe, kurze Zäpfchen aus Hartgummi, welche die relativ besten Schalldämpfer und wahre Menschentröster sind." In Theodor Lessing, "Über den Lärm," in *Nord und Süd. Eine deutsche Monatsschrift*, ed. Paul Lindau (Breslau: Druck und Verlag von S. Schottländer, April 1901), 80.

25. *Ohropax* Web site: www.ohropax.de (accessed on March 17, 2008).

26. For a detailed description of the First World War as the Loud War see Yaron Jean's chapter "The Sonic Mindedness of the Great War: Viewing History through Auditory Lenses" in this book.

27. R. Murray Schafer, *The Tuning of the World* (Toronto: McClelland and Stewart, 1977), 127.

28. Reinhard Strohm, *Music in Late Medieval Bruges* (Oxford: Oxford University Press, 1985), 8–9.

29. Steven Connor, "Sound and the Self," in *Hearing History. A Reader*, ed. Mark Smith (Athens: University of Georgia Press, 2004), 54–66.

30. Simon Schama, *Rembrandt's Eyes* (London: The Penguin Press, 1999).

31. Schafer, *The Tuning of the World*, 71.

32. To view other advertisement posters, please go to the *Ohropax* Web site at www.ohropax.de.

33. My own translation of Kafka's comments about *Ohropax* in a letter to his friend and companion, Felice Bauer: "Für den Tageslärm habe ich mir aus Berlin . . . eine Hilfe kommen lassen, OHROPAX, eine Art Wachs von Watte umwickelt." Franz Kafka, letter to Felice Bauer, April 5, 1915, in *Briefe an Felice*, ed. Erich Heller (Frankfurt am Main: Fischer, 1967), 632.

34. My translation of lines from Kafka's letter: "Es ist zwar ein wenig schmierig, auch ist es lästig sich schon bei Lebezeiten die Ohren zu verstopfen, es hält den Lärm auch nicht ab, sondern dämpft ihn bloß—immerhin." Ibid., 632.

35. My translation of lines from Kafka's letter: ". . . der Held [hat] ein ähnliches Leid, wie ich es habe, sogenannte Schlafkugeln, die er in Deutschland gekauft hat, Stahlkügelchen, die man ins Ohr rollen läßt. Es scheint aber leider eine Strindbergische Erfindung zu sein." Ibid., 632.

36. For these specific cuttings from early 1908, please refer to Lessing's newspaper scrapbook with their numerous articles on urban noise. Theodor Lessing's estate at the Stadtarchiv Hannover, No. 2555. Tying into Dr. Rubner's *Lärmmesser* invention, Sabine von Fischer's chapter "From Seat Cushions to Formulae: Understanding Spatial Acoustics in Physics and Architecture" in this book provides more in-depth elaborations on the scientific quantitative measurement of sound, its historical trajectory, and future applications.

37. Lessing, *Der Lärm*, 51.

38. Lessing, *Recht auf Stille*, 244.

CHAPTER 2

When Only the Ears Are Awake

Günter Eich and the Acoustical Unconscious

ROBERT G. RYDER

Imagine a world in which the dreams of others are not only accessible but newsworthy: a world in which journalists could gain access to the dreams of our political leaders or the dreams of everyday people around the globe in the course of a single day; where reporters could cite from these dreams, and one could see and hear the dream images of others on television or radio; a world in which such "dream reports" would be as significant as the summary of world events or national news. By finding out what a group of people dream about from a given region or country, one would gain access to their collective unconscious. If one compared what people are dreaming about on a global scale, it could be possible to catch a glimpse of what affects everyone, regardless of country or culture. Now imagine that one could only *hear* those dreams. Such would be the world that German lyricist, dramatist, and author Günter Eich (1907–1972) invited his listeners to with his most famous radio play, *Dreams* (*Träume*, 1951).[1]

Eich's *Dreams* has often been compared with the famous radio play in American history, Orson Welles's *The War of the Worlds*. Broadcast on Halloween, 1938, the play convinced thousands of listeners that aliens from Mars had invaded planet Earth. Welles's brilliant narrative method included breaking news coverage and on-site reporting, making it seem to "those just tuning in" that the aliens had landed and were wreaking havoc on cities across the country. Though Günter Eich's *Dreams*, by contrast, convinced no one that they were actually tuning in on people's dreams, it can be compared to Welles's *War of the Worlds*, because of how much controversy was generated during their original broadcasts.

The initial reaction of the German public to Eich's *Dreams*, which was broadcast at 8:50 P.M. on April 19, 1951, was overwhelmingly negative. During its premiere, the telephone operator at the Hamburg Northwest German Radio (NWDR) was flooded with callers complaining about its indecent content.[2] It is not difficult to understand why Eich's *Dreams* triggered so visceral a reaction in the German listening public: the five dreams unambiguously suggest scenes of deportation, execution, cannibalism, and the threat of being either hunted by an

unknown enemy or consumed from within for attempting to be content in a postwar consumerist society. Despite this inauspicious beginning of his postwar career, Eich went on to
write many radio plays and is now generally lauded as initiating the "golden age" of German
radio in the early 1950s. As Mark E. Cory wrote, the public anger provoked by Eich's *Dreams*
was "one measure of his achievement," while his other, "more telling measure of achievement . . . was the proliferation of dream plays, as studio after studio became a kind of
'acoustical dream laboratory.'"[3]

Many have discussed Eich's *Dreams* in psychological and sociopolitical terms, while
others have read it in accordance with reception theory. All of these critics have limited themselves either to the written page or to the play's effects on society. While it is necessary to
understand the impact the play had on its contemporary radio audience and the history of
German radio drama in general, what has been lost in previous critical analyses is, simply put,
its *acoustical* transmission. In 2007, the original broadcast was made available to the public
for the first time in over fifty-five years.[4] For a poet who once admitted that he perceived reality with his ears rather than with his eyes,[5] it is indispensable that one study Eich's plays with
one's ears as well. This chapter invites the reader not only to read, but to *listen* to the original
1951 broadcast and explore the relationship between its language and the voice that speaks
it, examining pronunciation, direction, and sound accompaniment.

The history of the German radio play, however, did not start with Eich's *Dreams*.[6] The first
German radio play, though it was neither called a *Hörspiel* (radio play) at the time nor did it
last more than fifteen minutes, was broadcast in 1924 by Hans Flesch. Titled *Zauberei auf
dem Sender: Versuch einer Rundfunkgroteske* (*Magic on the Air: Attempt at a Radio-Grotesque*),
it was broadcast exactly one year after the opening of the German airwaves to the public.[7]
Between Flesch's initial "attempt" at a radio play and Eich's full-fledged *Dreams* of 1951, the
radio play as a genre went through numerous alterations in form, content, and even name.
The presently accepted German word for radio play, "das Hörspiel," did not gain sure footing
in the parlance of Weimar-era radio culture until 1929, when it was defined in contrast to
another genre: the *Sendespiel*, which was a radio play based on a previously written drama or
text (like the term *Hörbuch*, or audio book today). The *Hörspiel* "was supposed to be a completely new work, composed exclusively for broadcast, which took into account the particu-
larities of a medium that was entirely acoustic."[8] The burgeoning radio culture of the Weimar
Republic, whose heyday lasted from 1924 to 1930, witnessed an explosion of acoustic and
radiophonic experiments from Walter Ruttmann's *Weekend* (1930) and Bertolt Brecht's
Lindberghflug (*Lindbergh's Flight*, 1929) to Alfred Döblin's radio adaptation of *Berlin
Alexanderplatz*. But Döblin's radio play, scheduled for the end of September 1930, never
aired, due at least in part to the changes in the political environment. As Peter Jelavich wrote,
this "marked a turning point in Weimar broadcasting: thereafter, radical right-wing ideas
were heard with increasing frequency on the airwaves, and the Nazis were able to stifle voices
critical to their views."[9]

But this did not mean that the Nazis eliminated the radio play genre. In his radio speech
in August of 1933, the newly appointed Minister of Propaganda, Dr. Joseph Goebbels, admitted that they would set aside "room for entertainment, popular arts, games, jokes, and music"
in radio. "But," he continued, "everything should have a relationship to our day."[10] To this end,
all radio plays produced from 1933 to 1945—and there were many—were heavily censored
for content and effect. While this particular history of the radio play has little bearing on this

chapter, it should nevertheless be recognized that Günter Eich himself wrote radio plays during the Nazi regime. Most of his plays during this time would fall under the category of the *Sendespiel* described above—that is, as adaptations of work by other authors. As Glenn Cuomo pointed out, Eich's reasons "for concentrating on adaptations in this period are clear enough, since such writing was particularly suitable for his situation. Adaptations required a minimum of creative effort on his part, making them quick and easy to produce."[11] But Eich also wrote a number of *Hörspiele* during the Nazi regime, and so the controversy persists over whether Eich's was "a passive assent, politicised by the conditions of dictatorship," or his multiple contracts with the Reich Radio Society (Reichs-Rundfunk-Gesellschaft, or RRG) involved "a more active attempt to support or even collaborate with the new regime."[12]

The particular focus of this chapter, however, is not concerned with entering into the critical debate over Eich's extent of conformity to the National Socialist ideology. Instead, this chapter is motivated by a reading of Eich's most famous postwar radio play, *Dreams*, and how it exemplifies specifically for radio art what I call the "acoustical unconscious." The term is a variation on Walter Benjamin's theory of the "optical unconscious," a term he pursued in two of his seminal essays, "Little History of Photography" (1931) and "The Work of Art in the Age of Mechanical Reproduction" (1935–1939). While Benjamin's particular reception of Freudian psychology is worth its own anthology of essays, it is obvious from the very combination of words, "optical unconscious" ("das optische Unbewußte"), that Benjamin modified Freud's fundamental insight for his own purposes. Only by listening to the relationship between voice and language, to vocal projection and the accompanying sounds is it possible to hear how Eich taps into an acoustical unconscious that forces listeners to awaken to and contend with the collective history of which they are a part.

RADIO PSYCHOLOGY

In his recent contribution to the history and theory of both German and American radio, titled *Das Radio*, Wolfgang Hagen concluded the first half of the book by emphasizing that both psychology and psychosis are necessary when developing an epistemology of German radio:

> My thesis is that, as a technical medium, radio articulates a reality and facticity of hearing voices from which we cannot escape and which radio wires us into at the same time. In this way, radio irreversibly broadens our means of perception and also our knowledge of hearing voices by referring us to the self-articulated ambivalence of hearing voices through the demand of the unconscious. . . . In distinction to America . . . the medium in Germany has absolutely no chance of eluding its strong psychotic inheritance.[13]

One of the leading scholars of German radio history today, Hagen is adamant that radio is not a medium of anxiety or psychosis per se; rather, it contains a "knowledge that articulates itself,"[14] a knowledge of hearing voices (*Stimmenhören*) particular to the medium and which is inextricably linked, as the thesis above indicates, to the unconscious. But precisely how this knowledge of hearing voices is connected to the unconscious is difficult to articulate.

Hagen discussed two characteristics of the unconscious that might help us to elucidate the relationship between the unconscious and hearing voices. First, following Freud and Lacan, Hagen wrote that "hearing voices is an act of the unconscious and is accompanied, determined and driven by the desire to want to hear voices."[15] Hagen relied here on the long and complex history of the psychoanalytical treatment of the human voice in order to connect the medium of radio to the unconscious. The second characteristic that Hagen attributed to the unconscious is Freud and Lacan's shared belief, "that the unconscious has a linguistic structure, that the unconscious is a speaking [*ein Sprechen*], that the unconscious speaks."[16] In short, Hagen described the unconscious both in terms of hearing voices and as a voice that speaks. Radio, it seems, is the voice of the unconscious. To put it another way, while Hagen explicitly stated that radio is not "a medium of anxiety or something like it,"[17] he nevertheless implied that it is a medium of the unconscious.

Hagen's second quality—that the unconscious speaks—leads us back to Walter Benjamin's influential essay, "The Work of Art in the Age of Mechanical Reproduction." Benjamin described the role of the camera in the following terms: "Clearly, it is another nature that *speaks* [*spricht*] to the camera than to the eye. Other above all in the sense that a space [*Raum*] interwoven with human consciousness gives way to a space interwoven with the unconscious."[18] This means that, while the naked eye sees a certain way, the camera is privy to another nature that speaks to it. This nature, of course, does not speak a language that can be "heard" acoustically, but it is "other" because the language that it speaks is accessible only through the medium *to* which it speaks. This is what justifies, for Benjamin at least, the optical unconscious: a technological medium or prosthesis is necessary for the optical unconscious to be thought. Photography and film have access to another kind of nature, one that the naked eye cannot perceive.

In conjunction with Hagen's thesis, the same can be said of acoustical media: another nature speaks to the microphone than to the naked ear. Citing Freud and Lacan's view that the unconscious is a language that speaks, Hagen offers all the necessary elements to develop the acoustical unconscious in terms of radio. If, for Benjamin, the optical unconscious in film amounts to a reorganization of conscious and unconscious perceptual data, such that in film we begin to see things that we have never *consciously* seen with the naked eye, for Hagen, the acoustical unconscious in radio offers a unique way of hearing voices and sounds that was previously unheard—and unheard of—until radio.

This is one side of the acoustical unconscious—one might say its technical requirement or "other nature" inspired by Benjamin's theory of the optical unconscious. But before concluding this section, I would like to dwell on one major point: when examining Benjamin's optical unconscious or proposing its acoustical variant, I am not referring specifically to the unconscious as such, but rather to a *becoming conscious* of what could not have been previously observed without the technological medium in question. To reiterate, the acoustical unconscious is the index for new modes of acoustical experience that become conscious in ways that previously could not have been experienced. This is what is meant when Benjamin writes that "film has enriched our field of perception (unsere Merkwelt bereichert),"[19] an observation that Hagen echoes sixty-five years later when he writes that "radio irreversibly broadens our means of perception (unsere Wahrnehmungsweisen erweitert)."[20] The optical and acoustical unconscious, as working terminology, thus presuppose extensions of perceptual experience. It would be misleading to suggest that we are concerned only with the unconscious per se, as if that were possible. Eduardo Cadava is right to say that, "for both Benjamin and Freud, neither the unconscious nor the conscious can be thought independently of one another—there can be no passage between them without there already being relays or paths that would facilitate such a passage."[21] Film and radio are media that facilitate such pathways. The concern is not so much the unconscious itself as the *awakening* to acoustical modes of perception previously left unheard.

AWAKENING TO DREAMSCAPES AND SOUNDSCAPES

While Benjamin was a prolific writer and a renowned essayist, it is not well known that he also wrote a number of radio plays, including a series of radio lectures for children (which he called *Hörmodelle*) and even a few unpublished texts about radio itself. In his two-page "Reflections on Radio" ("Reflexionen zum Rundfunk") written in 1931, Benjamin was specifically concerned with how radio had not been used properly in his day. He argued that instead of being given the chance to react critically, the radio public had been converted into "dull, inarticulate masses—a public . . . that has neither yardsticks for its judgment nor a language for its feelings."[22] He compared it to other cultural art forms and institutions, writing that, "Until now there has never been a genuine cultural institution that has not authenticated itself as such through an expertise *awakened* [*erweckt*] in the public based on the strength of its forms and technology."[23] Radio, for Benjamin at least, had the same potential as film, theater, or any other art form to authenticate itself, a process that can only be accomplished once the public *awakens* to its potential.

This returns us to Eich's *Dreams*. If every cultural institution involves a process whereby the public learns to judge art by awakening to its particular forms and technique—to its "other nature"—then the ability to judge requires that one is and remains awake.[24] Although it may sound paradoxical, the whole point of Eich's *Dreams* is to wake up. Two lines from the closing poem indicate the absolute wakefulness that Eich calls for: "Wake up, because your dreams are terrible! / Stay awake, because the horror comes closer."[25] These lines could stand in for the play as a whole, since all five dreams depict, in their own fashion, not just the nearing threat of *das Entsetzliche* (the horrible), but how we are powerless to escape it.

Before we go any further, it is necessary to distinguish what both Benjamin and Eich wanted to awaken in the public ear. As we have seen, Benjamin wrote about how the listening public of his day had not been given a yardstick by which to judge the medium of radio. Unfortunately, Benjamin would not live to experience the awakening of the "dull, inarticulate masses" of the listening public to radio art. Radio plays, especially in Germany, are generally regarded as epitomizing the aesthetics of radio broadcasting. One of the first national indications of this growing awareness in the public was the inauguration in 1950 of the Blind Veterans' Radio Play Prize (Hörspielpreis der Kriegsblinden), which remains to this day the most prestigious award given to radio plays in Germany. Even though Eich's plays from the 1950s helped to raise the awareness that Benjamin sought, Eich's *Dreams* was not specifically the historical turning point for the "inarticulate masses" to awaken. While Benjamin's call for awakening is pedagogically and aesthetically motivated, Eich's motivation in *Dreams* is fundamentally moral and sociopolitical. This is not to say that aesthetic and moral "awakenings" are mutually exclusive, but rather that Eich made use in *Dreams* of the emerging aesthetic awareness of radio to pursue his own political agenda. By emphasizing the all-too-human character of Nazi Germany's crimes and extending them into the moral malaise of Western culture as a whole, Eich used *Dreams* to criticize the listening public both for their passive acceptance of the former and desire to integrate into the latter. The most famous line of the play encapsulates this call to rise against submission: "Be different, be sand, not oil in the world machinery!"[26]

But why did Eich employ dreams to awaken his listeners to their bad conscience and moral proclivities? There are multiple reasons for this, but this chapter focuses on the three most important ones: a peculiar characteristic of the auditory sense, radio's affinity toward dreams, and the significance of dreams in psychology. These three parameters can more generally be categorized under phenomenological, radiophonic, and psychological headings, but all of them affect each other and combine to make the notion of dreams the most useful vehicle for Eich's message of wakefulness.

The first reason (the phenomenological) is because of what it means to listen. More than any sight that a viewer beholds, sounds penetrate all who hear them. Don Ihde writes in his *Phenomenology of Sound* that our auditory field and auditory focus is "not isomorphic with visual field and focus, it is *omnidirectional*":

> In the shape of the auditory field, as a surrounding thing, the field-shape "exceeds" that of the field-shape of sight. Were it to be modeled spatially, the auditory field would have to be conceived of as a "sphere" within which I am positioned, . . . If I hear Beethoven's Ninth Symphony in an acoustically excellent auditorium, I suddenly find myself *immersed* in sound which *surrounds* me. The music is even so *penetrating* that my whole body reverberates, and I may find myself absorbed to such a degree that the usual distinction between the senses of inner and outer is virtually obliterated. The auditory field surrounds the listener, and surroundability is an essential feature of the field-shape of sound.[27]

While these are not unique claims, they clarify just how indistinguishable the threshold is between the hearer and the heard. Unlike vision, where the perceiver and the perceived can be clearly demarcated, the acoustical realm more easily allows for the fluid *interpenetration* of perceiver and perceived. The breakdown of the boundary between inner and outer, subject and object, that defines the acoustical sphere, is one of the most intriguing characteristics that distinguish the auditory realm from the visual one. As demonstrated by the examples that follow in this section, the localizing of the listener in relation to what is being heard becomes especially problematic when there is the added ambiguity between reality and fantasy.

This leads to the second reason why Eich employed dreamscapes: because of their affinity to the medium of radio and to the genre of the radio play in particular. As Justus Fetscher wrote in a recent article, "The radio play's presentation of sound material is unable to distinguish the fictitious from the factual, dream from reality, the paranormal from the normal."[28] How much this affinity of the genre is due to its reliance on the omnidirectional auditory field described earlier is debatable. It is indeed one thing to be immersed in Beethoven's Ninth Symphony in a concert hall and another to listen to Eich's *Dreams* on the radio or through headphones. So while it is true that the lines between both subject-object and reality-fantasy tend to blur in the radio play, it does not follow that the lack of a subject-object dichotomy necessarily leads to a blurring of reality and fantasy. What is clear is that radio plays tend to "epitomize illusion and auditivity by playfully exploiting and challenging them, and thus making them conscious for the listeners."[29] To make auditory illusions conscious is analogous to the "other nature" of radio that we examined in the first section. To reiterate, this other nature speaks differently to the microphone than to the naked ear, and it is "other" above all because different, previously unconscious spaces stretch, expand, and overlap into conscious ones. Another way to say this is that the radio play in particular, with its specific presentation and organization of sound material, draws for us a different conscious and unconscious auditory map, one that superimposes dream and reality upon the same soundscape.

Last but not least, Eich made use of dreams because of their significance in the history of psychology, a history that began exactly fifty years earlier with Freud's *Interpretation of Dreams* in 1901. Freud indisputably legitimized the dream as an object of psychological study by developing his theory of dream analysis, an activity that Freud famously described as "the royal road" to understanding unconscious mental processes. Psychoanalysis involves the patient to awaken to his or her own unconscious desires and fears. Eich's *Dreams* cannot be thought of without psychology, and Eich confronted his *conscious* listeners with their bad dreams, asking them to wake up from them. He did not ask his listeners to interpret the dreams, nor did he offer any direct interpretation of the dreams himself. And yet, Eich amplified the already intimate connection between radio play and dreamscape not simply to make the auditory ambiguity all the more conscious, but to imbue this becoming conscious of an auditory illusion with moral obligation and political awareness. What links Freud's psychology to Eich's *Dreams* is the necessity to awaken to unconscious mental processes, but, whereas Freud wished to advance science, Eich was motivated by the advance of society and each citizen's moral responsibility within it.

These three key elements—the interpenetration of the hearer and the heard, the play between reality and fantasy, and the dream as symbolic barometer of one's hidden fears and desires—together help us to understand why Eich used dreams to pursue his agenda of social and political awakening in *Dreams*. German radio theory has always had to deal with the medium's affinity with the fantastic and the dream; Wolfgang Hagen's thesis that we read before concerning the role of the unconscious is no exception. But when defining the acoustical unconscious, I am not referring specifically to radio's *affinity* to dreams, but rather to how the medium rearranges our everyday soundscape to make us aware of sounds and voices that we would normally not be conscious of. The acoustical unconscious refers to a different way of perceiving the world through a particular medium. While this different mode of perception may elicit a dreamy, fantastical, or "other worldly" effect, the effect is less important than what is made conscious that previously was not and why. The following short analysis of the first of five dreams in Eich's radio play is meant as a model of reading—and listening to—particular elements like voice and sound accompaniment that signal a becoming conscious of that which was previously acoustically unconscious.

FIRST DREAM

Dreamt by Wilhelm Schulz, a German locksmith, between the first and second of August, 1948, the first dream of Eich's *Dreams* invites the listener to imagine a group of people in a freight car devoid of lights. The incessant noise of a slow-moving train and some other voices in the wagon are all we hear. The story revolves around the memories of an old couple, who can just barely remember when they used to live outside of the freight car. Two other generations of their family, their grown-up grandchildren and their great-grandchild, Frieda, also occupy the dark train car with them. It becomes clear that, while the old couple might have once had a happy existence beyond the freight car, everyone else has no recollection of the outside world, nor do they believe there is one.

As in many of his other plays, like *An Hour with the Encyclopedia* (*Eine Stunde Lexikon*, 1931) or *The Year Lazertes* (*Das Jahr Lazertes*, 1953), *Dreams* introduces characters that repeat a particular word or phrase. The old man and woman remember strange words from a temporally (and ever more spatially) distant world. One word in particular, "Löwenzahn" ("dandelion") is repeated because it, like the distant memory of the outside world, becomes increasingly difficult to remember with each passing minute. The old woman who first told her husband, "Dandelion—what strange words you use!"[30] asks him not long after:

> Very Old Woman: What is the flower called that you spoke about, the yellow one?
> Very Old Man: Löwenzahn.
> Very Old Woman: Löwenzahn, yes, I remember.[31]

As in the other radio plays just mentioned, Eich's focus on words and names that are either being constantly forgotten or mutating into similarly sounding words that bring with them new memories or meanings is a hallmark of his radio work, proving how attuned he was to the acoustical fragility of a word. This particular passage is not the last time the image of a yellow flower is mentioned, but it will be the last time its name is spoken; that is to say, the last time the word for the flower is remembered. Particularly significant is the way Eduard Marks, who played the old man in the original 1951 broadcast, articulates "Löwenzahn": he hesitates on and then repeats the first syllable, "Löw-" when answering his wife, as if he can barely remember the word. The breaking down of the word's articulation by Marks—which could never be recognized if one simply read the words on the page—further makes conscious the word's combination of "Löwe" ("lion") and "Zahn" ("tooth").

What ultimately breaks apart is the relationship between signifier and signified: words and names begin to peel away from their putative meaning and become meaningless sounds.[32] This exemplifies the unique play between diction and language made possible by radio. Radio's "other nature" allows a word, through its saying, to more easily split from its given meaning because of its attention to the purely auditory and phonetic construction of the word. Another way to say this is that, in radio at least, the conscious meaning of a word more easily gives way to a word's unconscious elements—its sound qualities, its inflection, rate, and intonation. Eich was very aware of this potential, which is one aspect of how radio sounds out the acoustical unconscious.[33]

Another example of the specific use of the voice in radio involves less a play between pronunciation and word than between vocal direction and displacement. A significant moment in the dream occurs when the characters recognize a hole in the wall, through which they can get a glimpse of the outside world:

> Very Old Woman: If there's a hole in the wall, we should be able to look outside.
> Grandson: Okay, I'll look outside.

Very Old Woman: What do you see?
Grandson: I see things that I don't understand.
Wife: Describe them.
Grandson: I don't know what words belong to them.
Wife: Why don't you look out anymore?
Grandson: No, I'm afraid.[34]

The very old man (*Uralter*) and very old woman (*Uralte*) subsequently look through the hole and recognize things they have not seen for forty years, including a field of yellow flowers. But by listening carefully to the voices in the broadcast during this passage, we realize that it is not the *diction* but the *direction* of the voice that is crucial. When the middle-aged grandson looks out of the hole, his voice changes considerably: instead of speaking to one or another family relative, he seems to speak *directly* to the radio listener by speaking closer into the microphone.

In 1951, director Fritz Schröder-Jahn used this recording technique whenever any of the characters "looked out" from the hole; it gives the acoustical impression that they are not just "looking out" but actually "speaking out" from the freight car in which they are imprisoned.[35] Two inferences can be made from this change of vocal direction and distance. First, the listener might conclude that the characters are speaking directly to him, as if his ears were pressed up on the other side of the hole, listening in. The idea that they could glimpse the outside world through the listener's ears describes a unique experience of synesthesia, whereby one looks into an ear to see out. According to this scenario, surreal as it may sound, the radio listener would be located outside of the freight train and therefore part of the outside world. This introduces the dimension of space into this acoustical experience: the listener feels physically transported into the play's space.

But a second, more sinister inference could be made: if one imagines the characters' voices not as external to oneself but as internal—speaking from *within* one's mind—then their view of the outside world merges with that of the listener. According to this interpretation, the listener's mind doubles as the dark freight car, so when the grandson looks through the hole, he is looking through the listener's eyes and speaking with his voice. The listener is therefore inclined to open his eyes and look out into the outside world *with* the grandson, as if the listener was the grandson, the very old man, and very old woman, confronting the outside world with them.

Whichever interpretation is correct—and the ambiguity of the auditory field allows for both interpretations simultaneously—Eich and director Schröder-Jahn split the position of the radio audience between these two scenarios: the radio audience is *both* outside of the freight car hearing in and inside the freight car looking out. This is what was meant before when "the usual distinction between the senses of inner and outer is virtually obliterated."[36] The fundamental displacement of the listener, involving at once participation and partiality, generates a crisis of localization whereby the listener can never fix a single place or position on which to stand, and as such is always on the alert, always listening for what is to come. In this example, displacement and alertness are generated not through the diction of the voice, but through its direction and distance.

This final example from the first dream of Eich's *Dreams* further complicates the issue of displacement, but this time not through the voice, but through another acoustical feature of the 1951 performance: the accompanying sound of the freight train heard throughout the dream. All five dreams feature a particular sound that not only lends structural unity to the dream as a whole, but is also integral to the narrative of that dream. In the final dream, for instance, the sound of termites devouring the insides of buildings and humans alike is heard both by the characters in the dream and by the listening audience, a technique often referred to as "point of audition" (as opposed to point of view) and further embellished in Eich's play of the same year, *F sharp with Overtones (Fis mit Obertönen)*.[37]

The acoustical mise-en-scène of the first dream, which involves the unmistakable sounds of a train rolling over tracks and the rhythmic sounds of a steam engine, immediately presents the listener with a general idea about where the voices are. The train itself could be anywhere, but it is clear that the voices are inside a train and that it is on the move. But as the dream unfolds, the incessant sounds that upon first hearing indicate a slow-moving freight train begin to suggest the sounds of someone sleeping. The low, rhythmic booms of the train as it moves over the tracks sounds like the beating of a heart, while the higher sighs of the distant steam engine conform almost uncannily to the deep breathing of a sleeper.

The suggestion that the sounds of a slow-moving train in a dream echo the sounds of the body as it experiences that dream—an echo that, again, can only be perceived by listening to the radio play—is not an unusual phenomenon. During sleep, it is natural that the body's unconscious perception of both internal and external stimuli determines, at least in part, what is dreamt. This phenomenon is usually recognized at the moment of awakening, when we realize, for instance, that the siren of the ambulance in our dream was really our alarm clock. What is unusual is when we are given the opportunity to recognize this process of unconscious translation by hearing both at the same time, that is, when the listener hears both the sound in the dream and the stimulus that is causing it to be a part of that dream. In Eich's first dream, radio listeners simultaneously hear the train and the sounds of the dreamer as his body unconsciously translates its internal sounds into the sounds of the train. This is the only instance in all of Eich's *Dreams* where the dreamer's presence is implied, however obliquely. It is important to understand that the train sounds are unconscious acoustical translations of the internal sounds of the dreamer's body while he is sleeping. Just as the sounds of a word begin to separate from its meaning when pronounced differently, and just as the listener is split between participation and partiality, the accompanying sound of "trainness" oscillates disjunctively between the sound of a train in dream consciousness and the sound of a body sleeping.

I would like to conclude by showing how the example of a train that is also the bodily sounds of the dreamer is reminiscent of a passage Benjamin wrote in *The Arcades Project*. The way a sleeper's internal bodily noises and feelings are translated into dream images acts as a model for how Benjamin thought of the dreaming collective and its urban body:

> Just as the sleeper . . . sets out on the macrocosmic journey through his own body, and the noises and feelings of his insides, such as blood pressure, intestinal churn, heartbeat, and muscle sensation . . . generate, in the extravagantly heightened inner awareness of the sleeper, illusion or dream image which translates and accounts for them, so likewise for the dreaming collective, which, through its arcades, communes with its own insides.[38]

The sound of a freight train generated by a dreamer's heartbeat and breathing echoes these remarks if we imagine that the dreamer of Eich's first dream—Wilhelm Schulz, German locksmith—represents the German dreaming collective. The consequence is that we hear the breathing of the sleeping collective as it translates the sounds of its internal organs into that of a train. This suggests that Eich's intention was for the German dreaming collective to awaken to itself by hearing itself dreaming. This example thus leads us to the notion of a *collective* acoustical unconscious, for in learning to hear consciously what its own body, with its "exceptionally heightened inner awareness,"[39] unconsciously translates into the dream, the German dreaming collective awakens to its own unconscious processes and is forced to contend with its own body as collective history.

Much more can be said about how the listeners of Eich's *Dreams* awaken to previously unconscious acoustical knowledge of voices and sounds, both in this dream and the four remaining ones.[40] By perfecting a radiophonic language that calls attention to the disjunction between word and sound, de-centers the listener, and discloses the unconscious translation of sounds into acoustical dream images, Eich systematically dismantles the ear, banishing through sound the private realms that would otherwise allow an individual refuge from what Frederic Jameson has called the omnipresence of history and the implacable influence of the social.[41] Explicitly calling for a future community that must no longer seek refuge in either its history or its dreams, Eich recruits a radiophonic language whose "other nature" speaks a different constellation of acoustically conscious and unconscious data. Subsequent readings of Eich's work would have to take into account awakening to this new configuration, to this mode of hearing when only the ears are awake.

NOTES

1. At the same time that Eich's *Dreams* was being broadcast, the Westdeutscher Rundfunk (West German Radio) was developing a new studio for electronic music. Brett Van Hoesen and Jean-Paul Perrotte's chapter discusses this type of sonic experimentation in greater depth.
2. Karl Karst's extensive notes in the dust jacket of the 2007 compact disc release includes transcriptions of a selection of callers' vehement reactions to the radio play. Also included on disc three is a "Musikalischer Epilog" by Hans Schüttler, who mixes concrete sounds and rhythmic beats with fragments of callers' reactions originally recorded in 1951. Günter Eich, *Träume* (Der Hörverlag, 2007). CD.
3. Mark E. Cory, "Soundplay: The Polyphonous Tradition of German Radio Art" in *Wireless Imagination: Sound, Radio, and the Avant-garde*, eds. Douglas Kahn and Gregory Whitehead (Cambridge, MA: MIT Press, 1994), 351.
4. The recent release on compact disc also includes a new dramatization of the radio drama performed and recorded in 2007, allowing us the rare opportunity to compare the vocal and theatrical techniques in the original broadcast with those used today.
5. Justus Fetscher, "Blindness and 'Showside': Non-Visual Aspects of German Radio and Radio Plays in the 1950s," *Monatshefte* 98: 2 (2006): 250.
6. The end of Yaron Jean's chapter points to the increasing importance of the radio after World War I. Here I focus on one aspect of radio's use: the *Hörspiel*.
7. For a detailed description and analysis of Hans Flesch as *der Hörspielmixer* see Daniel Gilfillian's *Pieces of Sound: German Experimental Radio* (Minneapolis: University of Minnesota Press, 2009), especially pages 67 to 75.
8. Peter Jelavich, *Berlin Alexanderplatz: Radio, Film, and the Death of Weimar Culture* (Berkeley: University of California Press, 2006), 82.
9. Ibid., 93.

10. Joseph Goebbels, "Radio as the Eighth Great Power," ed. and trans. Randall Bytwerk et al. German Propaganda Archive, www.calvin.edu/academic/cas/gpa/goeb56.htm (accessed December 15, 2010). "Wir wollen der Unterhaltung, der leichten Muse, Spiel, Scherz und Musik bereitesten Spielraum geben; aber alles soll eine innere Beziehung zur Zeit haben." Joseph Goebbels, *Signale der neuen Zeit. 25 Ausgewählte Reden* (München: Zentralverlag der NSDAP), 205.

11. Glenn R. Cuomo, *Career at the Cost of Compromise: Günter Eich's Life and Work in the Years 1933–1945* (Amsterdam: Rodopi, 1989), 66.

12. Matthew Philpotts, *The Margins of Dictatorship: Assent and Dissent in the Work of Günter Eich and Bertolt Brecht* (Oxford: Peter Lang, 2003), 197. The texts of both Cuomo and Philpotts are excellent English resources for Günter Eich's life and work during the Nazi regime.

13. "Meine These ist, dass das Radio als technisches Medium eine Realität und Faktizität des Sprechen-Hörens artikuliert, der wir uns nicht entziehen können, und an die uns das Radio gleichsam ankabelt. Insofern erweitert das Radio irreversibel unsere Wahrnehmungsweisen und auch unser Wissen über das Stimmenhören, indem es uns auf die durch das Begehren des Unbewussten selbst artikulierte Ambivalenz des Stimmenhörens verweist . . . Im Unterschied zu Amerika . . . hat das Medium in Deutschland gar keine Chance, seinem starken psychotischen Erbe zu entkommen." Wolfgang Hagen, *Das Radio: Zur Geschichte und Theorie des Hörfunks—Deutschland/USA* (München: Wilhelm Fink Verlag, 2005), 136–137. Translations mine unless otherwise noted.

14. "Dieses Wissen artikuliert sich." Ibid., 136.

15. "Stimmenhören ist ein Akt des Unbewussten und von dem Begehren begleitet, bestimmt und getrieben: Stimmen hören zu wollen." Ibid., 134.

16. "dass das Unbewusste eine Sprachstruktur hat, oder genauer: dass das Unbewusste ein Sprechen ist, das(s) das Unbewusste spricht." Ibid., 134.

17. Ibid., 136.

18. "So wird handgreiflich, daß es eine andere Natur ist, die zu der Kamera als die zum Auge *spricht*. Anders vor allem dadurch, daß an die Stelle eines vom Menschen mit Bewußtsein durchwirkten Raums ein unbewußt durchwirkter tritt." My emphasis. See Walter Benjamin, *Gesammelte Schriften*, vol. 1 (Frankfurt am Main: Suhrkamp Verlag, 1974), 500. English translation found in *Selected Writings*, vol. 4 (Cambridge: Harvard University Press, 2003), 265. Since most—though not all—of the Benjamin passages cited have been retranslated at least in part, subsequent citations will be referenced first by the German edition (GS), then by the Harvard University Press publication of the *Selected Writings* (SW).

19. Benjamin, *GS*1, 498; *SW*4, 265.

20. Hagen, *Das Radio*, 136.

21. Eduardo Cadava, *Words of Light: Theses on the Photography of History* (Princeton, NJ: Princeton University Press, 1997), 99.

22. "stumpfen, unartikulierten Massen—das Publikum im engeren Sinn . . . das keine Maßstäbe für sein Urteil, keine Sprache für seine Empfindungen hat." Benjamin, *GS*2, 1506; *SW*2, 543.

23. "Nie hat es noch ein wirkliches Kulturinstitut gegeben, das sich als solches nicht durch das Sachverständnis beglaubigt hätte, das es kraft seiner Formen, seiner Technik im Publikum *erweckt hätte*." My emphasis. See Benjamin, *GS*2, 1506. In the official translation of this sentence in the *Selected Writings*, "erweckt" is translated as "created" (*SW*2, 544).

24. Much more can be said here in terms of Benjamin's theory of awakening, especially the way the human body is central to his definition of consciousness. I will address this issue briefly at the end of this article.

25. "Wacht auf, denn eure Träume sind schlecht! / Bleibt wach, weil das Entsetzliche näher kommt." Günter Eich, *Gesammelte Werke*, vol. 2 (Frankfurt am Main: Suhrkamp, 1973), 321.

26. "Seid unbequem, seid Sand, nicht das Öl im Getriebe der Welt!" Trans. Egbert Krispyn, *Günter Eich* (New York: Twayne Publishers, 1971), 73.

27. Don Ihde, *Listening and Voice: The Phenomenology of Sound* (Athens: Ohio University Press, 1976), 75. Original italics.

28. Fetscher, "Blindness and 'Showside,'" 246.

29. Ibid.

30. "Löwenzahn—was du für merkwürdige Wörter gebrauchst!" Eich, 291.

31.
    Uralte: "Wie hieß die Blume, von der du vorhin sprachst, die gelbe?
    Uralter: "Löwenzahn."
    Uralte: "Löwenzahn, ja, ich erinnere mich." Ibid., 291

32. This reaches its thematic height and ethical significance in the dream when the grandchild, a grown man, argues with the old man that he should not speak of such meaningless words. Ibid., 292.

33. Parallel to this potential of words splitting from their meaning is the equally disjunctive tendency in Eich's radio plays of voices that split from their (oftentimes barely) established identity. It would be worth pursuing, for instance, how separation itself becomes the constitutive factor between word and meaning, voice and identity.

34.
    Uralte: "Wenn ein Loch in der Wand ist, müßte man hinausschauen können."
    Enkel: "Gut, ich schaue hinaus."
    Uralte: "Was siehst du?"
    Enkel: "Ich sehe Dinge, die ich nicht verstehe."
    Frau: "Beschreib sie."
    Enkel: "Ich weiß nicht, welche Wörter dazu gehören."
    Frau: "Warum schaust du nicht weiter hinaus?"
    Enkel: "Nein, ich habe Angst." Ibid., 294.

35. Director Alexander Schuhmacher did not use this vocal technique in the 2007 production of this dream. He did, however, entirely modify the soundscape of this dream from the earlier version. A particularly unique example of this is the use of a high-pitched tone to sonically imitate the *Sonnenstrahl* (sunbeam) streaming through the hole when it is first discovered.

36. Ihde, *Listening and Voice: The Phenomenology of Sound*, 75.

37. For the theoretical implications of comparing "point of audition" with "point of view" shots in film, see Michel Chion's book, *Audio-Vision* (New York: Columbia University Press, 1994). It should be pointed out that these "point of audition" sounds used in Eich's *Dreams*, whether they are drums in the distance (fourth dream), the heavy approach of footsteps (third dream), or even the sounds of the train speeding up (first dream), are amplified as each dream comes to an end. This technique implies the increasing threat to the listener's safety, a threat that Eich explicitly describes in the line from the closing poem already cited.

38. "Wie nun der Schläfer . . . durch seinen Leib die makrokosmische Reise antritt und die Geräusche und Gefühle des eigenen Innern . . . Blutdruck, Bewegungen der Eingeweide, Herzschlag und Muskelempfinden in seinen unerhört geschärften innern Sinnen Wahn oder Traumbild, die sie übersetzen und erklären, zeugen, so geht es auch dem träumenden Kollektivum, das in Passagen in sein Inneres sich vertieft." Benjamin, *GS5*, 491; *AP* 389.

39. "seinen unerhört geschärften innern Sinnen." Ibid.

40. For instance, the diction at the end of the first dream is significantly different between the 1951 and 2007 radio productions.

41. Frederic Jameson, *The Political Unconscious. Narrative as a Socially Symbolic Act* (Ithaca, NY: Cornell University Press, 1981), 20.

Defining Space through Sound

Battlefields and Concert Halls

A s Goodyear's chapter on urban noise illustrated, sounds do not occur in a vacuum; rather, they are intimately connected with the spaces in which they occur and with the environments in which they are perceived. When those frustrated by the urban din in German cities of the early 1900s could not leave the physical space to escape the noise, they sought out novel ways to change their space by blocking out unwanted sounds—using earplugs— and thus creating their private soundscapes. Robert Ryder discusses dream spaces that are not tangible and only exist in the spaces of the radio play by German author Günter Eich, into which the listeners feel physically transported. While these chapters show how sound affects the way that one perceives a space, the converse is also true: a space changes the perception of sound. The two chapters in Section II examine both inside and outside spaces and consider how sound can be used to understand or organize knowledge about a space (in one case, a battlefield), and how the perception of sound impacts the way that a space is specifically designed (such as a concert hall).

Examining the different soundscapes of three distinct battlefields (in the air, on the ground, in the sea), Yaron Jean approaches World War I from a sound perspective; drawing on information about military history, he demonstrates how this complex historical event was perceived by those involved in battle, even—or especially—when vision was obscured by fire, smoke, clouds, or water. The soldier was forced to map out the battlefield in front of his ears and to learn how to distinguish between the sounds of danger and sounds of safety. Jean calls this alertness and the ability to immediately distinguish between the two—and to then act instantly on this decision—"sonic mindedness." Through the auditory "lenses" of the three battlefronts, Jean shows to what extent the sensory experience of the Great War as a technological war relied on the transition from the visual to the acoustic. In this context, sounds could save lives.

Just as sound creates distinct spaces of safety or danger, as demonstrated by Jean, so, too, can sound create a space that is harmonious or discordant in less dire circumstances.

The sounds in concert halls might not save lives, but these sounds, too, clearly define a space. Sabine von Fischer, a journalist and architect, explores the physical relationships between sounds and their spaces. Her history of selected modern concert halls is also a history of architectural acoustics, as she explains the ways that building material, the shape of a space, and its reverberation time all affect the way the listener perceives that soundscape. Moving beyond the physical measurement of sound waves, von Fischer asks how the quantitative values of the science of acoustics are related to qualitative understanding of experience in the social sciences and the arts. In a more general sense, von Fischer is concerned with how sound affects our experience of an architectural space.

CHAPTER 3

The Sonic Mindedness of the Great War

Viewing History through Auditory Lenses

YARON JEAN

The famous photographer Robert Capa once noted that he chose to be a photographer because, as a young Jewish immigrant from Hungary, nobody spoke his native language. For him, photography served as a universal language to express emotions and feelings beyond the scope of the written word. During his short and stormy career as a photojournalist before his death in 1954, Capa's photographs became in many respects the visual *lingua franca* of the modern war and its horrors. His images from the first half of the twentieth century changed the conception of both photography and journalism. Like photographic images, sound, too, can function as a language to communicate detachment from a specific mother tongue. The study of sounds can provide an auditory lens through which one can seek to understand historic events. An "ear-witness" can convey his associations of given sounds with a given place and share his experiences with others. The establishment of such sound environments as a common language to describe the combat experience of the First World War in Germany (1914–1918) from the perspective of individuals involved in the war is the focus of this chapter.

Because of new technological developments and their large-scale employment, the First World War was significantly louder than its predecessors. Its increased volume led to a major shift in auditory perception *on* the battlefields: war was not only *seen* anymore, for the extensive use of new technology presented an obstruction to vision.[1] The large-scale employment of indirect and rapid fire on the battlegrounds nearly dissolved the visual presence of the enemy who was now merely considered a "target *area*." Blinded by smoke and explosions and under rapid and indirect fire, the modern infantry soldier found himself in a sightless world. Yet his sense of hearing compensated for the loss of vision; in order to survive the hostile situation, he gradually learned to listen and to tune his ears to the soundscapes of war. Although sight was lost on the battlefields, its metaphors and tropes continued to fuel the auditory perception of the soldiers on the front, leading to an amalgam of senses. What did the First World War sound like and how did certain sounds influence the experience of it?

What was the significance of hearing in the modern battlefields? How did the "auditory lens" help soldiers conceptualize the three major German battlefronts? And how can this help us understand the First World War as a seminal catastrophe, which defined the course of German history?

The Great War is considered by many to be an historical watershed for German history and, like other collective traumas, it imprinted its long-term influences in a relatively short period. The modern war as a prototypical historical event is an already established scholarly topic. In their illuminating discussions, Paul Fussell, Samuel Hynes, and Marc Ferro have changed the way we understand the First World War and perhaps war in general:[2] not only as a matter of large-scale military engagement between states, armies, and ideologies, but rather as a social and cultural turning point in a time of general crisis. These scholars suggested new ways to observe war not only as one major, solid event, but rather a dynamic and abstract occurrence that consisted of many separate situations labeled collectively as a war. This separation is an important notion when considering the fact that the First World War was fought on three major battlefronts, which will be examined separately in this chapter: the battlefronts on the ground, in the sea, and in the air.

An inspection of the soundtracks of these three distinct battlefronts is the first step in "hearing" the war. In answering these questions, one must also inquire into the mechanisms that translated individuals' auditory experiences of the war into collective cultural experiences. Kept alive in the cultural archive of memory, these auditory experiences later played a dominant role in the Weimar Republic.[3] Viewing the battlefields of the First World War through "auditory lenses" enables us to illuminate the complex relationship between sounds and their meanings. No less significant, it encourages us to suggest ways to interweave soundscape history within the broader context of political, social, and cultural change. The concrete situation of the battlefield serves as a suitable historical framework to provide a shape to the abstract and fuzzy character of sounds and noises and assist in pinpointing them within a clear context of time and place.

THE AUDITORY LENS AND SONIC MINDEDNESS

Sounds (including noises) are first and foremost a matter of physiological reception. "The vibration of the air comes to be a sound first by encountering an ear," [4] noted the famous German scientist and philosopher Georg Christoph Lichtenberg (1742–1799) in the late eighteenth century. Unless these faculties are disabled, the human ability for sensory experience of the world crosses boundaries of time, place, gender, and class. Yet what context is needed to give these sensory experiences their unique meaning? Can an individual's sound experience of war be translated into a (version of a) collective cultural experience? To identify representative examples of the sound experience of war, one must look for common markers of experience. The highly dangerous situation in the battlefield with its immanent sense of fear and uncertainty seems to be the most dominant element of any experience of battle and therefore suggests itself as a starting point.

Being "under fire," especially in the modern battlefield of the First World War, meant daily exposure to danger and its sounds, such as the thunder of explosions, shells, and machine-gun fire; sounds of safety, on the other hand, could be found as well, such as all-clear sirens.

The modern soldier was at all times able to decode all heard sounds into one of these two categories to differentiate between safety and danger in the extreme and hostile situation of the battlefield. Motivated by the universal human desire to survive, the soldier developed the ability to tune his ears in order to immediately categorize the heard battle sounds and instantly act on a decision—an ability that I call wartime sonic mindedness. Surrounded by loud explosions of artillery and the rattle of rapid fire on the front (or confronted with deafening noise at the ammunition factories in the hinterland), many experienced the loud sound vocabulary of the modern war machinery for the first time. Though only a minority was directly exposed to the sounds of war as soldiers on the front, many others were affected by the sounds of war as civilians and therefore developed wartime sonic mindedness as well. They, too, based their actions on the distinction between sounds of danger and sounds of safety; a habit that, once acquired, they did not lose after war, and one that helped shape the interwar period.

THREE THEATERS OF WAR

I present three modes of auditory perception during the First World War personified by three different German soldiers: (1) the modern infantry soldier who learned to tune his ears to the noisy soundscapes of the modern battlefield, (2) the member of a submarine crew who had to create his isolated soundscape based solely on auditory perception due to a lack of vision underwater, and (3) the pilot in the air who faced a completely different kind of soundscape (or lack thereof) as his eye from above discovered a soundless image of the battlefield. Each of the three battlefields—on the ground, in the sea, and in the air—limited the sensory environment in a way that forced the soldiers to redefine their modes of perception; only by adjusting to their new role could they act. These three theaters of war can give us a three-dimensional perspective of the sound environment of the Great War in a way that can help us explain not only *what* people heard, but also, and no less important, *how* they heard and how that influenced their perception of the war at large. This shift in perception, from visual to auditory, led to the new sonic mindedness and a unique sound vocabulary at each battlefront.

Noisy Grounds

A few years before the outbreak of the First World War, German military experts warned about the dangers of the coming armed conflict in a publication of 1907: "The bigger and more complicated armies become, the deeper the misunderstanding gets between the real war and military training in times of peace."[5] Indeed, the acoustic impact of the newly introduced artillery and automatic weapons could not be practiced, for these sounds came in at a volume that could, and still can, hardly be imagined (see Figure 3.1). To help auralize the sounds on the ground consider the following numbers: At the beginning of the war in 1914, there were about 7,680 artillery cannons of different types on the German side. In 1918, the records show that about 2,800 artillery batteries fired more than ten thousand shells in a month.[6] Consequently, the sound of artillery became the soundtrack of the battlefield, or, to

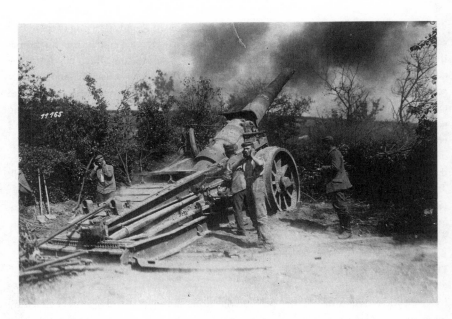

Figure 3.1
German artillery (17 cm cannon) in France, July 1917.
Bundesarchiv, Photo 102-00277A. Photographer unknown.

use the words of a British officer in the war, "As the master of the battlefield, [the artillery's] thunder was like a gigantic force that never stopped, day or night."[7]

The new warfare technology had dire consequences because it shifted the focus of the battle from duel fighting to a mass engagement, as one could no longer identify individual enemies but rather blurry areas or groups of people. As vision lost its focus, sound came to the fore in the Loud War.[8] Yet volume is not only a quantitative value but is also perceived qualitatively, as positive or negative. Ludwig Scholtz, a field medic volunteer on the Eastern front, articulated the meaning clearly conveyed by sound when he described the rattling of machine guns as unfamiliar and inspiring a sense of foreboding.[9] The dominance of sound as a defining marker in the battlefield experience did not limit itself to a nonmediated encounter with an unfamiliar soundscape. Gradually, the soundscape caused the modern soldier in the trenches to tune his ears to the unfamiliar situation and adjust, thereby assisting him in surviving in battle. After a while, he could easily distinguish between the sounds of friends and of enemies, solely by hearing sounds of explosions. Nuances in the sounds of artillery became important; they could make the soldier feel protected or threatened. He could determine his distance from the enemy by hearing an explosion or gunfire, and this helped him decide how urgent the situation was. This tuning of ears also separated the experienced soldiers from new recruits. Whereas the former could "read" the sounds and immediately act depending on their classification, the inexperienced soldier was still confused—for him, the soundscape of the battlefield consisted of hostile sounds only; he had not yet trained his ears to differentiate between the various sounds of danger and the sounds of safety.[10] This acoustic division served as a precondition for the infantry soldier to survive the extreme situation of the battlefield.

This was particularly true for the trench warfare on the Western and Eastern fronts where sight was lost behind barbed wire fences, mounds of earth, and the smoke of explosions.

The increasing significance of auditory over visual perception on the battlefield drew scholars' attention already during the war. In 1915, the *Zeitschrift für Sinnesphysiologie* (*Journal of the Physiology of the Senses*) published a study that described the influence of acuity of vision at day and night on the auditory perception of the human ear. The research concluded that the accuracy of aural identification was lower during the day when vision could take over. The acuity of hearing increased again after darkness when visibility decreased.[11] A year later, in the article "Das Ohrlabyrinth als Kompass" ("The Inner Ear as Compass"), another scholar went even further to suggest that the soldiers on the front used their ears as a kind of acoustic compass to locate sounds in space.[12] However, for those at sea, the rumbling thunder of the ground front was replaced with the noisy silence of the deep, creating a different rubric of wartime sonic mindedness among the submarine crews.

Blinded Eyes

There is no doubt that one of the most remarkable fronts in the First World War was the underwater front. Although the idea of an underwater weapon was not new, it was the German submarine offensive during the First World War that gave the submarine its symbolic character in the history of naval warfare. The use of ultramodern technologies in order to fight underwater ignited the public imagination in all of the warring nations. Ironically, the massive usage of submarine warfare was established as a compromise between ambitious strategy on the one hand and lack of suitable battleships on the other. Therefore, one can go a step further and argue that submarine warfare from its very beginning was not established through objective capabilities, but was based on its psychological effect as a kind of *Wunderwaffe* (wonder weapon) that would win the war much more in the public opinion and much less on the battlefield itself (see Figure 3.2).

Yet how did the submarine contribute to the development of sonic mindedness on the battlefront underwater? The answer relates directly to the auditory experience of the fighting while inside a submarine. A submarine crew member recounts that being in a submarine meant fourteen days of nightmare consisting of alarms, sounds of explosions, depth charges, and propeller noises.[13] While the difficulty of living inside a confined space of a submarine is not questioned, it is interesting to examine the manner in which its unique sound experience contributed to submarine warfare becoming such a powerful symbol.

With the ability of the submarine to dive into the (supposedly silent) deep, the visual detachment in the isolated soundscape of the underwater experience was a given. The absence of the visual, however, cannot be equated with an absence of sound: underwater warfare was not silent at all. Not only were there lots of noises and voices inside the submarine, but the crew actually maneuvered the submarines based on sound: they "saw" through a hydrophone (the predecessor of modern sonar), a technical device that measures the distance from the submarine to the bottom of the sea or to another ship by means of sound waves. It consisted of a sensitive sound detector and a complicated localization device. The wireless operator in the submarine had to turn the microphone to the coming noise in order to locate it on a given coordinate plane. The true mark of expertise was not the ability to

Figure 3.2
Submarine "U-10" built at the Germaniawerft in Kiel, Germany.
Library of Congress, Prints & Photographs Division, LC-B2- 3292-11.

locate underwater noise in general, but rather the acoustic ability of the hydrophone operator to distinguish between the sounds of friend and foe. Hearing the enemy underwater was
for the crews almost the only way to visualize and observe the battle situation both under and
above the water. Sounds, therefore, functioned both as a tool to locate the enemy and for
survival in the deep.

The hydrophone operator's acoustic skills, acquired after many hours of practicing, had to
be even better than those of the other crew members. For instance, many hydrophone opera-
tors learned to distinguish between the propeller sounds of heavy convoy vessels, which
meant potential "prey," and the "angry" and hectic propeller sound of an enemy cruiser,
which meant possible danger. Another important issue was the ability to reconstruct the
acoustic map as a visual one in order to locate the enemy: in other words, the operator translated his acoustic findings into visuals to present the results to the rest of the crew. In order to
transform his ability to hear into the crew's ability to act, the operator first had to convert
what was heard to what could be seen. This sound imaging was also a way to translate the
battle experience into a concrete situation. While the noises of danger meant for the submarine crew the need to avoid the enemy, the very same noises meant for the cruiser the chance
to win the battle. The key point for both sides was the ability to locate the presence of the
other through its sounds.

Here again, one can divide the sonic mindedness in the submarine into two sound categories: the sounds of safety and the sounds of danger. The sounds of safety for the crew members could be identified with the routine procedure of living in a submarine, like the rhythmic
rattle of the engines or the reassuring, humming noise of the ventilators. Another significant
sound of safety in the submarine was the sound of the gramophone. During the long sea

journeys many crews played their favorite tunes while on board. In this sense, the crackling sound of gramophone records heard all over the submarine in the middle of the ocean was for many a sound of comfort and served as a reminder of the civilian lives left behind.

The sounds of danger, on the other hand, were associated with notions of emergency and threat. Most of the time, it began with a screaming alarm accompanied by the deafening roar of pressurized air and seawater mixing in the diving tanks while the submarine prepared to dive. Usually the convoy vessels were escorted by cruisers and submarine hunters. Consequently, in most cases, it was only a question of time until the submarine was discovered. This was also the time when the submarine took advantage of its unique abilities by diving even deeper into the sea. At this point, all over the submarine, one could easily hear the beeping sound of the hydrophone acoustically searching for the sounds of the enemy. As danger came closer, however, the crew could hear it as the heavy propeller noise of enemy cruisers reached the submarine from above. Interestingly, the submarine crew had two ways of hearing the enemy: through sounds produced directly by the enemy and through their own sounds (produced by the hydrophone). Because of the confined space of this "sound chamber" and reduced sounds from the outside, the acoustic experience was amplified.

In times of safety as in times of danger, one of the major acoustic landmarks (or, sound-marks) in the submarine was the engine room, a space where sound and place were brought together. Two sound sources should be noted here: the combustion engines for normal cruising and the electric motors for underwater use.[14] As long as the submariner could hear the diesel engines, he could assume that everything was all right. Or as one of the bridge officers of the U-202 put it: "We are having a good trip and the diesel engines are singing their monotone song."[15] Contrary to the "monotone," and maybe even boring, sound of safety, the humming sound of the electric motors was perceived by many crews as an acoustic sign of emergency. In the First World War, the submarines were not capable of staying underwater for an extended amount of time. That meant that the submarines spent the majority of their time cruising on the water surface; it was only in times of danger or emergency that they were forced to dive. Therefore, in the sound vocabulary of the submarine crews, the changing of the sound environment from diesel motors to electric motors meant also a change from routine procedure to an emergency and time-sensitive situation.

Underwater, the submarine crew could hear different sounds. Because of the sound-transferring capabilities of the water, they had to "sharpen their ears" to better listen to the sounds of the enemy. But to avoid discovery, the submarines had to cover their tracks, i.e., reduce their noise stamps. This mode of cruising, known as *Horchfahrt* (listening cruise), consisted of reducing the submarine's machine sounds to the absolute minimum. In addition, all crew members were asked not to make unnecessary noise. This was especially critical if the submarine had already been discovered by the enemy and was targeted. Once a submarine was hit and many of its systems began to collapse, the sounds of danger would mix with the interior sounds of safety to create an even more alarming acoustic blend.

Blinded Ears and Visual Deafness

Like the war in the sea, the war in the air did not represent the lion's share of the fighting in the First World War and subsequently did not change the course of war. Still, along with

Figure 3.3
Biplane fighter aircraft Albatros C III flown by Ernst Udet and others.
Bundesarchiv, Photo 104-0321. Photographer unknown.

submarine warfare, it is considered one of the most culturally influential dimensions of battle that ignited the public imagination and further contributed to what Peter Fritzsche called an "air mindedness" in the Weimar Republic.[16] Yet how did aerial warfare during the First World War contribute to the establishment of a sonic mindedness in a way that influenced many during and after the war? As shown in the previous "theaters of war," ground and sea, new technology influenced warfare and its sonic mindedness—a notion that holds true for flight as well: in the air, the introduction of the fighter plane created a new form of aerial and visual perspective (see Figure 3.3). The airplane changed the common division between front and hinterland, as everything could be quickly accessed. Significant for this chapter, airplane warfare meant for the pilot that he could see everything, yet what he saw was neither accompanied nor followed by sound. The noise inside these airplanes was so loud that it masked the sensory experience of the pilot in a way that made the battleground beneath look soundless and frozen. Consequently, the pilots experienced a new kind of sensory split between seeing and hearing that, along with the creation of an almost unlimited visual aerial perspective from above, also demanded acoustic detachment between the pilot's eye and the sounds of his targets on the ground. This sensory split between sound and image gradually translated into an emotional split, alienating the pilot's eye from his other senses. The result was mainly a soundless screening of the visual surface beneath, colored by the endless roaring thunder of his own engine.

In his memoir *Mein Fliegerleben* (1935), Ernst Udet, one of the major aviation pioneers in Germany in the interwar period and a former fighter pilot, used the visual metaphor of a huge aquarium to describe his experience of the ground battlefront from the air.[17] For Erwin Boehme, one of the most famous German pilots in the First World War, flying over the front and observing the soundless explosions from above seemed unreal.[18] Unfortunately for this examination, both Udet and Boehme elaborate on their magnified visual impressions, but do not remark on heard sound events. The famous acoustician Henry Watt noted at the turn of the century that hearing means experiencing.[19] Does this mean in the case of the fighter pilots in the First World War that no hearing also meant no experiencing? We have to assume that they did hear sounds, such as the engine of their own machine, another plane passing by, or faint explosion sounds from afar, yet it seems as if either the sounds are not remembered at all or they are considered of secondary importance. Alternatively, perhaps the sound experience inside the plane cannot find its place within the entirety of the visual perception. What were the mechanisms that created this shift in the auditory perception? What influenced the pilots' sonic mindedness during the war?

Here again, the engine (more accurately, its sounds) plays a major role in the pilot's soundscape. Most of the fighter planes in the First World War were equipped with a single rotary internal combustion engine that produced much noise and vibration. At the time, the planes were mainly one- or two-seater biplanes with an open cockpit. The latter meant that the overall noise was increased by the sounds of the propeller and the whistle of the wind as well as the rattle of the machine guns. Due to the open cockpit, pilots wore heavy flight gear consisting of a helmet, scarf, goggles, and a flying jacket. Many pilots suffered from hearing problems and ear infections caused by the severe flight conditions in a cold and unpressurized atmosphere.[20] Considering the fact that the successful use of wireless communication was just beginning,[21] one may conclude that the pilot was sonically almost completely isolated from his fellow soldiers and only existed in his private soundscape.

Historically, we can observe the year 1916 as a turning point in the history of military aviation and its sonic mindedness. Until that year, the main purpose of the airplane was to perform reconnaissance missions. One of the reasons for the limited role of the airplane was the fact that there were no suitable heavy armaments for them to carry. This reality was about to change when the synchronized machine gun was developed in 1916. A simple chain wheel locked the machine gun whenever the propeller blade crossed the line of fire. Thus, a new warfare technology emerged in the middle of the First World War that allowed the pilot to fly and shoot. The connection between the flight direction and the fire direction historically established the major role of the airplane in the First World War as a fighter plane. This new role had a major influence on the auditory perception of the aviator as well. Now looking (instead of listening or hearing) was cemented as the primary sense needed in order to win the battle. Simply put, once the pilot had reached his destination, he mainly concentrated on maintaining eye contact with the target area viewed through the airplane's gun sight. This further prioritization of visual over auditory perception in the air battle might also explain why neither Udet nor Boehme mentioned (or even remembered) the soundscape of air battle in the First World War.

The evolution of air battle with regard to the pilot's sound environment was also influenced by another technological limitation that was discussed in the previous section on submarines, namely the inability of the early airplanes to stay in the air for an extended amount of time. Due to small fuel tanks and limited engine power, most of the fighter planes in the First World War could remain in the air for less than an hour. This meant that most of the time, the fighting experience of the pilot consisted largely of time on the ground in long stretches of waiting between flights. Contrary to the infantry and the submarine, the pilot experienced the battle only in short, intense periods of time. Therefore, pilots could sometimes perceive their experiences in the battle only retrospectively. Once back on the ground, they were able to reflect upon and reconstruct the battle in the air.

The sonic detachment the pilot experienced during the air battle, due to the noise of the engine, wind, and machine-gun fire, stood in stark contrast to the sounds of safety on the ground. Because the periods during which the pilot experienced sounds of safety quantitatively outnumbered the amount of time he experienced sounds of danger, the sounds of safety at the airfield functioned as a voiceover that masked and reshaped the soundless memories of the battle. As a result, World War I pilots carried a very different sonic memory of battle into Weimar-era civilian life than did their fellow soldiers on land or at sea.

SONIC MINDEDNESS AND ITS AFTERMATH

One of the major difficulties of the early cartography in the thirteenth century was the inability to find the correct perspective of the globe. After all, how can we illustrate something we are unable to see in its entirety? This problem was largely resolved in 1569 when Flemish cartographer Gerardus Mercator (1512–1594) developed a relative system to draw maps. Later known as the Mercator Chart, this system provided a reliable method of projecting three-dimensional objects onto two-dimensional maps and significantly contributed to the development of modern nautical navigation. Applying this example to the period under discussion, one could see how the First World War symbolically played a similar role in suggesting ways to project the fuzzy character of sound onto the matrix of the war's soundscapes. Furthermore, through the auditory lenses of the three theaters of war, one could learn to what extent the sensory experience of the Great War as a technological war relied upon the transition from the visual to the aural in a way that established a new kind of wartime sonic mindedness based on the learned distinction between sounds of safety and sounds of danger. In this sense, hearing sounds in times of war not only suggested new forms of sonic experience but also established a new sonic epistemology that was based on using the sense of hearing to avoid dangers associated with sound.

As a large-scale European crisis, the First World War with its sounds also served as a bridge between the soundscapes of the nineteenth century and the soundscapes of the twentieth century. As a result of the extensive use of warfare technology during the First World War, many throughout Europe confronted for the very first time a new connection between "mass warfare sounds" and "mass dangers." This was notable on three different battlefronts that developed and depended on three different modes of auditory perception.

The echoes of this sonic mindedness during wartime could also be heard in the Weimar Republic when many compared noises in big cities like Berlin with the ominous roar of yesterday's battlefields. Even without this comparison, it must be noted that the shift from the sounds of war to the war of sounds in the civil "battlefields" of the Weimar Republic assumed a much larger role in the contexts of the sonic mindedness in the interwar period. This new importance of sounds and hearing-listening, which also created a unique interrelation between sound and sight, was fully recognized in the interwar period. Only a few examples of the many interwar sound technologies that were developed or at least significantly improved as a result of the war will be mentioned here. Alongside the development of the cinema and mass consumption in the Weimar Republic, one can see the commercial development of the radio, the telephone, and the gramophone as electro-acoustic turning points that were influenced by the war and therefore increased the collective sound experience in German society at that time. The introduction of commercial radio broadcasting in Germany in November 1923 and the large scale use of telephone and wireless communication are two examples. Furthermore, the technological (and increasingly commercial) ability to preserve past sounds—especially voices—by imprinting them on mass-produced records is another major change in the way sound and place were perceived in the interwar period. Not only was sound more important than before, it even became a commodity that was bought and sold and was distributed and listened to internationally. The new role of sound in the Great War preceded this development and made it possible.

Mediated by a new mass sonic consumption, people transferred their already learned sonic mindedness from the war experience into the living rooms of the Weimar Republic, when the chaos of the former battlefields were civilized and transformed into the soundscape of civilian society. But this came with a price: the simple sonic division between sound of danger and sound of safety was gradually incorporated into the civilian "battlefields" of modernity in the postwar era until one could not distinguish anymore between symbolic fronts and imagined homelands. As Ernst Udet put it: "When I sit in the club and listen to gramophone sounds from the briefing room, I really do not know whether I am in a café in Berlin or in the middle of a war."[22]

NOTES

1. In the introduction to this book, Florence Feiereisen and Alexandra Merley Hill illustrate to what extent the cultural superiority of the human eye over the human ear predominated in the course of Western civilization since ancient times. The sense of hearing was only employed when vision was obstructed. In the context of this chapter, it is particularly interesting to discover when the soldiers involved in World War I relied on their sense of hearing: imminent threats caused a shift in primary senses and therefore a return to premodern, almost primitive times.

2. Paul Fussell, *The Great War and the Modern Memory* (Oxford: Oxford University Press, 1977); Marc Ferro, *Der grosse Krieg 1914–1918* (Frankfurt am Main: Suhrkamp, 1988); Samuel Hynes, *A War Imagined: The First World War and English Culture* (London: Bodley Head, 1990).

3. For the indirect influences of the sonic experience of the First World War on the establishment of sound art during the Weimar years, see the chapter by Brett Van Hoesen and Jean-Paul Perotte in this book.

4. "Die Erschütterung der Luft wird erst Schall, wo ein Ohr ist." Quoted in Ulrike Freiling, "Sprachsinnlichkeit, Wahrnehmung, Erkenntnis und Sprache in den Schriften George Christoph Lichtenbergs," (Ph.D. dissertation, Marburg Univ., 2001), 145, http://archiv.ub.uni-marburg.de/diss/z2001/0395/ (accessed June 30, 2010).

5. "Je größer und komplizierter die Armeen werden, desto größer wird das Missverständnis zwischen dem wirklichen Kriege und unsere Friedensübungen." Quoted in Friedrich von Bernardi, *Organisation und Ausbildung der Kavallerie für den modernen Krieg* (Berlin: Verlag Ernst Siegfried Mittler und Sohn, 1907), 15.

6. Ernst von Wrisberg, *Wehr und Waffe, 1914–1918* (Leipzig: KF Koehler, 1922), 16ff.

7. Bernard Fitzsimons, *The Big Gun: Artillery 1914–1918* (London: Phoebus, 1973), 22.

8. For a fictionalized account of the battlefield on the ground, see *All Quiet on the Western Front* by Erich Maria Remarque. This passage captures the variety of sounds in this theater of

war: "The thunder of the guns swells to a single heavy roar and then breaks up again into separate explosions. The dry bursts of the machine-guns rattle. Above us the air teems with invisible swift movement, with howls, pipings, and hisses. They are smaller shells; and amongst them, booming through the night like an organ, go the great coal-boxes and the heavies. They have a hoarse, distant bellow like a rutting stag and make their way high above the howl and whistle of the smaller shells." Erich Maria Remarque, *All Quiet on the Western Front* (New York: Random House, 1958), 59.

9. Ludwig Scholtz, *Seelenleben der Soldaten an der Front: Hinterlassene Aufzeichnungen des im Kriege gefallenen Nervenarztes* (Tübingen: JCB Mohr, 1920), 109.

10. Remarque captures this contrast between new recruits and seasoned soldiers, particularly with regard to their reactions to sound: "Every man is aware of the heavy shells tearing down the parapet, rooting up the embankment and demolishing the upper layers of concrete. When a shell lands in the trench we note how the hollow, furious blast is like a blow from the paw of a raging beast of prey. Already by morning a few of the recruits are green and vomiting. They are too inexperienced." *All Quiet on the Western Front*, 106.

11. D. Bachrach, "Über die Hörschärfe zu verschiedenen Tageszeiten," *Zeitschrift für Sinnesphysiologie* XLIX: 2 (1915): 99, quoted in *Archiv für Ohrenheilkunde* 97 (1915): 262–263.

12. A. Güttich, "Das Ohrlabyrinth als Kompass," *Deutsche Medizinische Wochenschrift* 38 (1916), quoted in *Berliner Klinische Wochenschrift* 43 (May 15, 1916): 528.

13. Michael Salewski, *Von der Wirklichkeit des Krieges: Analysen und Kontroversen zu Buchheims Boot* (Munich: Deutscher Taschenbuch Verlag, 1976), 31.

14. The rumble sounds of combustion engines colored the urban experience in Germany even prior to the outbreak of the First World War and were considered by many, such as the German-Jewish philosopher Theodor Lessing (1872–1933), to be sonic symptoms for cultural decline. During the war, these sounds changed into sonic markers of safety. For the seminal contribution of Lessing to the cultural identification of noise in the context of late imperial Germany, see the chapter by John Goodyear in this book.

15. "Wir machen eine gute Fahrt, und die Diesel machen ihr eintöniges Lied." Quoted in Edgar Spiegel von und zu Peckelsheim, *U-202: Ein Kriegstagebuch* (Berlin: August Scherl, 1916), 11.

16. Peter Fritzsche, *A Nation of Fliers: German Aviation and the Popular Imagination* (Cambridge, MA: Harvard University Press, 1992).

17. Ernst Udet, *Mein Fliegerleben* (Berlin: Ullstein, 1935), 57.

18. Letter from January 14, 1916 quoted in Johannes Werner, ed., *Briefe eines deutschen Kampfliegers an ein junges Mädchen* (Leipzig: K.F. Koehler, 1930), 15–18.

19. J. Henry Watt, *The Psychology of Sound* (Cambridge: Cambridge University Press, 1917), 1.

20. Werner T. Scott, "Airplane Deafness and Its Prevention," *Military Surgeon* 52: 3 (1923): 300-301. Quoted in *Zentralblatt für Hals- Nasen- und Ohrenheilkunde* 3: 4 (1923): 470.

21. F. Herath, "Funktelegraphie und Flugzeug" in *Der deutsche Rundfunk* 3: 44 (October 31, 1925): 2825–27; Hans Schlee, "Erlebnisse aus dem Anfängen der Funktelegraphie in Luftfahrtzeugen" in *Der deutsche Rundfunk* 3: 46 (November 15, 1925): 2986–87.

22. Ernst Udet, *Kreuz wider Kokarde*, (Berlin: Braunbeck, 1918), 61, 91. This chapter is based on the first chapter of my doctoral dissertation "Hearing Maps: Noise Technology and Auditory Perception in Germany 1914–1945," submitted to the Hebrew University in Jerusalem in 2005. I would like to thank Till van Rahden for his careful reading of previous versions of this chapter and Florence Feiereisen, Alexandra Merley Hill, and the anonymous readers for their helpful comments and insights. Finally, I owe special thanks (in alphabetical order) to Dan Diner, Joel Miller, Wolfgang Schieder, and Moshe Zimmermann for their intellectual contribution to my dissertation project. Unless otherwise indicated, all translations are mine.

CHAPTER 4

From Seat Cushions to Formulae

Understanding Spatial Acoustics in Physics and Architecture

SABINE VON FISCHER

S paces for musical performances are sites of extended debates about whether the natural sciences can measure and predict sonic and sensual experience. A film score can underline and heighten the drama of a story. Similarly, in a concert hall, a symphony's crescendo can evoke sensations that are no less intense. What happens in space that makes emotions fly? Sound waves are reflected and absorbed by the enclosing surfaces of a room, pitch and timbre change, reverberations last longer or shorter. While physicists are capable of quantitatively measuring these parameters, the question remains how their effects on our emotions can be evaluated. When is something "music to our ears"? Can good acoustics be defined solely with reference to physical properties, or must one appeal to subjective impressions, such as the reactions of musicians and audience?

ARCHITECTURE BETWEEN TECHNICAL AND SOCIAL SCIENCES

In the course of the current "sensual turn," as claimed by anthropologists and historians,[1] the sonic dimension of space has become a focus of interdisciplinary research, beyond the physical measurement of sound waves. At the core of these controversies lies the question of how the quantitative values of the science of acoustics are related to qualitative understanding in the social sciences and the arts. Architecture has always been connected with the technical and the social sciences, and spatial configurations are central to the sounds we perceive. When considering sounds in architecture, we are challenged by a variety of scenarios, such as the ocean of resonances of a grand orchestra in a concert hall, the echoes of our steps in a hallway, the hum of ventilators in an office space, and the background music in department stores. While the profession of the sound designer in the film industry is just a few decades old—with acoustic consultants for shopping and transit spaces being an even younger line of work—architects have always, intentionally or not, created sonic environments. A musical performance brings the aural to the foreground; even if the visual remains part of the scenario, it is the quality of the sound that is critical. In designing an architectural space, the aural space confronts us with all possible ambiguities of spatial boundaries, for the tactile, visual, and auditory components each perform according to their own rules. These ambiguities and the complexity of the task, along with budgetary constraints, often result in the exclusion of auditory considerations in the architectural design process.

In its initial stage, the science of architectural acoustics, which is not much older than one hundred years, was applied exclusively to theaters, operas, and concert halls. Over the decades, it entered and regulated the construction of apartment blocks, office buildings, hotels, and shopping malls. Today, it is not only the physical construction of a building that affects the sound, but also electro-acoustic technology, which inserts another level of ambient sound into the space. While independent from the physical location, sound technology can enhance existing qualities of a space, or even shape a space. However, when sound first became a scientific discipline and one connected with space, architects confronted it with great skepticism.

Recent investigations imply that the "sensual" and the "sonic" turns have indeed arrived in architecture; the era of the uncontested primacy of the visual seems to have come to an end. The number of publications dedicated to the other senses attests to this. In their *Spaces Speak, Are You Listening?* for example, Barry Blesser, a digital audio engineer, and Linda-Ruth Salter, a social scientist, explore how one experiences space by attentive listening, which they extend into the broader notion of "auditory spatial awareness."[2] The book does not investigate a specific culture or time period, but regards the presence, impact, and aura of sound as a general phenomenon. While much of Blesser and Salter's writing is based on the notion that most aural architecture is not intentionally designed but results from a combination of natural, incidental, and unwitting factors,[3] it is all based on the belief that there is a physical explanation for the acoustic experience. According to Blesser and Salter, the challenges in creating sound environments are to bring together the many specialized disciplines that shape our surroundings, as well as to find appropriate applications of sound technologies—which, in their estimation, are at hand. Such trust in the capacities of scientific calculation is the result of developments in the twentieth century, when architectural acoustics and electro-acoustics entered the scene. What remains to be resolved are the social and philosophical questions, which these technologies trigger.

In this chapter, I focus on German and Austrian examples of concert halls, which successfully created aural environments and can be read as benchmarks in the erratic development of the acoustic dimension of architecture. In this development, a tension existed between the traditional understanding of a coincidental, even superstitious or mystical quality of an architectural space on the one hand, and the modern approach of a scientific, measurable relationship between sound waves and the materials with which they must interact, on the other.

THE DEPTH OF THE MATERIAL

When the Viennese architect Adolf Loos (1870–1933) published "Das Mysterium der Akustik" ("The Mystery of Acoustics") as a newspaper article in January 1912,[4] he pleaded for the preservation of Vienna's Bösendorfer Hall from the standpoint that a reconstruction elsewhere would never reproduce the acoustic qualities of this concert hall on Herrengasse 6 in Vienna's city center.

> I was asked whether the Bösendorfer Saal should be preserved. I presume what prompted the question was the idea that reverence for the past demands we should not demolish a hall that has played such an important role in the musical history of Vienna. But it is not a question of reverence for the past, it is a question of acoustics.[5]

In 1872, Ludwig Bösendorfer, piano maker, patron of the arts, and one of the most colorful and original of Viennese personalities at the time, had taken over the equestrian stables of the Palais Liechtenstein and had converted the riding hall into a concert hall of nearly six hundred seats.[6] The discipline of architectural acoustics did not yet exist as such and was more of a trial-and-error approach at first: Bösendorfer himself—wearing his inimitable top hat while riding a pony and listening to his friend shout from the other end of the hall—decided on the position of new interior walls and during construction moved the rear wall three times until the acoustics satisfied his ear.[7] The large windows that remained over the newly added wooden siding in the hall were reminiscent of the previous life of the building; while the hall itself was not spectacular, its dimensions and surfaces were chosen with care. The concert hall in the converted riding stable gained a reputation as an outstanding venue and, at the time, even became Vienna's most popular concert hall. It was praised for "its beautiful simplicity, which made a 'very intimate yet noble impression' and contributed to the 'inner collection of listeners.'"[8] Accounts of the time pleaded that the hall was of the same significance as Vienna's Großer Musikvereinssaal, yet exceeded its acoustics.[9] The success of this daring challenge to one of Europe's prime concert halls might have been the result of subjective judgment; however, the list of musicians who performed in the Bösendorfer Hall reads like the *Who's Who* of the European music scene of the time, among them pianists Anton Rubinstein, Franz Liszt, Moriz Rosenthal, Eugen d'Albert, Johannes Brahms, Ignaz Paderewsky, Bruno Walter, Teresa Carreño, Emil von Sauer, Arthur Schnabel, Ernst von Dohnányi, Béla Bartók, and Edvard Grieg; violinists Pablo Sarasate and Georg Hellmesberger; composers Johannes Brahms, Anton Bruckner, Hugo Wolf, Max Reger, Gustav Mahler, and Richard Strauss; and many more.[10]

In "The Mystery of Acoustics," an enthusiastic plea for the conservation of the concert hall, Loos expressed his skepticism over the new science of architectural acoustics. It was a widespread belief at the time that the acoustic performance of a space could not be calculated or predicted, because music was not a technical discipline but rather an art form. At the turn of the century, physical acoustics were not integrated into architectural practice—if at all, acoustics were determined empirically. The idea that reverberation time could be calculated with a formula, based on dimensions and surfaces of a space, must have seemed to many a modern fashion rather than a law of nature.

> Until now *every* new hall has had poor acoustics. . . . Have our ears changed? No, it is the material the hall is made from that has changed. For forty years the material has absorbed good music and has been impregnated with the sound of the Philharmonic and the voices of

our singers. There are mysterious changes in molecular structure which until now have only been observed in the wood violins are made of.[11]

According to Loos, the building material and its tuning over time are essential to the acoustic performance of any space—therefore mere copies of the geometry of famous concerts halls must be doomed to fail.

In Loos' reasoning, the high quality of music to which those walls were exposed over the course of time was responsible for the outstanding acoustic performance. He believed that, like the wooden body of a string instrument, a concert hall can never sound perfect from day one; the depth of the walls of a concert hall "soak up" (or "absorb") the music being played and are "impregnated" by the singing voices over time. He suggested "mysterious changes in molecular structure" that defied scientific explanations (until today). In the case of Vienna's Bösendorfer Hall, music resounded on masonry walls under the heavily loaded floor slab of the library above, with no need of adjustments by sound absorbers. When Loos praised the acoustic performance from the depth of the bare walls, he overlooked the fact that the Bösendorfer Hall was said to perform at its best when two-thirds occupied,[12] which equals the absorbing body surface of four hundred people in the audience.

FROM MYSTERY TO MEASUREMENT

The key turning point from "mysterious processes" to measurements in architectural acoustics had already come about in 1900 when American physicist Wallace C. Sabine (1868–1919) had published his formula of reverberation time, and it is very likely that these papers had traveled across the Atlantic Ocean to Vienna long before Loos published his polemic newspaper article in 1912. Already in May 1911, at the latest, the physicist Gustav Jäger had presented his experiments of reverberation measurements at the Imperial Academy of Sciences in Vienna.[13] It is not documented but it is likely that Loos had learned of the recent scientific developments, which were to impact architecture thoroughly in the decades to come.

Reverberation is the sum of sound reflections from all surrounding surfaces. In an exterior space, a sound pressure wave bounces back from a wall or a building facade; in an interior space, sound can travel much longer, from surface to surface, and create extended reverberations. Sound reflections that occur with a delay are referred to as echoes. It is important for the scope of this chapter to keep in mind that the sound waves hit our eardrum directly or by reflecting off surfaces such as walls, ceilings, furniture, floors, and even other people. Reverberant sound as the collection of these reflected waves dies away quicker when the sound energy is absorbed by the surfaces of the room, furnishings, and bodies. In a very simplified way, the process of hearing can be described as sound waves traveling from their source to our outer ear. Here, they are then channeled along the ear canal to our eardrum. The vibrations the eardrum sends off are transformed into nerve impulses, which are then interpreted and recognized by the hearing center of the brain as certain sounds. Spaces of total absorption, such as in anechoic chambers of acoustic laboratories, but also in the air on top of a mountain, can be described as "acoustically dead." The room is considered "acoustically live" when the sound lingers before dying away. Highly reflective surfaces (such as concrete or glass) lengthen the reverberation time. The trick is to find a balance—a "live" room without echoes or too much reverberation time.

The optimum reverberation time for an auditorium depends on its intended use. For a medium-sized all-purpose auditorium where music and speech should be heard clearly and distinctively, one to two seconds is desirable. As a rule of thumb, the smaller the room, the shorter the reverberation time should be. The bigger the auditorium, the longer the sound waves take to travel to their receptors' ears. For example, Paris' Notre Dame Cathedral has a reverberation time of 8.5 seconds. Sacral music written for pipe organs is often conceived for such reverberant spaces. Speech, on the other hand, will be difficult to understand, as the same sounds would remain audible for 8.5 seconds. (Imagine hearing even three words, each 8.5 seconds in duration, quickly spoken after one another!) Commonly, lecture halls have a reverberation time of less than one second to make sure that all spoken information can be parsed and understood.

It is not only the size and shape of a hall that influences its reverberation time; it is also the hall's surfaces and construction materials. When in 1895, at the age of twenty-seven, the aforementioned physicist Wallace C. Sabine was asked to investigate the miserable acoustics of Fogg Museum's lecture hall at Harvard University, he quickly discovered that the reverberation time of the lecture hall was not proportional to its volume. During his patient and exhaustive experiments conducted at night, when no other sounds would disturb the measurements, he found out that the length of added curtains and the number of seat cushions in the hall—borrowed during these nights from the nearby Sanders Theater—had an impact on the reverberation time as well.[14] Thus the seat cushion became the initial "unit" of his experiment. Since cushions have different sizes, shapes, and fabrics, Sabine introduced the "open window-unit" as his standard measurement; its definition is based upon a one-square-foot area of open window—an equivalent surface of no reflections, which thus is equivalent to a complete sound absorber. Soon thereafter, the "Sabin" was used as a standard unit of absorption in the early twentieth century, until it was replaced by "equivalent absorption area,"[15] which is used in science today.

In tables of absorption coefficients, one can find different absorption coefficients for various materials. This coefficient typically also changes with frequency, so the reverberation time is likewise frequency dependent. While the new metric measure has replaced Wallace C. Sabine's initial unit, the "open window-unit" or "Sabin" created more of a narrative. To give a few examples: one square foot of thick Oriental carpet equaled 0.25 Sabins, and four square feet of the same carpet equaled one Sabin; a seat cushion from Sanders Theater equaled 0.7 Sabins; one square foot of brick equaled about 0.02 Sabins; and one adult human, sitting in an audience, equaled about 4.7 Sabins.[16] Sabine was able to calculate the relations of the different parameters and came to his famous formula, which relates surface areas (according to the absorbing quality of each material) to the total volume of the space. In solving the acoustic problem of Fogg Hall as a young assistant professor, he had created the new field of architectural acoustics. The Sabine Formula for reverberation time became the main parameter of room acoustics.[17] It is still applied in room acoustics today, yet it is complemented with considerations of the ratio of direct sound and early reflections to the overall sound.

In 1912, when Loos wrote his text defending the acoustic mystery of the Bösendorfer Hall, the understanding of sound propagation was a very young science. Loos mocked the idea that sound paths could be predicted like "billiard balls bumping through space." These physicists "drew straight lines from the sound source to the ceiling and assumed that sound would be sent on its way by bouncing off the board in the very same angle. All these constructions," he concluded "are nonsense."[18] By writing this in such a polemical manner, Loos possibly wanted to expose his understanding of the modern science, which accounted not only for the geometric behavior of sound, but also for the energies contained in a wave of sound. Loos thought of himself as a modern man and did not categorically oppose the sciences, yet he was a skeptic toward anything that could be thought of as just fashionable. This might be the explanation of why he countered the new science of architectural acoustics with such mystical arguments as the quality of the "tuning over time" that "impregnates" the walls and essentially forms the sound of a space. To underscore his argument, he claimed that all halls ever built sounded poor on the occasion of their first concert.[19] In his plea for the preservation of the Bösendorfer Hall, he played up his doubts that the reconstruction of the Bösendorfer Hall could ever constitute the "same space," even when rebuilt identically. Nevertheless, the Palais Liechtenstein was demolished after the final concert on May 2, 1913, to give way to a high-rise of the property's new owner. The last performance featured Beethoven's String Quartet in F Major, Schubert's String Quintet in C Major, and Haydn's Variations on the National Anthem. The famous Bösendorfer Hall was never reconstructed.[20]

In 1900, when Wallace C. Sabine first published his findings on reverberation time, a new era of concert hall design, devised by scientific principles, began. In the same year, Boston's Symphony Hall was inaugurated, designed by McKim, Mead, and White with advice on acoustics by Sabine and inspired by the rectangular geometry of the Old Leipzig Gewandhaus. Its reverberation time was estimated by Sabine through his formula, and it was the first concert hall to be designed according to quantitative findings. The reverberation time was later measured by various acousticians as ranging from 1.2 up to 4 seconds, depending on the occupancy and the frequency measured.[21] While praised by many, especially for the clarity of the tones, a music critic of the *Boston Evening Transcript* wrote about the opening night on October 15, 1900: "Everything was clean-cut and distinct, the tone was beautifully smooth, and, so to speak, highly polished; but it had no life."[22] Like several others, as Emily Thompson recounts in *The Soundscape of Modernity,* the critic resisted "the very idea of a scientifically controlled sound, as it contradicted his own romantic conception of the unpredictable nature of all music."[23] It is the same resistance that Adolf Loos would express twelve years later in Vienna: music could not simply be calculated beforehand in the realm of science, but it had to be of a different, more artistic or even celestial nature.

When we say that something is "music to one's ears," we mean that it is pleasant to hear. This does not mean that we actually hear music as a culturally specific art form or as a new dimension of experience, but what has been said fulfills expectations and is in accord with our (aesthetic) values. Ironically, even the acclaimed Symphony Hall in Boston at first was received with doubt by the audience: the music played on the opening night was not "music to the ears." Thompson assumes that the ears of the audience were not ready to hear the well-tempered resonances of a modern concert hall. It was only after some time that Boston's Symphony Hall was recognized as one of the world's greatest concert halls, and after a few decades, architectural acoustics became an internationally recognized discipline of science; was considered in some architecture curricula; and, in the postwar period, led to the founding of institutes of technical acoustics.

PROPORTIONS AND SHAPES

Designing a space for sound means assigning a permanent geometry to volatile matter. Since Vitruvius, considerations of volume and resonance and, since Alberti, proportional studies are part of every architect's education; yet, the forms that result from these foundations could not vary more. One popular preconception among architects of the twentieth century is that a space for music has to adopt wave-like shapes, materializing the immaterial form of sound waves. Another geometric concept is the wedge shape, which has largely been informed by visual criteria: the frontal stage is visible from all angles, as in a cinema. The form seems to take the visual more into consideration than the acoustic. Each of the many possible formal concepts has produced a number of acoustically acceptable and remarkable concert halls, as well as many of lesser success. In *Concert Halls and Opera Houses—Music, Acoustics and Architecture*, a rigorous and comprehensive assessment of one hundred concert and opera halls, the acoustician Leo Beranek compared volumes, dimensions, geometries, materials, acoustic measurements, and verbal judgments on internationally renowned music auditoriums. The geometries vary greatly from rectangular to elliptical, rounded, irregular, or fan shaped—and opinions on them range no less—yet rectangular halls repeatedly appear among those rated "superior" or "excellent."

The hall that most tenaciously turned over the dogma of the rectangular hall is the Berliner Philharmonie, home to the Berlin Philharmonic Orchestra, designed by architect Hans Scharoun (1893–1972) and according to the advice of acoustician Lothar Cremer (1905–1990), an exterior view of which is shown in Figure 4.1. It is everything but a box: none of the walls are parallel, and its "music in the center" spatial concept was rated as "a most

Figure 4.1
The exterior of Scharoun's Philharmonie.
Photograph by Frank Swenton, 2010.

dramatic room" and as "one of the models of successful acoustical design."[24] Others have said and written that the design was primarily informed by visual criteria and that the acoustic qualities have been neglected.[25]

In 1956, Scharoun, a key figure in twentieth-century architecture in Germany by virtue of his contributions to 1920s avant-garde architecture, as well as his postwar buildings, won the competition for a new concert hall on a site located at the edge of Berlin's Tiergarten with an unprecedented layout. The building with its curved roofline over the two multifaceted concert halls and foyers was asymmetrically and freely formed, unlike any other famous concert hall at the time. The building was partially received as a late expressionist variation of Scharoun's earlier, more classically modernist period; however, the only thing that can be said with certainty is that it is unique in its form and expression. Today, the Philharmonie complex inaugurated in 1963 is on a different, yet nearby, site, just a few steps west of where the Wall had divided Berlin (1961–1989). The complex features one larger and one smaller concert hall; the form of the large hall however, the key space of the project, remained faithful to the initial concept. In his 1957 article "Music in the Middle" ("Musik im Mittelpunkt"), Scharoun explained his competition entry with the following words:

> The next consideration was this: is it mere coincidence that, whenever people hear improvised music, they immediately gather around in a circle? This quite natural process whose psychological aspect everyone can comprehend, one would have to transfer into a concert hall setting—that was the task the architect had set for himself. The music should also be the spatial and visual focus. This was the starting point for the form of the Philharmonie. . . . Last but not least, the design was made spatially and technically feasible only through advances in acoustic science. "New territory" was conquered and developed here in close collaboration with the acoustic engineer, Professor Cremer.[26]

The asymmetrical layout of seats enveloping the center, as seen in Figure 4.2, placed only about a tenth of the audience behind the orchestra; the majority listened from either in the front or from the side; this takes into account the directionality of the human voice and of certain instruments. Early reflections off wall sections around the orchestra disperse directional sound to all listeners. The staggering of the terraced layout averts focus points as they occur in circular and elliptical auditoriums and helps deliver the music in such a manner that all members of the audience receive both direct and indirect sound.

Like a "hillside vineyard," as Scharoun described it in his own words,[27] the concert hall unfolds around the stage in the center—an idea that Frank Gehry also adopted for his Disney Concert Hall in Los Angeles of 2003, a structure often criticized for compromising acoustics in favor of the visual, just as its Berlin predecessor had been criticized. The terraced layout can be seen in the architectural plans for Scharoun's hall, in Figure 4.3.

That fact that the hall was completed in 1963, seven years after the jury's vote for Scharoun's project and after long debates primarily about its unprecedented form, is largely indebted to the persistent support throughout the competition and planning process of the Berlin Philharmonic's acclaimed conductor Herbert von Karajan (1908–1989):

> Music as the focal point: this was the keynote from the very beginning. . . . Here you will find no segregation of "producers" and "consumers" but rather a community of listeners grouped

Figure 4.2
The interior of the Berliner Philharmonie's larger hall.
Photograph "Philharmonie Innen." © Lauterbach/Berliner Philharmoniker.

around an orchestra in the most natural of all seating arrangements. . . . Man, music and space
come together in a new relationship.[28]

This, of course, prompts a series of questions: should a concert hall be designed for the eye at
all? Does the visual impression impact our hearing? On the one hand, it was the unusual
layout of the "music in the middle" that aroused criticism; on the other hand, the expressive
shapes and presence of the hall's acoustic devices for reflecting sound into the entire space
were unknown in classical concert hall layouts. Already during the 1950s, after the jury's
decision for Scharoun's project, not everyone reacted enthusiastically. "Not all concertgoers,"
as the *Spiegel* reported in its 1957 article "Achteckige Philharmonie" ("Octagonal
Philharmonic Hall"), "wish to be reminded by visible constructions—acoustic reflectors—
that the miracle of hearing is a physical process controlled by science, just as the spectator of
a theater performance is not keen to have the headlights visible before his eyes."[29] Karajan,
though, claimed that the enveloping, revealing layout was especially adequate for the performance style of his orchestra. Austrian by descent, Karajan conducted the Philharmonic
Orchestra for thirty-five years and remains a legend for his animated appearances, which led
to the nickname of the orchestra as the "Circus Karajani."

Despite Karajan's praise and the international acclaim of the Berlin Philharmonie, each
concert experience remains a subjective one; it is subject to personal taste whether the spectacle of Karajan's directing had a suitably formidable setting in Scharoun's building, which
placed the music in the center, or whether one finds it disturbing to witness a concert as a
collective event. Scharoun's reasoning of the immediacy of the musical experience, granted

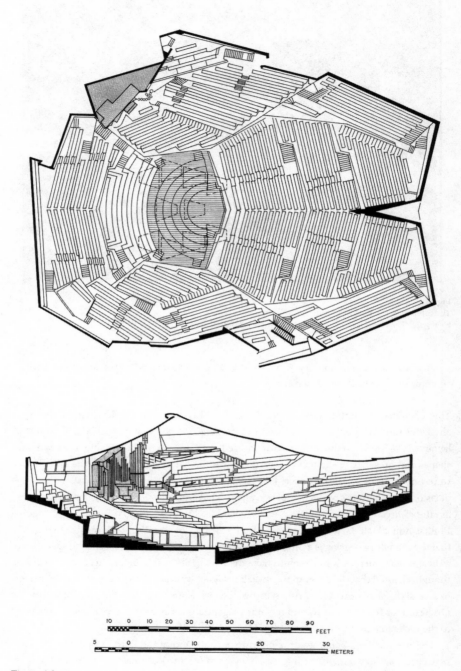

Figure 4.3
Architectural plan of the interior of the Berliner Philharmonie's larger hall. Image from Leo Beranek's *Concert Halls and Opera Houses: Music, Acoustics, and Architecture*.
Reproduced with permission of the author.

by the spatial layout (none of the 2,335 listeners is more than thirty-two meters away from the orchestra), cannot be achieved by any rectangular hall, not even by smaller halls of the nineteenth century.

Despite the criticism of some, the design of the relatively large Berlin Philharmonie of 21,000 cubic meters with its 2,335 seats accomplishes an exemplary time of 1.5 to 2.4 seconds of reverberation for the different frequencies and occupancies.[30] Yet it must be noted that additional acoustic reflectors were added to the hall's ceiling in the 1970s to adjust the reverberation of sound toward the orchestra, another important factor determining the quality of music; an orchestra that cannot hear its own playing is not able to perform well.

Not only according to audiences and musicians, but also to experts of technical acoustics, does the verdict of which hall is the best one remain undecided. The acoustic engineer Leo Beranek, one of the most prolific acousticians of our time, attempted in the 1996 edition of his in-depth documentation of seventy-six existing concert halls to establish a rating based on many factors such as scientific measurement and judgments by professional and lay listeners; however, in the second edition of the work that appeared eight years later, extended to one hundred halls, he had dropped the ratings in favor of a critical discussion of the parameters at hand for the evaluation of the quality of the opera and concert halls.

In Beranek's rating of 1996, the Berlin Philharmonie scored in the "B+" category, which accommodates more than half of the halls. Only nine halls were ranked "superior (A+)" and "excellent (A)," among them Amsterdam's Concertgebouw, the aforementioned Boston Symphony Hall, New York's Carnegie Hall, and Vienna's Großer Musikvereinssaal. Beranek rated the majority of his examples as "good to excellent" (B or B+), as a result of the experts' range of opinions that allowed for no definite conclusion. In other words, from lack of agreement among the experts, many halls ended up with a midrange rating.[31] Despite Beranek's admirable effort to provide all available information on size, shape/geometry, and material; conducting the acoustic measurements; and interviewing conductors, musicians, and audiences, much of the halls' acoustic quality remains, as Loos had described it in 1912, a mystery. Because it was long demolished when Beranek conducted his research, the Bösendorfer Hall, a simple rectangular hall inserted into a riding school, remains a myth beyond the inexplicable qualities of sound.

It comes as no surprise, then, that many acousticians today refer to the "shoebox" auditorium not only as a traditional solution, but as the only one. Recently built famous examples are the ones in Lucerne, Switzerland or Lahti, Finland by the late Russell Johnson (1923–2007) and his firm Artec. They demonstrate that even relatively large concert halls can have excellent sound quality and yet be flexible in serving multiple musical purposes. Their walls are neither an illustration of sound waves nor of any rhythm or angle, but enclosures of a space with the purpose of reflecting a previously determined amount of the array of traveling sound. Reverberations in "shoebox" auditoriums can be predicted with more accuracy than in irregularly shaped spaces and can be adjusted or enhanced with movable elements, secondary chambers, or other means. The possibility of electro-acoustic augmentation of the natural sound of a space had appeared at the horizon of technological innovation since the 1930s, but was not considered appropriate for a concert hall, where the purpose of attending is to hear live instruments, not loudspeaker playbacks.

Today, especially as newly designed concert halls (often for economic reasons) become larger and larger, creating longer paths, and thus extended delays for traveling sound, hidden loudspeaker amplification seems to be gaining acceptance among engineers. Blesser, a digital audio engineer himself, fundamentally questions the term "natural acoustics" when it comes to the debate of electro-acoustic support for musical performances. In his argument, even before the appearance of loudspeakers, "acoustic interventions of sound-dispersing statues, stand-reflecting ceiling panels, sound-diffusing walls, and sound-absorbing panels" rendered the sonic landscape of a room "artificial."[32]

Magnificent twentieth-century spaces for music with freer forms than the shoebox model, such as the Berlin Philharmonie or the Sydney Opera House by Jorn Utzon (1973), do not follow the standards of architectural acoustics. It seems that they derive their complex harmony from the simultaneity of physical, visual, and aural space. At the source of the intuition that has guided these and other architects must be the awareness that, while architecture relies on the three physical dimensions of space, sound occurs in the fourth dimension of time: it is a time-based phenomenon, temporal and ephemeral, and therefore a quality which architecture can never reproduce, but only enable.

TEMPORAL AND SPATIAL SENSATIONS

Architectural space is determined on an architectural drawing before any tone resounds inside of it. Therefore, designing a space for music is always an anticipation of the future. Time, the primary dimension of all sounds, cannot be built into the walls; it will enter when the music starts playing. In anticipation, yet without prejudice, architecture can enable a sound experience that is not only "music to one's ears" but a real sensation in time and space. Architects will always have to move in multisensory dimensions, hoping that the ambiguities among physical, visual, and aural space aesthetically heighten each other as constructive, rather than destructive interferences. It is no coincidence that according to *Merriam Webster* "aural" contains two meanings: the first definition is "of or pertaining to the ear or to the sense of hearing" and is from the same origin as the second, which is "of or pertaining to an aura."

Loos claimed in his text that one must also consider time to "fine tune" the concert hall; that is, architecture is not only defined by the results of geometry and surface. This notion of an ambient quality makes him a notional antecedent to contemporary architects like, for example, the Viennese architect and sound artist Bernhard Leitner who since the 1970s has explored the space-forming capacity of sound,[33] Berlin architect Gabi Schillig with her extended interest in ephemeral space and new materials,[34] or the Swiss architect Philippe Rahm. Rahm's recent writings and interventions on "physiological architecture" reflect a careful study of the way that a person interacts with and is affected by the environment, or the "electromagnetic, biological, and chemical interaction between architecture, the environment, and our organism."[35] Nearly a century before the emergence of physiological architecture, Loos had made us aware that architectural space is concerned with a wider range of parameters than just meters, which are represented proportionally in plan and section on a sheet of paper. Yet unlike Loos, this younger generation of architects is not shy about merging phenomenological truth with scientific facts and certainly puts more faith in modern technologies than Adolf Loos did in his times: sensorial experience is measured by and dependent on degrees Celsius or Fahrenheit, meters per second, lux, kelvin, decibel, hertz, and so on.

Today, with the help of ray tracing and other extensive computer simulations, acoustical engineers can compute spatial acoustics in great detail. Yet, is this enough? Does it capture the "mystery of acoustics"? Will a quantitative measurement ever encapsulate the aural experience? Most real-world acoustic calculations, therefore, still depend widely on empirical methods; even when these methods are more sophisticated than Ludwig Bösendorfer riding his pony through his hall—the "mystery of acoustics" sustains itself in many ways.

NOTES

1. Wolfram Aichinger et al., eds., *Sinne und Sinneseindrücke in der Geschichte* (Innsbruck, Wien, München: Studien Verlag 2003).
2. Barry Blesser and Linda-Ruth Salter, *Spaces Speak, Are You Listening? Experiencing Aural Architecture* (Cambridge, MA: MIT Press, 2006), 13.
3. Ibid., 5.
4. Adolf Loos, "Das Mysterium der Akustik," 1912. In Adolf Loos, *Trotzdem, 1900–1930* (1931, Wien: Georg Prachner Verlag, 1997), 116–117. The date of January 1912 was assigned by Adolf Loos himself retrospectively as described in the foreword to *Trotzdem*, 15. All translations are mine, unless otherwise noted.
5. "Man hat mich gefragt, ob der Bösendorfersaal in Wien erhalten werden solle. Der frager ging wohl von der voraussetzung aus, dass es eine frage der pietät wäre, einen saal, der in der musikgeschichte eine so große rolle gespielt hat, nicht zu demontieren. Aber diese frage ist nicht eine sache der pietät, sondern eine frage der akustik." Loos 1931, 116. English translation by Michael Mitchell from: Adolf Loos, "The Mystery of Acoustics," in Adolf Loos, *On Architecture* (Riverside, CA: Ariadne Press, 2002), 108.
6. Christina Meglitsch, *Wiens vergessene Konzertsäle. Der Mythos der Säle Bösendorfer, Ehrbar und Streicher*, Musikleben 12 (Wien: Peter Lang Verlag, 2005), 97.
7. Ibid., 123.
8. Christina Meglitsch summarized the public responses: "Seine schöne Einfachheit, die einen 'sehr traulichen und doch noblen Eindruck' machte und zu der 'inneren Sammlung der Zuhörer' wesentlich beitrug." Ibid., 95.
9. Christina Meglitsch quotes the final success to establish the former stable as a concert hall as follows: "[D]er Bekanntheitsgrad und die Beliebtheit des Saales [wuchs] so stetig, dass er als gleichbedeutend—die Akustik jedoch weit übertreffend—mit dem Grossen Musikvereinssaal in die Geschichte einging." Ibid., 103.
10. Ibid., 104–105.
11. "Aber bisher war jeder *neue* saal schlecht akustisch . . . Haben sich unsere ohren geändert? Nein, das material, aus dem der saal besteht, hat sich geändert. Das material hat durch vierzig jahre immer gute musik eingesogen und wurde mit den klängen unserer philharmoniker und den stimmen unserer sänger imprägniert. Das sind mysteriöse molekularveränderungen, die wir bisher nur am holze der geige beobachten konnten." Loos 1931, 117. English translation by Mitchell, from *On Architecture* 109.
12. Meglitsch, *Wiens vergessene Konzertsäle*, 124.
13. Gustav Jäger, "Zur Theorie des Nachhalls," aus den Sitzungsberichten der kaiserlichen Akademie der Wissenschaften in Wien, math.-naturwissenschaftl. Klasse, Bd. 120, Abt. IIa, Mai 1911. In this report, Jäger repeatedly refers to Wallace C. Sabine's publication in the *American Architect and Building News* of April 7, 1900.
14. Emily Thompson, *The Soundscape of Modernity—Architectural Acoustics and the Culture of Listening in America, 1900–1933* (Cambridge, MA: MIT Press, 2002), 33–36.

15. Deutsche Gesellschaft für Akustik e.V., "Akustische Wellen und Felder," March 2006, http://www.dega-akustik.de/publikationen/DEGA_Empfehlung_101.pdf, section 5.1.8, page 47 (accessed January 6, 2009).

16. Robert Sekuler, "Reverberation and the Art of Architectural Acoustics," *Homepage*, November 29, 2002, http://people.brandeis.edu/~sekuler/SensoryProcessesMaterial/reverberation.pdf (accessed January 6, 2009).

17. The Sabine formula as applied today is: T = 0.161 V/A, where T is the reverberation time, V is the volume of the room in cubic meters, and A is the absorption area in square meters. The formula that Wallace C. Sabine had published on May 5, 1900 in the third sequel of *Architectural Acoustics* in the *American Architect and Building News* was k = 0.171 V, which in principle corresponds to the current formula.

18. "Sie zeichneten gerade linien vom tongeber nach der decke und meinten, daß der schall wie eine billiardkugel im selben winkel von der bande abspringe und seinen neuen weg nehme. Aber alle diese konstruktionen sind unsinn." Loos, "Das Mysterium der Akustik," 116.

19. "Aber bisher war jeder *neue* saal schlecht akustisch." Loos, "Das Mysterium der Akustik," 117.

20. In 1983, the Bösendorfer piano company formally opened a new salon for concerts on the ground floor of their factory on Graf Starhemberg Gasse in Vienna's fourth district, which is now commonly known as the Bösendorfer Hall, see its Web site at www.boesendorfer.com. Other than the name, this hall bears no resemblance to its predecessor.

21. Leo Beranek, *Concert Halls and Opera Houses. Music, Acoustics and Architecture* (New York: Springer, 2004), 586.

22. Quoted in Thompson, *The Soundscape of Modernity*, 53.

23. Ibid., 54.

24. Leo Beranek, *Concert and Opera Halls. How They Sound* (New York: AIP Press, 1996), 245.

25. Jürg Jecklin, "Raumakustik im Wandel der Zeit—Zum Verhältnis von sichtbarem und hörbarem Raum," *werk, bauen und wohnen* 12 (2006): 8–13.

26. "Ist es ein Zufall—war die nächste Überlegung—dass überall, wo improvisiert Musik erklingt, sich Menschen sofort zu einem Kreis zusammenschließen? Diesen ganz natürlichen Vorgang, der von der psychologischen Seite her jedem verständlich ist, müsste man in einen Konzertsaal übertragen—das war nun die Aufgabe, die sich der Architekt gestellt hatte. Musik sollte auch räumlich und optisch im Mittelpunkt stehen. Davon ausgehend ergab sich die Gestaltung des Neubaues der Philharmonie. Dass der Entwurf in räumlicher und technischer Hinsicht heute realisiert ist, verdanken wir nicht zuletzt der Vorleistung der akustischen Wissenschaft. In enger Zusammenarbeit mit dem Akustiker, Prof. Cremer, wurde hier 'Neuland' erobert und erarbeitet." From: Hans Scharoun, "Musik im Mittelpunkt: Bemerkungen zum Neubau der Berliner Philharmonie, 29.7.1957," quoted in Hans Scharoun, *Bauten, Entwürfe, Texte*, edited by Peter Pfankuch (Berlin: Mann Verlag, Akademie der Künste, 1974), 279. Translation of some passages by Pamela Johnson. In Peter Blundell Jones's detailed study of the design process, Lothar Cremer appears as permanently skeptical about music in the round; later however, Cremer called Scharoun the "most accommodating architect he ever worked for," in Peter Blundell Jones, *Hans Scharoun* (London: Phaidon Press, 1995), 182.

27. "Der Saal ist wie ein Tal gedacht, auf dessen Sohle sich das Orchester befindet, umringt von den ansteigenden Weinbergen." Scharoun, *Bauten, Entwürfe, Texte*, 292. Others have described the layout as a terraced landscape, or leaves around a blossom.

28. From Herbert von Karajan's letter, when he was consulted by the judges of the architectural competition in 1956, quoted in Blundell Jones, *Hans Scharoun*, 178.

29. "Nicht jeder Konzertbesucher . . . habe den Wunsch, durch eine 'sichtbare Konstruktion'—den Klangreflektor—daran erinnert zu werden, daß das Wunder des Hörens ein physikalischer, von der Wissenschaft gesteuerter Vorgang ist, so wenig wie der Zuschauer einer Theateraufführung die Scheinwerfer . . . sichtbar vor Augen haben möchte." In "Achteckige Philharmonie," *Spiegel* 5 (1957), www.spiegel.de/spiegel/print/d-32092771.html (accessed July 8, 2010.)

30. As listed in Beranek, *Concert Halls and Opera Houses,* 603.

31. Ibid., 57–58.

32. Blesser and Salter, *Spaces Speak, Are You Listening?* 198.

33. See www.bernhardleitner.com.

34. See www.gabischillig.de.

35. Formerly the partnership of Décosterd & Rahm. Jean-Gilles Décosterd and Philippe Rahm, *Physiological Architecture = Architecture Physiologique* (Basel: Birkhäuser Verlag, 2005).

SECTION THREE
East and West
Sounds in the Shadow of the Wall

S ection I illustrated and discussed the creation of private and collective spaces of sound that either escaped the noisy urban environment (Goodyear) or tapped into an acoustical unconscious that forced the listeners of Eich's radio play *Dreams* to awaken to and to cope with the collective history of which they are a part (Ryder). Section II focused on how the experience of space influences the experience of sound. Section III moves forward in history, addressing the context of the Cold War era's soundscapes while asking: Did East and West Germany sound different? Do socialism and capitalism produce different acoustic experiences? An analysis of the strongly divergent land- or cityscapes of the former GDR and FRG would indicate market- and industry-related differences that should result in different soundscapes. For example, the Trabant, by far the dominant make of car in East Germany, was acoustically distinguishable from the variety of car makes and models available in the West. The chapters in this section use two very different approaches, one literary and one journalistic, to investigate the different soundscapes of East and West Germany. By extension, they examine the connection between sound and identity by asking whether divergent soundscapes necessarily mean divergent identities.

Curtis Swope's reading of Wolfgang Hilbig's novel *Das Provisorium* sets up the dichotomy of industrial sounds from the East (a boiler room in a Leipzig factory) and the Western sounds of consumerism (hotels and street life in Nuremberg, Munich, and Zurich). C., the protagonist in *Das Provisorium*, finds himself in the midst of these conflicting soundscapes and both positively and negatively affected by them. While C.'s experiences in the West are riddled with paranoia, due to constantly ringing telephones, and distaste, inspired by the aural waste of pornographic noise, his experiences in the East offer a different perspective. Imbued with neither silence nor with positive sound, the industrial setting in the GDR both comforts C. and threatens him with sonically induced anxieties. Swope concludes that the sonic ambivalence of these experiences suggests a corresponding ambivalence of identity in *Das Provisorium*'s protagonist.

Nicole Dietrich also examines the sounds of the East versus those of the West, yet she concentrates on Berlin. "An attention to sound," Bull and Back argue, "helps put the city in motion and alerts us to how places change as they are animated by sound. Sound and movement are closely related in the navigation of the urban experience."[1] In Dietrich's analysis, the city is alive, yet living two lives joined by a common dead zone, the Berlin Wall. Approaching this investigation from the perspective of a radio journalist, she presents interviews with citizens of the former East and West Germany on the specific sounds that they associate with the former GDR. By using the descriptions of these ear-witnesses, she illustrates that the two geographically divided German spaces in fact shared one common air- or soundspace. Her chapter is furthermore an example of how aural sensations are linked to feelings of longing and belonging, here, in both an urban and a national context.

NOTE

1. Michael Bull and Les Back, eds., *Auditory Culture Reader* (Oxford: Berg Publishers, 2003), 299.

CHAPTER 5

From the Boiler Room to the Hotel Room

Sound and Space in Wolfgang Hilbig's
Das Provisorium *(2000)*

CURTIS SWOPE

Wolfgang Hilbig, a renowned contemporary German novelist and poet who passed away in the summer of 2007, gained little official notoriety in his native East Germany (the German Democratic Republic, or GDR). He nevertheless became something of a legend in the 1970s underground literary scene in his home state of Saxony and in the Prenzlauer Berg neighborhood of East Berlin. The (in many ways well-grounded) image of Hilbig as an experimental modernist writer oppressed by communist authorities moved west with the publication of a volume of his poems, *Abwesenheit* (*Absence*), in 1979 by a major West German publisher. Hilbig himself would follow in 1985, when the East German government issued him a visa for travel to the capitalist West Germany (the Federal Republic of Germany, or FRG). When the Berlin Wall fell in November of 1989 and, less than a year later, the two Germanys were united into one (a series of events referred to as the *Wende* or turning point), Hilbig set to work on the novel *"Ich"* (*"I"*, 1993), which would establish him as one of Germany's new leading writers. Though Hilbig never collaborated with the East German secret police, the infamous Stasi, *"Ich"* traces the psychological breakdown that may have followed had he done so. Hilbig's next, again semiautobiographical, novel, *Das Provisorium* (*The Temporary Solution*, 2000), sketched the psychological torment of an East German writer in West Germany from 1985 to the Wende.[1]

Having lived in and written about three different Germanys, Hilbig was uniquely positioned to explore in his work the extent to which the Wende represented a major historical break. He was acutely aware of the different levels of technological progress in East and West. When asked in a 2001 interview whether he used a pen, typewriter, or computer to give his lavish prose textual form, he replied: "I use a mechanical typewriter and note with a certain anxiety that it is slowly falling apart, because there aren't any more to be had."[2] This assertion reflects the technophobia of a writer committed to print media at the turn of the millennium. Yet, in light of Hilbig's years of labor as a lowly factory stoker in Saxony's industrial zone, and in light of his bumpy landing in the high-tech everyday world of the FRG, the clash between mechanical typewriter and computer comes to stand for two distinct material cultures: East and West—each with very different horizons of sensory experience.

In examining this aspect of Hilbig's prose, this chapter focuses on images of sound and space in the different sonic landscapes of capitalism and socialism as represented in *Das Provisorium*.[3] The novel follows the protagonist, worker-cum-writer C., as he descends into alcoholism and wallows in his own sexual anxieties at peep shows and in hotel rooms. Narrated from the perspective of the early 1990s, C.'s journey is rendered in what essentially is a set of disordered flashbacks to and memories of different moments in his life. These moments span from his time in Leipzig just before receiving his travel visa in 1985 to his experience of changes at the Leipzig train station after the Wende. Key narrative threads, though linked only loosely, include C. ending his relationship with his girlfriend in the East; his relationship and ultimate breakup with Hedda, a woman with whom he lives in Nuremberg before the Wende; his visit to friends in Munich; his stint at a Bavarian alcoholics' retreat; and reflections on his work in a factory boiler room in the GDR, prior to 1985.

The interplay of sound and space in the novel subverts simplistic assumptions about the different fields of sensory experience in East and West and about the Wende as a radical historical rupture. Hilbig uses both Eastern and Western soundscapes, with their differing technological origins, to critique instrumental regimes of power across ideological borders and to underscore the inevitability of complicity with such regimes.[4] In both these cases, initial critique yields first to alienation then to subsumation of the self into the power structure. In the capitalist world, resentment against street music and subway noise in the Nuremberg cityscape and fear of telephones and doorbells in a Munich apartment give way to auto-erotic subjugation to pornographic films in a Zurich hotel room. In the socialist East, the writer-protagonist laments the militaristic hum of machines in a factory and the Stalinist bleating of functionaries, but goes on to celebrate the hisses of a coal-fired boiler that spur his creative energies. During the novel's climactic scene after the Wende, the protagonist lies drunk in the Leipzig train station where the sound of jackhammers preparing the station for renovation is subsumed by the visual experience of the newly corporatized space (see Figure 5.1). In these parallel narrative threads, Hilbig's text twice rearticulates the classic modern crisis of subjectivity, first in a highly modernist guise which represents the main figure's objectification by and alienation from technologies of power in nonrealist prose and next in his acceptance and conscious reenactment of his loss of self. The result is a text that draws on different intellectual and aesthetic traditions to criticize multiple paths of modernization in the twentieth century and sees post-Wende Germany not as a break from the past but as yet another flawed statist project.

To better understand Hilbig's critique and the possible antidotes he offered to modern statism, this chapter shows how his participation in the 1995 WORTspielRÄUME project, which saw motion-activated tape recordings of his works placed into the old GDR mailboxes of the former East Berlin, prefigured the problems of his novel. The project used sound to address the relation between agency and authorship on the one hand and technologies and systems of power on the other. It involved the shaping of a soundscape by a literary and artistic collective using the physical infrastructure of the GDR mail system and tried to shape

Figure 5.1
Leipzig train station.
Photograph by Curtis Swope, 2007.

spontaneous, democratic listening publics through the use of sound technology. Like the novel, the installation revived modernist gestures, in this case the creation of alternative public spheres, to critique sets of problems like dominant media forces and top-down reshaping of urban spaces that had been inherited from past iterations of German statehood. The Wende for Hilbig was not so much a reshaping of modernity in a way demanding new tactics, but rather another problematic phase of modernization that challenged artists and writers to rehearse anew strategies of critique from radicalizing subjectivity to thematizing its demise to seeking alternative forums of expression by appropriating the technologies of power themselves. *Das Provisorium* and WORTspielRÄUME are a complementary two-pronged articulation of these dilemmas.

FOCUS ON SOUND

The scholarship on Hilbig has tended to emphasize vision as a category for understanding his figures' relationship to spaces and to dominant systems more generally.[5] R. Murray Schafer, a theorist of sound, would likely see this as an example of "visual bias." "In the West," he explains in *The Soundscape: Our Sonic Environment and the Tuning of the World* (1977), "the ear gave way to the eye as the most important gatherer of information about the time of the Renaissance, with the development of the printing press and perspective painting."[6] Yet, ears work differently from eyes. Having no earlids, they receive information even as the body sleeps. The ears' mere "hearing" becomes conscious "listening" during a process in which a psychological filter in the brain selects which sounds are desirable and which are not.[7] Despite sound's distinctive qualities, however, scholars describing what is heard must rely on spatial terminology just as much as scholars describing what is seen. Sound, even in the very signifiers used to analyze it, is linked to space, because noises, even more so than sights, have a range beyond which the body cannot perceive them. The borders of such ranges define acoustic spaces, within which sounds can gain meanings through place-specific social practices.

In Hilbig's *Das Provisorium*, sound's inherent spatiality becomes a vehicle for showing how modern systems of power operate on individual subjects. Hilbig was a self-taught student of Kafka and learned from his works how to catalog processes of isolation, disorientation, and self-destruction in a world of modern technology and invasive bureaucracy.[8] This modernist technique, combined with a focus on sound, enabled him to represent his earlier protagonists as punching bags for the verbal garbage of the GDR's mainstream media and midlevel civil servants.[9] *Das Provisorium* traces an individual's identity loss and sonic disorientation in both East and West. Through this focus on sound, Hilbig participated in renewed debates about how systems of control operate (namely visually *and sonically*) at a time when West Germany's swallowing of the East was (and still is) forcing a reorganization of Germany's power structures. Most of the GDR's citizens had Western television in their apartments before 1989. After the Wende, the roar of BMWs echoed in their streets and the sounds of Western muzak filled their stores. Hilbig channeled the gaps and disjunctures of this economic transition by applying inherited literary and artistic techniques to a treatment of the relation between sound and space. In so doing, he pointed to the painful similarities between the GDR factory boiler room and the FRG chain hotel room and provided a dual antidote to *Ostalgie* and Western triumphalism.

NUREMBERG: CONFLICTING STREETSCAPES

At the novel's opening, in September of 1989, C. finds himself in Nuremberg. The capitalist streetscape's electronic sounds appear at first to be the object of stinging critique, but their status soon becomes ambiguous. C.'s hazy psychic filter makes it unclear whether the loudspeakers and rumbles he hears rising up through the pavement from the subway system below are real or imagined:

> And under the pavement the subway cars went shooting by, released now and again hosts of shoppers under the organizing voices of the loudspeaker system, directed them to the closely spaced escalators which catapulted the streams of people directly into the brightness of the shopping district.[10]

The controlled monotony of Western consumer desire here resonates in the very paving stones of Nuremberg's alleys.[11] C.'s aversion to the electronically mediated sound of the loudspeakers appears at first to critique the technology of sonic power as it militaristically regulates mindless subjects in the consumerist space of the capitalist streetscape. This is reinforced when C., immediately after hearing the loudspeakers, observes a man and woman who, leaving their table suddenly, appear to obey the dominant rhythms of consumerism, "as though there had been a warning bell in their heads."[12] The young people have internalized the mechanisms of power in a Nuremberg consumer streetscape that C. apparently despises.

Yet C.'s independence from the directed sounds of consumer culture is called into question when he encounters a young man playing guitar in a Nuremberg public square. C. dismisses this nonconsumerist gesture as "show-off music" and thinks greedily of the recently purchased record he carries under his jacket.[13] The electronic mediation of the phonograph is preferable here to the immediacy of the streetscape's ad hoc music. What could have devolved into a one-sided critique has become defused through counterimages that deliver a multiplicitous view of the Nuremberg streetscape's sounds. This matches Hilbig's own intentions for the novel as expressed in interviews after its publication, in which he asserted that any political implications grow organically from the central purpose of faithfully recreating the psychic experience of a GDR writer-worker on the streets of FRG cities.[14] This does not mean that he denies the power of critique, merely that the ambiguous meanings of electronic sounds cannot be taken simply as weaponry in a preconceived attack on capitalism.

PHONE IN THE APARTMENT: BETWEEN LIFELINE AND ASSAULT

The soundscape of C.'s Nuremberg apartment offers a similarly ambiguous set of meanings. His (electronic) telephone connects C. to an outside world that demands his emotional energy, yet paradoxically reinforces his distance from that world and exposes his inability to meet those demands. Early in the novel, Hilbig uses a phone conversation between C. and the girlfriend he left behind in Leipzig to reveal how electronic mediation dematerializes the body. As the two speak, her face fades in his mind. C. desperately tries to conjure a "real" image of her, but by the end of the call, he can refer to her only as "the voice in Leipzig."[15] The presence of this mediated sound in C.'s apartment in Nuremberg should be a bridge between his former life in the East and his current life in the West. But while the communication technology of the electronic age can cross borders, it cannot surmount the internal dislocation of the transplanted writing subject. The disembodied voice coming through the receiver—or perhaps better said, C.'s consciousness of its disembodiedness—leaves the soundscape of his apartment a spatio-sonic depravation chamber alien to both his Eastern upbringing and to the lively Nuremberg streetscape he is equally divorced from. The East-West opposition dissolves within a provisional, private space, which belongs to neither side of the divide.

The telephone becomes C.'s outright enemy in his friend's apartment in Munich, which occurs during the relationship with Hedda. After leaving, C. recalls his visit there, recounting the few images that remain in his memory. Chief among them is an early morning phone call that he perceives as a sonic assault: "He searched the three rooms desperately for the telephone, which did not want to cease ringing; finally, he had the receiver in his hand and identified himself. A woman's voice, which spoke sentences that didn't want to end and talked far too quickly, forced its way to his ear."[16] The voice is that of the woman who owns the apartment telling C. that he needs to vacate the place quickly because she and her husband need it. The ring of the doorbell makes matters worse as C., befuddled and disoriented, tries to grasp the import of the ongoing phone call. The soundscape of the apartment is hostile, its electronic gadgets allowing the outside world to deliver malicious pinpricks in C.'s aural skin.

Yet this communicative prodding mitigates the critical energy of the main figure's psychic sensitivity to the sounds of the electronic age; the whole scenario has been planned by C.'s Western girlfriend as an intervention to carry him off to an alcoholism recovery center near Munich. There is a gap here between C.'s sensory perception of the efforts to get in touch with him and the reality of his own near-demise as a result of his addiction. Because of this gap, any critique of the soundscape targets both the world of mediated communication and C.'s psyche itself. The former is guilty of reinforcing C.'s estrangement while the latter embraces a spatial isolation within which communication technology becomes a personal device for self-torture rather than a mode of establishing contact with people offering help.

However, C.'s failure to accept electronic mediation as a potential lifeline in this case does not prevent him from doing so in others. When he turns to his record player to drown out the sound of the butcher's dogs, whose barks fill the courtyard behind his Nuremberg apartment, he implicitly affirms the value of electronic sounds he had previously devalued. The dogs' yelps recur as a *leitmotiv* throughout the novel, by the end of which C. has imagined them as mythic "cerberuses" in the "vestibule of hell."[17] Their sound reduces his apartment to a "tripartite cell, in which he breathed dust and felt besieged by the tireless barking and shrieking."[18] The sound of his electronic record player and a recently purchased album by the Paul Butterfield Blues Band help reassert some measure of sonic authority by drowning out the canine howls. Within the apartment, electronically mediated rock and roll is a weapon, though ultimately futile, against the inner demons projected by a broken self onto the world around it. The sounds within private space, just as the sounds on the Nuremberg street, cut both ways and elude fixed categorization.

ZURICH HOTEL ROOM: CONQUERING VISION

The sonic space of the Zurich hotel room, where C. stays during a book tour, becomes an extension of the apartment, or perhaps an extreme form of the problems it had posed. At first, the room is a site for reinforcing the cocoon of isolation the apartment had established. After a book reading, the weather outside is beautiful, but C. sits in his room with curtains drawn, choking on the stench of cigarette smoke and his own alcoholic vomit. The telephone penetrates even this den of self-destruction: "The telephone screamed constantly; journalists wanted to speak to him; his hosts wanted to invite him to a restaurant; trembling with horror he waited for the noise to stop."[19] The telephone's invasion into the hermetic space threatens to burst the bubble of C.'s self-imposed separation. In his adopted echo chamber, C. finds that his weak body spares him human contact; he picks up the phone when Hedda calls, only to find that a "bellowing coughing fit" issues from his mouth rather than the usual greeting.[20] The noise of his aching chest inserts his body's self-induced infirmity into the electronic medium of the telephone to cut that body off from further contact.[21] C. sonically counter-colonizes the communication technology that has imposed itself on his quasi-private time in the hotel room.

C. carries a certain amount of this curious critical energy to the pay-per-view pornography he registers for and watches in the room. Sound proves more reliable than vision in this endeavor. At first, C. deconstructs the scenes, as his eyes and ears help him expose the mechanisms that lie behind the images. Maintaining an ironic distance, he thinks of suggestions he would give to the cameraman for filming bodies not made for filming: taping the man's scrotum to his thigh to get it out of the shot and creating a hole in the floor to film the couple from below. C.'s arousal, however, conquers his critical vision as the sex scene approaches its climax. His ironic distance from the visual aspects of the film fades as he is captivated by the image of the male penetrating his female partner from behind. Yet C. can maintain some critical distance through sound. He mocks the availability of both English and German language for scenes whose sound consists largely of "moaning and an even more wretched-sounding music."[22] He can still deride the lack of synchronization between moans and facial expressions, as he speculates that the sounds must be coming from cameramen forced to stand on their heads to capture the absurd shots.[23] The pornography's sounds, in a way not unlike the telephone's, ultimately become penetrating and estranging distractions that must be eliminated so that C.'s uncritical, unseeing prostration before the image can proceed.[24] While watching, he "even trie[s] to mute his coughing" and turns the TV's volume down so that he can barely hear the women's "swinish squeals."[25] C. thus exerts control over his sonic environment, in essence designing a soundscape of silence, the purpose of which is to render the space of the hotel room as purely visual as possible in order to enact the self-immolation of his fetishistic loss of vision. The attack on sound here, manifest in the production of silence, is a signal that critical alienation has given way to the deafness of a subject willingly extinguishing itself in the technologies of power.

C.'s memories of the GDR's industrial soundscapes, which he associates, at least initially, with personal creativity, stand in stark contrast to the West's ringing telephones and pornographic noise.[26] Though the West's consumer noise, which according to C. penetrates the "ear canals" and "brain cells" of citizens within its reach, is juxtaposed to the East's industry, both seek to tear down autonomous subjectivity.[27] The initial association of the GDR soundscape with personal creation finds its chilling flipside in the hum of industry's machines, which C. compares to a "column of tanks on the march."[28] This is on the one hand a reference to the GDR's growing militarism in the 1980s as an escalated nuclear arms race replaced détente. On the other, it is a link to the original sin of socialist militarism in the East as inherited from Stalin, who also bequeathed a legacy of cultural control. C. is assaulted accordingly by "verbal cannonades of Stalinist cultural functionaries."[29]

IN THE BOILER ROOM: CREATIVE SOUNDS

The factory where C. works before 1985 is cast in similar terms.[30] He recalls sitting in the break room before the workday, listening to the manufacturing process: "The different voices of the machines closed ranks into a victory-assured drone which made the plant quake in its foundations. The factory howled, as though an arsenal of airplane motors had been spurred into action."[31] The sounds of militarism reverberate through the physicality of the factory space itself. Space and sound become one as GDR industry is rendered in an almost expressionist sound imagery that converts a space of production, when projected though the lens of the writing subject, into a hellish war machine. C.'s interpretation of the sounds grafts the long-suffering experience of a writer forced into—yet cultivating—spatial isolation onto the hum of factory machines and uses modernistic techniques against a state stuck in the technological modernity of early twentieth-century heavy industry. The hindsight of knowledge of the twentieth century's greatest horrors, constantly recurring in the novel in C.'s boxes of books labeled "Holocaust and Gulag," casts the fallout of that modernity into high relief and makes its perpetuation in the Eastern bloc all the more atrocious.[32]

Yet when C. is working the nightshift alone in the boiler room, the factory takes on a different sonic guise:

> In the hall's darkness his steps crunched on the leftover metal filings, a walk of spirits too clearly heard, which doubled and tripled itself in the reverberations of this mammoth cathedral, whose religion was work. A few months ago he himself had worked here still; now he knew a cell full of glowing energy lurking in the netherworld beneath the concrete floor, a cell he ruled—and he was suddenly the secret God of this cathedral.[33]

The sound of C.'s steps, their crunch, converts them into the steps of a ritualized movement through a spiritual space. The sound echoing off the walls triggers a set of sonic associations in C.'s mind that transform the factory into a cathedral. Having earlier established the factory as a key site of the GDR's militaristic power structure, C. subverts this structure by tapping into its sonic energies and stylizing himself as their center. Sound is a psychological trigger for this fantasy of power—the echoes of C.'s footsteps make him a priest of industrial technology.

In the boiler room, industrial sounds, as both symbols and material manifestations of industrial modernization, become a vehicle for C.'s reflections on his creative process and enactment of complicity with industrial modernity. He shovels coal into the furnace and uses this experience of working in heavy industry as fuel for his own metaphors.[34] The burning coal produces steam that hisses with aggressive, mechanized energy: "In the fire channels, the fire had swollen to a drone, regular like a locomotive, like a ship's engine; from above, out of the gloomy work halls, could be heard the punches, echoing like whips, with which the steam was shooting through the piping."[35] Here, C. physically produces the powerful sounds of the GDR's industrial religion, itself representing the dying throes of nineteenth-century industrial might.[36] He also writes about this process of production in a modernist prose that rehearses his own personal story of casting off the formal strictures of socialist realism. If that literary mode had blindly celebrated gleaming new factories, Hilbig here trolls his memories for those now-ruined factories not only visually, but also sonically. C.'s exploration of the sounds he remembers in the GDR's industrial spaces and their association with his creative production entails a self-reflection alien to socialist realism's assumption of an easy relationship between the world of the text and the world of reality. This modernist technique applied to the GDR's industrial soundscape makes visible the troubled historical trajectory of one path of technological modernization in the twentieth century.

Hilbig writes here not only about industrial labor, but also about his writing's dependence on that labor in recognition of his complicity in the GDR's destructive industrial regime. C. is indeed seduced by the force of an outmoded industrial modernity, imagining himself as its perpetrator and perpetuator. His willingness to celebrate the industry's sounds becomes a ritual in which sound is not an estranging distraction to be eliminated but rather the central symbol of a momentary fantasy of power. C. recognizes his literary creativity's unholy alliance to industrial production—he compares heaving coal into the furnace to burning the "scythian forests of his childhood."[37] The writing of such fantasies in which personal advance is linked to the destruction wreaked by technology exposes complicity with a system that allows such destruction to continue. The celebration of sonic power here mirrors the complicit deafness of the hotel room scene. There, he turned the television volume down and restrained his coughing, building a soundscape of silence and performing his loss of subjectivity. In the GDR boiler room it is the orchestration of the powerful sounds of hulking machines that that allows C. to enact a parallel loss of self. Taking place after the Wende, the novel's closing image reinforces, not surprisingly, the Western paradigm of deafness, as an echoless jackhammer rattles in the distance, followed by silence. Again, the absence of sound signals the step from the modernist exploration of alienation from a sonic environment to the performance of a silent authorial death in a newly corporatized space.

SOUND SPACES

None of the sonic environments in the novel presents a one-sided picture. In fact, each set of sounds in each of the novel's key spaces affect C. both positively and negatively. The electronic sounds of Nuremberg's loudspeakers grate on him—but so too does the less mediated, more spontaneous sound of the street musicians. The telephone in his Western apartment is a lifeline and a penetrating distraction. The clanks and drones of GDR industry are associated with both militarism and creativity. Such oppositions are constructed not only within the spaces, but between the various spaces of East and West, of industry and electronics. The sounds of the East, from cultural bureaucrats to the GDR war machine, and the sounds of the West, from the noise of consumerism to the manufactured groans of pornography, plague C. in equal measure. He can reinvent industrial sounds to enact creative rituals just as the electronic blare of the record player can help him drown out barking dogs. The ringing telephone in the private spaces of C.'s isolation preys upon him as much as the train station jackhammers in the public sphere. The monstrous industrial sound of the East and the ultimate deafness in the West offer parallel forms of performed complicity. The effect of these oppositions is to leave C. no escape. In visual terms, Hilbig strips away the curtain of illusion from before C.'s eyes only to reveal that no authentic truth lies behind it.[38] In sonic terms, this means that neither one particular sound nor one particular sonic environment is privileged above any other. Eastern and Western spaces contain sounds that penetrate C.'s psyche, subjecting him to their force as manifestations of dominant power systems, whether authoritarian-socialist or banal-consumerist. Both Eastern and Western systems offer opportunities for sonic performance of self-destruction. This leveling of oppositions provides a sobering comparison between communist and capitalist modes of modernization on the one hand and industrial and electronic modes on the other.

This bleak view of both phases of technological modernity and the states they produce reaches its sonic apex at the alcoholics' retreat near Munich to which C. is driven. There, the value of human speech, of sonic language itself, is called into question. The wails and moans of those suffering from the nightmares of detoxification form an uncanny chorus whose music is the sound of pure torture. C., suffering himself, imagines that the unintelligible yelping sounds of the men going through withdrawal form a sonic wave that spreads out over the whole compound, loading its every wall with "vibrations like electric energy" in a "dialogue with an equally speechless God."[39] C. claims no understanding of these sounds and makes no attempts at offering an interpretation. The most impenetrable of all of Hilbig's space-sound explorations in the novel, this sequence is remarkably free of electronic, industrial, or, for that matter, historically locatable sounds. The groans of the alcoholics tap into an eternal narrative of human suffering removed from mere quibbles of technological change. The fears driving their nightmares remain personal. What unites them, however, is a speechless rage that must be spewed forth in order to regain speech, until once more they turn to drink to kill their ability to communicate.[40] C. acknowledges here that his will to drink is linked to his desire to destroy speech, to eliminate language, as he links the patterns of his own self-destruction to the destruction of the linguistic structures that characterize modernity itself, both industrial and electronic. The will to self-immolation is the will to destroy the dominant powers that rely on language to construct their authority.

Still, this critique of modernization does not make Hilbig a knee-jerk anti-Enlightenment thinker by any means.[41] Even though all the soundscapes of the novel are folded into the ritual of C.'s destruction, each possesses the possibility for a moment of critical agency. His participation in the sonic situationism of French poet Marc Delouze's WORTspielRÄUME project in Berlin in May and June of 1995 helped enact this agency extratextually, establishing a decidedly interventionist relationship to a public sphere dependent on language's ability to communicate. The project was conceived by Delouze in conjunction with the leaders of the Orplid literary group in Berlin, of which Hilbig was a member, as a response to the astounding pace and scale of Berlin's post-Wende reconstruction. In order to offer a kind of historical counterweight to the growth of new neighborhoods, the project's designers hid taped recordings of the work of French and German authors from Balzac to Heiner Müller, from Voltaire to Hilbig inside the public mailboxes of the former GDR, then still intact in the neighborhoods of the former East Berlin. When passersby came within several meters of the boxes, the recordings inside were activated and the sound of, among other works, Wolfgang Hilbig's novels came floating out to the bewildered pedestrian. Most prominent and popular were the boxes along Karl-Marx-Allee, which were particularly entertaining to children (see Figure 5.2).[42]

More intriguing, though, is that Hilbig's sonic and spatial co-appropriation of the one-time Stalinallee for the forging of a spontaneous literary public, using the material apparatus of the much controlled, much spied-on GDR mail system, was started as a response to the forces of capitalism as they reshaped the city. The project's recolonization of a soundscape once dominated by Eastern bureaucrats, now dominated by the noise of consumerism, anticipated the critical oppositions Hilbig would set up in Das Provisorium, which he was just beginning around the time of the installations. Yet these installations allowed Hilbig's texts to transcend those oppositions by using sound to engage an ad hoc public on the GDR's most famous boulevard, ideally causing listeners to reflect on their surroundings and their own participation in the ever-changing soundscapes. If Hilbig's novel would explore the relationship between sound and space and create sonic environments that left the main figure subsumed by his own complicity with systems of power, then taking the sound of his prose to the streets could transform those texts into activist attempts to undercut the dynamics of complicity the characters within those texts enacted. Literature's sound in a material space rich in symbolism is an activist flip side to the destructive, and equally symbolic, sonic environments Hilbig constructed in Das Provisorium. But both the novel and the sonic installation share the use of techniques inherited from various modernist (and postmodernist) literary and artistic movements in order to point to sets of problems the Wende has by no means erased. In fact, Hilbig's prose and his urban intervention treat the Wende and the new German Republic as iterations of long-standing problems relating to modern systems of control and

Figure 5.2
Karl-Marx Allee.
Photograph by Curtis Swope, 2007.

possibilities for aesthetic critique. As such, both text and literary installation are contributions to critical post-Wende discourses that seek to engage the present by turning to modernity's troubled past trajectories, exploring the burden of catastrophic histories, and self-consciously reviving aesthetic techniques harnessed to criticize those histories as they were unfolding.

NOTES

1. Though there is as of yet no scholarly biography of Hilbig, who died in Berlin in June of 2007, much scholarly work on his prose has taken a biographical approach. See Thomas Beckermann, "Eigenwillige Ankunft. Einige Anmerkungen zu Wolfgang Hilbig vor seiner

ersten Buchveröffentlichung," in *Wolfgang Hilbig: Materialien zu Leben und Werk*, ed. Uwe Wittstock (Frankfurt am Main: Fischer Taschenbuch Verlag, 1994), 93–113; Churaithong Thongyai, "Zwischen Naivität und Strategie: Eine Untersuchung zur literarischen Laufbahn Wolfgang Hilbigs," in *Literarisches Feld DDR: Bedingungen und Formen literarischer Produktion in der DDR*, ed. Ute Wölfel (Würzburg: Königshausen & Neumann, 2005), 91–103; Gabriele Eckart, "Autobiographie als radikale Selbstkritik in Wolfgang Hilbigs Roman *Das Provisorium*," *Germanic Notes and Reviews* 35: 1 (Spring 2004): 30–44. Translations are mine unless otherwise noted.

2. Quoted in Jürgen Krätzer, "'Für einen Schriftsteller, der einen Text schreibt, ist die Welt immer auf irgendeine Weise provisorisch': Ein Gespräch mit Wolfgang Hilbig," *Die Horen: Zeitschrift für Literatur, Kunst und Kritik* 46 (3 [203]) (2001): 144–145. "Ich benutze eine mechanische Schreibmaschine und sehe mit einer gewissen Angst, daß diese langsam auseinander fällt, denn es gibt keine mehr."

3. For a journalistic approach to the sonic difference between East and West, see Nicole Dietrich's chapter in this book.

4. Julia Hell has linked Hilbig to modernism's estranging literary devices but has insisted that, whereas Brecht estranges in order to reveal a truth, Hilbig believes there is no single truth to be revealed. Julia Hell, "Wendebilder: Neo Rauch and Wolfgang Hilbig," *Germanic Review* 77:4 (2002): 279–303, 285. While she does not call this technique "postmodern" or "poststructuralist" others have. See Rhonda R. Duffaut, "The Function of Poststructuralism in Wolfgang Hilbig's Novel *Ich*," in *Rückblicke auf die Literatur der DDR*, ed. Hans-Christian Stillmark and Christoph Lehker (Amsterdam: Rodopi, 2002), 371–88. Paul Cooke explicitly rejects any claim that Hilbig is "postmodern." Paul Cooke, "Countering 'Realitätsverlust': Wolfgang Hilbig and the 'Postmodern Condition,'" in *The Writers' Morality/Die Moral der Schriftsteller*, ed. Ronald Speirs (Oxford: Peter Lang, 2000), 123.

5. Julia Hell, "Eyes Wide Shut: German Post-Holocaust Authorship," *New German Critique* Winter 88 (2003): 9–36. Many other studies explore the visual aspects of Hilbig's prose. See Erk Grimm, "Im Abraum der Städte: Wolfgang Hilbigs topographische 'Ich'-Erkundung," *Text + Kritik: Zeitschrift für Literatur* July 123 (1994): 62–74; Hell, "Wendebilder"; Genia Schulz, "Graphomanien: Zur Prosa Wolfgang Hilbigs," *Merkur: Deutsche Zeitschrift für europäisches Denken* 41:5 [459] (May 1987): 413–18.

6. R. Murray Schafer, *The Tuning of the World: Toward a Theory of Soundscape Design* (Philadelphia: University of Pennsylvania Press, 1977), 10. Schafer goes on to assert that this had ramifications for the ways in which cultures imagine God. Sound had played a much greater role in conceptions of divinity prior to the Renaissance. Schafer, 10–11.

7. Ibid., 11.

8. Hilbig's modernist gestures have been compared to Kafka's. See Beckermann, "Eigenwillige Ankunft"; Helmut Böttiger, "Monströse Sinnlichkeiten, negative Utopie. Wolfgang Hilbigs DDR-Moderne," *Text und Kritik* 123 (1994): 52–61; Hans-Dieter Schütt, "Kafka in Meuselwitz," *Neues Deutschland*, March 19, 2003; Angelika Winnen, *Kafka-Rezeption in der Literatur der DDR: Produktive Lektüren von Anna Seghers, Klaus Schlesinger, Gert Neumann und Wolfgang Hilbig* (Würzburg: Königshausen & Neumann, 2006).

9. Key among these is the protagonist of *"Ich."* Space is a central trope here. See Jennifer Marston William, "Spatial Language and Dissolving Dichotomies in Wolfgang Hilbig's '*Ich*,'" *Germanic Review* 80:2 (2005): 164–78. William focuses specifically on the ambiguity of the East-West border in the main figure's psyche.

10. Wolfgang Hilbig, *Das Provisorium* (Frankfurt am Main: S. Fischer, 2000), 9. "Und unter dem Pflaster jagten die U-Bahnen herbei, entließen unter den ordnenden Stimmen der Lautsprecheranlagen wiederum Scharen von Käufern, dirigierten sie auf die dicht bestandenen Rolltreppen, welche die Menschenstöme direkt in die Helligkeit des Einkaufsviertels katapultierten."

11. Hilbig had already used vibrations in stone to represent Berlin in *"Ich."* There, the narrator sits in the catacombs beneath the city listening to the metaphoric hum of urban life in the concrete around him. See Wolfgang Hilbig, *"Ich"* (Frankfurt am Main: S. Fischer, 1993), 20. The vibrations of urban stone in *Das Provisorium* seem more realist because they are caused by the subway. Yet the detail with which C. renders the noises of people and vehicles below him suggests that sonic imagination is at work as much as realist "hearing."

12. Ibid., 10–11, "als hätte es in ihren Köpfen ein Klingelsignal gegeben."

13. Ibid., 15. "Vorzeigemusik."

14. Krätzer, "Für einen Schriftsteller," 149. Though critical of consumer culture, Hilbig acknowledged his participation in it. In a 1998 interview he noted his expensive reading glasses and recent purchase of three sweaters at half price. He even praised Westerners for their control of consumer instincts, citing by contrast Easterners' unhealthy lust for new cars. See B. Kern, "Die verdächtige Pünktlichkeit der Züge," *die tageszeitung*, February 19, 1998, 27.

15. Hilbig, *Das Provisorium*, 18–19.

16. Ibid., 40. "Verzweifelt suchte er in den drei Räumen nach dem Telefon, das nicht aufhören wollte zu klingeln; endlich hatte er den Hörer in der Hand und meldete sich. Eine Frauenstimme drang an sein Ohr, die nicht enden wollende Sätze sprach und viel zu schnell redete."

17. Ibid., 22–23, 158, 308. "Zerberusse," "Vorraum der Hölle."

18. Ibid., 307. "dreigeteilten Zelle, in der er Staub atmete und sich belagert fühlte vom unermüdlichen Bellen und Keifen."

19. Ibid., 129. "Dauernd schrillte das Telefon, Journalisten wollten ihn sprechen, seine Veranstalter wollten ihn ins Restaurant einladen, zitternd vor Entsetzen wartete er darauf, daß das Läuten wieder aufhörte."

20. Ibid., 131. "ein brüllender Hustenanfall."

21. Though Hilbig himself resisted readings that saw C.'s plight as a medical "case study," such an interpretation is valuable. Christine Cosentino has lumped *Das Provisorium* into the category of twenty-first century studies in illness. For Hilbig's view of the "case study" reading see Krätzer, "'Für einen Schriftsteller.'" For an actual "case study" reading see Christine Cosentino, "Christa Wolfs *Leibhaftig* und Wolfgang Hilbigs *Das Provisorium*: Zwei 'Krankenberichte' an der Jahrtausendwende," *Germanic Notes and Reviews* Fall 34: 2 (2003): 121–27.

22. Hilbig, *Das Provisorium*, 170. "Gejammer und einer noch jämmerlicher klingenden Musik."

23. The sounds of the pornography, consumerism, and Stalinist bureaucrats alike fit into Hilbig's well-documented fascination with visual detritus. Like images of the GDR's poisoned countryside, the sounds of the pornography become emblematic testaments to the side effects of blind faith in progress. For Hilbig on "waste" see Alan Corkhill, "Scarred Landscapes: Wolfgang Hilbig's Ecocritique," *AUMLA: Journal of the Australasian Universities Language and Literature Association* 96 (November 2001): 173–88.

24. Julia Hell has taken C.'s scopophilia as the structuring element of the narrative. She sees C.'s loss of "seeing" as part of Hilbig's comment on a "radical loss of any sense of epistemological privilege" that in turn structures his take on authorship in the wake of the Holocaust. Hell, "Eyes Wide Shut," 21.

25. Hilbig, *Das Provisorium*, 175. "versucht sogar gedämpft zu husten," "schweinische Quieken."

26. One reviewer has seen Hilbig's equation of Western capitalism with technology and sex as something of a cliché. The reviewer saves Hilbig from this charge by reading the insufficiency of this critique as part of the novel's larger aesthetics of self-doubt. I accept this and would add that the cliché is undone by the ambiguity of Hilbig's dichotomies, which ultimately calls them into question. Gerrit Bartels, "Innenraummonster," *die Tageszeitung*, March 23, 2000, 4.

27. Ibid., 180. "Gehörgänge," "Hirnzellen."

28. Ibid., 271. "eine Kolonne von Panzerfahrzeugen i[m] Marsch."

29. Ibid., 275. "die verbalen Kanonaden stalinistischer Kulturfunktionäre."

30. This section is concerned with the sound of the factory specifically and of industry more generally. In Chapter 7, David Tompkins considers how the importance of industrial labor became part of socialist realist music.

31. Ibid. 284–285. "die verschiedenen Stimmen der Maschinen schlossen sich zusammen zu einem siegesgewissen Dröhnen, das den Betrieb in seinen Grundfesten erzittern ließ. Das Werk heulte, als habe man ein Arsenal von Flugzeugmotoren in Gang gesetzt."

32. Hilbig has been included among GDR writers who criticized their state's hyperrational planning and in so doing criticized modernity more generally, particularly its environmental destruction. This was a theme for Hilbig in slightly lesser known and shorter works from the late 1980s and early 1990s including some of the stories in *Arbeit am Ofen* (Frankfurt: S. Fischer, 1994). See Alan Corkhill, "Scarred Landscapes."

33. Hilbig, *Das Provisorium*, 287. "Im Dunkel der Hallen knirschten seine Schritte auf liegengebliebenen Metallspänen, ein Geisterschritt, der überdeutlich zu hören war, der sich verdoppelte und verdreifachte im Widerhall dieser riesenhaften Kathedrale, deren Religion die Arbeit war. Vor wenigen Monaten hatte er hier selbst noch gearbeitet, jetzt wußte er um eine lauernde Zelle voller glühender Energie im Jenseits unter dem Betonboden, die er beherrschte, und er war plötzlich der geheime Gott dieser Kathedrale."

34. The boiler room had been central to Hilbig's prose prior to *Das Provisorium*. Helmut Böttiger has called the space the "focal point of all associations" in Hilbig's work ("Mittelpunkt aller Assoziationen"). See Böttiger, "Monströse Sinnlichkeiten," 56. This is not the case in *Das Provisorium*, in which the boiler room is but one among a network of sonic spaces, each of which is harnessed in the larger critique of Western and Eastern modernization projects. Yet given Hilbig's obsessive rendering of the boiler room's sounds in his 1990 short story "Über den Tonfall" ("On Sound"), it is not surprising that this is one of the richest passages in *Das Provisorium*.

35. Hilbig, *Das Provisorium*, 292. "In den Feuerkanälen war der Brand zu einem Dröhnen angeschwollen, gleichmäßig wie ein Eisenbahnzug, wie eine Schiffsmaschine; von oben, aus den noch finsteren Werkhallen, hörte man die peitschend nachhallenden Schläge, mit denen der Dampf durch die Rohrleitungen schoß."

36. Erk Grimm, writing about Hilbig's prose before *Das Provisorium*, sees the boiler room scenes as re-creations of the sensory experience of nineteenth-century industry. I agree, but would add that *Das Provisorium* sees these sounds as relics that nevertheless shaped the consciousness of generations of GDR citizens. Inasmuch as those citizens still reflect that experience, the boiler room scenes do not replicate the nineteenth century as much as they explore current political and social problems in a time of historical transition. See Grimm, "Im Abraum."

37. Ibid., 291.

38. Hell, "Wendebilder," 285.

39. Ibid., 44–47, 48–49. "Vibrationen wie elektrische Energien", "Zwiesprach mit einem ebenso sprachlosen Gott."

40. Ibid., 48–49.

41. Cooke and Corkhill have shown as much.

42. Gaby Hartel, "Grass bröckelt im Amselgang," *die tageszeitung*, May 20, 1995, 32. For more on Delouze's larger project of sonic and textual intervention see Marc Delouze and Daniel Fournier, *La Diagonale des Poètes 1982–2002: vingt ans d'intervention* (Genouilleux: éditions la passe du vent, 2002). For more on the reception of the Berlin project, particularly in the GDR-built housing estate of Marzahn, see Alexandra Mundt, "Briefkästen 'sprechen an,'" *Berliner Zeitung*, June 15, 1995.

CHAPTER 6

Berlin Sounds
Audible Cartography of a Formerly Divided City

NICOLE DIETRICH

Sometimes silence can be enriching. While talking, it is difficult to concentrate on smells, touches, and sounds. Being silent is the precondition for being open to the variety of sensations that a human being can absorb. This chapter is informed by radio journalism, in that it deals with sound memories and the absence of speech, while at the same time relying on the instrument of language to express the tension between speech and ambient sound. This tension, typical for any radio interview, demonstrates how enriching sound can be to a story and how powerfully its absence can be felt; as thematized in the introduction of this book, it is difficult to put sound into words, yet articulating remembered sounds provides a better understanding and a more vivid memory of the past. The interviews in this chapter speak to the importance of using sounds to remember and to the meaning(s) of silence.

SENSUAL GEOGRAPHY

With regard to urban space, one often forgets that the city is not only perceived visually but invites its inhabitants on a sensual journey. Rolf Lindner, professor of European Cultural Anthropology at the Humboldt University Berlin, conducted a visual, acoustic, tactile, and olfactory study of three selected streets in that city (Ackerstraße, Adalbert-Straße, and Karl-Marx-Straße) from April 2006 until September 2007[1] and presented the research findings in three parallel exhibitions at the Museum Mitte am Festungsgraben, the Kreuzberg Museum, and the Gallerie Saalbau in Neukölln. On his accompanying Web site *Sensing the street. Eine Straße in Berlin*, Lindner wrote: "A street in Berlin: the chirping of birds and the roaring of exhaust pipes, graffiti-colorful and concrete-grey, head scarf and leather jacket, East and West next to each other: the Adalbertstraße [in Berlin-Kreuzberg] is a landscape of sensual oppositions."[2]

This chapter focuses on the role of sound in acoustically reliving Berlin between 1961 and 1989. An investigation into the city's soundscapes opens new layers of experiencing the urban context and leads to a deeper understanding of the city. In order to hear these sounds, one has to listen carefully. Yet the nature of listening is a complicated and complex one, as Barry Truax points out in his book *Acoustic Communication*:

> We should recall that whereas hearing can be regarded as a somewhat passive ability that seems to work with or without conscious effort, listening implies an active role involving dif-fering levels of attention—"listening for," not just "listening to."... A general characteristic of cognitive processing that seems to lie at the basis of listening is the detection of difference. Sound is predicated on change at every level.... Therefore, we may characterize the first stage of cognitive processing as the detection of change. Detail is important, but only when it presents new information.[3]

Sound, sound environments, or soundscapes in this chapter do not refer to noise, oral history, or music. Instead, the focus is on ambient sounds and specific sources of signals. An ambient sound is an acoustic summary of whatever encloses the listener, though it does so unintentionally.[4] Listeners are touched by something that is not embedded in chords and tunes like music and is not encoded linguistically like language.[5] The main difference between music and ambient sound lies in the individual's choice of what kind of music to listen to, as opposed to the lack of agency one has in being exposed to the noises around oneself. It is these sounds, seemingly insignificant to the listener, which nonetheless affect one, regardless of one's decision, choice, taste, or will.

The term "ambient sound" (or "soundsphere") addresses what producers of radio docu-mentaries, such as the author of this chapter, refer to as an "acoustic atmosphere." While it can easily cause problems during an audio production and in the process of editing, it is also painfully missed when it is not there. For example, while recording the soundscapes of Mumbai, Lisbon, and Detroit in order to create a mimetic city portrait for the radio, one should not try to artificially create these ambiences. Every city has its own characteristic "city sound" like it has its own architecture, its own pace, and its own social dynamics.

Yet many choose to alienate themselves from the sounds of their city. In his critique of urban human behavior, composer and theorist John Cage observed:

> Many people in our society now go around the streets and in the buses and so forth playing radios with earphones on and they don't hear the world around them. They hear only what they have chosen to hear. I can't understand why they cut themselves off from that rich experience which is free. I think this is the beginning of music.[6]

Music means "com-posing" audible elements whereas ambient sounds position themselves arbitrarily in space. What Cage considered the beginning of music is the aforementioned phenomenon of audible presence. Usually these sounds are filtered out as annoying and interfering. Since they have no obvious purpose or, arguably, relevant information they are disregarded as bothersome occurrences, useless for communication or—even worse—as harmful particles of acoustic pollution. These phenomena are—contrary to Cage's rehabilita-tion of them as musical components—still considered to be the opposite of music.[7]

Furthermore the appearance of ambient sound is beyond the control of the listener. The English language is able to express this often unsolicited obtrusion with the dual meaning of the term "volume";[8] sound occupies a certain space and acoustic intensity when perceived. In particular, ambient sound radiates unasked, bounces back intangibly with sources often tricky to localize. In short, these sounds are ephemeral and present at the same time; they are neither fictitious nor intentionally made by an author or composer and very rarely created according to a plan or set of rules. This kind of audible emergence is best described as an unintentional encounter that questions both the positioning of the self (the listener) as well as the other (the source). Ambient soundscapes are hard to decipher due to the fact that their elements are hard to separate. The ear filters out what it already knows and tries to find order in chaos: when one thinks of a cobblestone street with people, cars, radios, and dogs, the loudest source—probably the old car with its rusty exhaust pipe—will get the most attention, but it will mix with the barking of the dog and the sounds of high heels stepping on the cobblestones. In other words, it is hard to completely separate one source from the other, even more so if they are unknown sources. Thus, the conscious perception of these ambient sounds depends on the listener's position in space, on the closeness to the source, and on the meaning of the sounds for the listener in terms of danger or irritation or other information.[9]

Professional radio journalists are used to handling sounds differently, simply because radio enables the sounds to speak for themselves. Any kind of sound is respected, as all sounds add layers of meaning to what one produces for radio. In radio, sound is even more crucial than in television because there is no visual backup. Just imagine hearing a voice that tells a story: how much more effective is it when there is the "right" sound in the background? With the "right" sound, radio journalists can alter the meaning of what this person is saying, they can manipulate the level of attention, they can frame certain utterances acoustically and, by doing so, create multiple layers of perception and meaning. These impressions emotionally and directly affect the listeners.[10] Knowing this from my work in the studio, I wanted to explore how the ambient sounds of the everyday influence one's life. This chapter, then, leaves the studio and ventures out into the streets of Berlin, seeking to explore the power of auditory socialization. It asks, how can seemingly meaningless background noise become extremely meaningful in a city in which space is heavily politicized? And what role does sound play with respect to memory?

This chapter presents research findings of how aural sensations are linked to feelings of longing and belonging in an urban context.[11] Berlin seemed to be an ideal playground to learn about parameters of auditory socialization: two urban entities between 1961 and 1989, the German Democratic Republic (GDR) in the East and the Federal Republic of Germany (FRG) in the West, were geographically close yet ideologically far away. Consequently, they produced different typical city sounds following the rules of industrial design, media taste, technological development, and local accents. In regard to Berlin before, during, and after 1989, the following questions were of interest: What did the East and the West sound like? Which sounds are still recognized and identified with specific places? Which of them have been lost and are sorely missed? Can one still hear the difference between East and West today? For this research, historians, sound artists, anthropologists, and scholars of literature and theater were consulted, as well as the inhabitants of both the former East and West of Berlin. I recorded the interviews and collected sound samples from the Deutsche

Rundfunkarchiv Potsdam-Babelsberg (the German radio and television broadcast archive), a historic catalog of atmospheric or ambient sounds, as basic material for various radio documentaries that were then produced for Austrian Public Radio (ORF, Ö1).

FOUNTAINS: EAST GERMAN SOUNDMARKS IN THE CITY

Interviewees from the former East Berlin often stated that the sounds they missed from their neighborhoods the most were those of fountains. Before 1989, fountains were fundamental icons for meeting places in public parks and squares, and many of them were erected in East Berlin as prestigious signs of the regime. In the decade after 1989, most of them were shut down or deconstructed due to the city's financial collapse and privatization of water supplies. The East Berliners interviewed for this project reacted very emotionally to the sound of those fountains' water; a sound that made them calm and provided the soundtrack for social exchange. They emphasized its contemplative quality in the middle of the urban rush.[12] The concrete fountains had become metaphors for the antagonism of natural harmony and artificial, technical environments. They were also remembered as a public luxury. Fountains in West Berlin were neither so numerous nor so popular and therefore not missed. Nor were they associated with a specific place; in other words, they were not *localized*.

In the last few years, some of the fountains in the Eastern parts of the city were reopened, not with public funding but instead by private initiatives, recognizing that spaces with fountains are recreation areas within the city. I visited one of them close to Jannowitzbrücke in Berlin Mitte. In the noisy desert of Plattenbauten (industrial apartment blocks) and heavy traffic, a group of people were hanging out at a tiny fountain, not bigger than a bath tub, easy to miss. Because the district around Jannowitzbrücke is a heavily trafficked area, they had to stand close together to hear one another's words. All of them, I soon found out, lived in the nearby Plattenbauten and were frequent visitors of the pub (also called Jannowitzbrücke) situated right in front of the fountain. Some were retired, some held jobs, while others indicated they were between jobs. What they all shared was their common past in the GDR and the fact that they identified with and were proud of this site, because they associated it with their former country.

Pub owner Barbara Lauenburg stated:

Well, water is pleasant, a joy like flowers, you know, Berliners love the water. That's why we have so many fountains in Berlin, I mean, did you know Berlin has more bridges than Venice? Water is for people from Berlin-Brandenburg what the mountains are for Austrians or Swiss, it has the same effect. You sit down in between the houses, you listen to the fizzing and spluttering, you see the light reflecting and mirrored in the water, after some time you calm down, the sound of the water becomes louder, begins to dominate your senses. It creates an atmosphere, it means relaxing in a sea of concrete. . . .

I remember meeting at Straußberger Platz [in Berlin-Lichtenberg, N.D.] or at the Neptunbrunnen at Alexanderplatz, close to the TV tower. It was a spectacle, an attraction: the fountains would rise up five or six meters high, the cascades would flow. That was impressive, a meeting point for everybody. Or the Märchenbrunnen close to Königstor at Friedrichshain. It contained sculptured figures, all from fairy tales of the Brothers Grimm, very appealing for children. People loved these sites. The children gathered, they played here, it was peaceful. . . .

I am an old East Berliner, living in East Berlin since 1976, and I can tell, coming from the countryside: fountains compensate for the lack of nature in a city. Once they are torn down, something is missing. Living in a city means stress and lots of angry people. Sitting in front of a fountain makes people relax, I forget about how much shit happens in the lives of most of us. And I forget about the ugliness of my surroundings, because my ears take over. . . .

In GDR times, water didn't play a role. We had enough of it, and it was a source that belonged to everyone. It was part of local culture. You cannot separate water, you cannot own it, so you cannot privatize it. That's what I think, but the city agents think differently; they have sold what cannot be sold. It was ours. It is ours. And I miss the water games, the fresh and cool air surrounding the water, the noise it made when you approached it, it is a sound that is loud and pure at the same time, it is the sound of infinity. You know, West Berliners cannot appreciate these "modest" sources of public pleasure, because they lack the experience of social warmth and solidarity. That's what they envied us for but would never admit. And now they want to teach us that we have to learn that nothing is for free, anything must be paid for. . . .

Fountains are a part of Berlin, they belong here like the tram or the river Spree. When they are shut down, they are a disgraceful image. A fountain is there to work, let the water run. As long as our fountain didn't run—that was for fifteen years, shut down shortly after eighty-nine—it was used as a trash bin. The area became noticeably dilapidated. That was frustrating. For seven years now, I have been active in the fountain initiative, mobilizing the neighborhood, raising money, inspiring sponsors like a nearby brewery, the Berlin water supply, an insurance company, as well as an advertising company which declared itself as "the" Berlin fountain sponsor in return for advertising space. I learned that a fountain like our Pfauenbrunnen is good for business. It prettifies and stimulates.[13]

Lauenburg and the other anonymous East Berliners described the sound of the fountain as "peaceful" and did not seem to pay attention at all to the ongoing traffic jams—quite contrary to my own perception of this high-traffic area with the roaring of engines, shutting of car doors, and honking of horns. Instead, their ears "took over." It is interesting to note that, with the exception of the "ugliness of the surroundings," none of them mentioned specific negative sounds associated with the GDR. On the contrary, their ears harbored memories of the pleasure of sitting around a fountain in a public place, making them nostalgic about the agreeable sounds they were familiar with and rejecting the memories of sounds that were not so positive or meaningful.[14]

Today, by claiming the fountain's sounds as something specifically East German, they claim the entire unified space around the fountain to be East German—a sound and therefore a space the West Berliners would not appreciate or even understand. The shutting down of the fountains and the accompanying lack of their sound was, for them, yet another example of how the West took over the East. Most fountains were not disassembled, but, by shutting off the water, the city water supply stripped the fountains of their function. They were transformed from a nurturing place of relaxation for adults and children into abstract sculptures, seemingly useless. The fountain could not work as a visual landmark as its sounds made it into a soundmark. Sound created and triggered memory and led to a combined perception of acoustic and physical sensations: by reminiscing about the sounds of her "safe haven," the fountain, Lauenburg also recalled "fresh and cool air surrounding the water." The shutting down of the water, from the perspective of the interviewees, was equal to taking away their meeting space altogether, or to stripping them of their past. They associated water with community life, and its sound was equated with relaxation, the coming together of families, and the warmth of community during GDR times.

With the fall of the Berlin Wall and the reunification, many distinct acoustic features like the fountains have vanished, unless they were preserved for historical or archival reasons. Sounds that were supposedly typical for East Berlin before 1989, such as the jingles of Radio Moscow or RIAS,[15] megaphones and parades in public spaces, cobblestone streets, tramways, or the wide streets with specific echoes, were all mentioned as features of sound distinction in the divided city. The tiny reopened fountain behind the Jannowitzbrücke seemed to be one of the few aural souvenirs kept from the GDR available to everyday people (i.e., those without access to sound archives)—in other words, a constant reminder of the happy times of the past.

SOUNDS OF TRAFFIC: NAME THAT CAR!

After witnessing how people had claimed the sounds of fountains as something specifically East German, I sorted through the German radio and television broadcast archive, listening to many hours of street sounds, sirens, public announcements, parades, media jingles, technical devices such as toasters or tape recorders, and many other sounds to develop an aural survey for my interviewees. A series of tests was designed to find out what other sounds Ossis (East Germans) and Wessis (West Germans) would recognize as distinctively "theirs." Would people claim sounds depending on their auditory socialization? Would Ossis and Wessis separate themselves based on their acoustic memory? After being confronted with various sound bits, both groups were asked to identify sounds: GDR sirens, copy machines, home appliances, factory sounds in the neighborhood, doorbells, ringing telephones, and the like. The sound of traffic—car horns, car doors, and the sound of engines—seemed particularly interesting after interviewing Dirk Jacob, who had grown up in the West and who was responsible for the sound design in German films like *Good-bye, Lenin!* (2003), *Knallhart* (2006), and *Requiem* (2006). Jacob was convinced that traffic sounds are the most important acoustic ingredient to make a film historically "authentic" and credible. Such sounds, he stated, he would never "fake" digitally; rather, he reconstructed them by using archival material or reactivating original vehicles, like recording real trucks such as the Robur 80 on the set. "You should not pay attention to the sound, the sound should have an effect by itself," he said. "Sound acts subliminally. You realize the difference when you watch a film and turn it off. So is the difference between East and West, too: a noticeable—however subliminal—fact."[16]

The interviews started off with cars, since only a few car brands like Trabant, Wartburg, and Skoda S100 were available in the GDR; in light of this limited availability, it seemed that all interviewees would be familiar with the sounds. I met with two men and one woman from the former East: a lawyer, an archive employee, and a teacher. They listened to a few of the sound samples from the archive and were then asked to identify the sounds produced by car doors, motorbikes, and car engines. Here are two responses:[17]

> This is a motorbike MZ, a two-cycle engine, a typical GDR motorbike, no doubt, whether from the seventies or eighties. Well, and there, the banging of doors, maybe a Wartburg, the muffled sound is definitely not a Trabi, that I know, you feel that in your stomach, you know. . . .

> I couldn't tell, I have heard that sound before but I couldn't name it . Oh, that is outing me as a Wessi! Now somebody said "Kerstin," and the way she said that is clearly Eastern. This exact German, the tonality, you cannot miss that, neither as a Wessi nor as an Ossi, but from the sound of the cars alone, I cannot tell.

Many people from the East were able to easily distinguish among different car brands. They also showed an obvious pride in these car sounds. In comparison, people who grew up in the West were not able to identify the various car doors except for the Trabi—a car often cited in Western media as synonymous with the Eastern bloc. They were not familiar with any of the other car brands' sounds. "Oh, that is outing me as a Wessi" was a typical phrase heard in this game of search, recognition, and error—a game well suited to assess what is acoustically familiar and therefore part of local identity and sovereignty.[18]

In both of the following examples, sounds associated with traffic actively triggered East Berliners' childhood memories:

> Or in this song from the radio in the background ["Blaue Fahnen nach Berlin"], I wonder if it is from the fifties or from the "Deutschlandtreffen 64" . . . ah, now they are singing "nach Deutschland wehen." That must be from the fifties then, an FDJ [Freie Deutsche Jugend, N.D.] song, when the term "Deutschland" was still used; later that changed. 1964 Deutschlandtreffen, I was nine years old at that time, but for my elder siblings that was a huge event . . . well, radio sounds at the gas station, the words make it easier to identify the car park [laughs]. . . .
>
> There are a few traffic sounds, I remember, that have vanished completely, yes indeed. For example a street where nothing happens except a Trabi chugging around the corner. This hardly exists anymore. Or, there are no more Skoda S100s. When you were riding this Skoda S100, at a speed of exactly eighty kilometers per hour, it produced a roaring that would absorb all other frequencies, so you would be almost deaf. When I was a child, I enjoyed that so much, I would incite my mother: "Stay on eighty, stay there," and then came this strange roaring, where no voice could persist, as the basic frequencies of your voice were sucked, and you yourself were almost vibrating.

This investigation of the connection between sound and memory showed that the memories triggered even caused the interviewees to relive the physical sensations of that time. Again, all memories were positive—none of the interviewees remembered the adrenaline rush when suddenly hearing sirens of ambulances or the impatient honking of horns in traffic. In addition, none of the car sounds were perceived as isolated objects, but rather seen in the context of the entire soundscape, along with radio sounds and a human voice. As in the case of the fountains, the selectiveness of human memory should be examined: which sounds are still remembered today, and more interesting, which ones are not?

AT THE BORDER: SOUND INSULATIONS AGAINST THE WEST

Learning about the sounds of and within a privatized space such as a car led to exploring the sounds of public transportation, as many more people in both East and West Berlin used the city's transit system on a daily basis. What were the soundscapes on the tram and in the stations? Was there something specifically East or West German about these sounds? Before 1989, the train station Berlin-Friedrichstraße in Berlin-Mitte (see Figure 6.1), a giant transfer station for trains above and under ground and covered by an impressive roof made of glass and steel, was situated on GDR territory. All other stations on the Western lines that ran through East Berlin territory were sealed off. These "ghost stations" through which trains passed without stopping were nevertheless heavily guarded. Berlin-Friedrichstraße, however, served as a transfer point for West Berlin municipal railways and the subway (line U6). When a West Berlin passenger got out at Friedrichstraße station, he or she could transfer from one platform to another but was not allowed to leave the station (and enter the GDR) without the appropriate papers.

Figure 6.1
Train Station Berlin-Friedrichstraße.
Photograph by Nicole Dietrich, 2010.

Annette Scharnberg, who lived and worked as a psychoanalyst in West Berlin before the fall of the Berlin Wall, commuted from her apartment in West Berlin through East Berlin to her workplace in West Berlin. As the train passed through the East, she recalled:

On my way to [Berlin-]Wedding, I went through the East and I remember that everything there sounded a bit different. The underground itself sounded different, too. Instead of going fast and stopping periodically, it went really slowly through the guarded ghost stations. There was a specific sound to this slowness, somehow hollow, maybe because they were emptier. This hollow clack, clack, clack. A different resonance cavity. I think it is like in some films . . . steps approaching you across a big dark room: clack, clack, clack. This hollow sound—I think that stands for something threatening. A hollow sound in the emptiness. And it was emphasized by this light, too, a bluish kind of light. Sound and light together created a very special experience that was a bit threatening but also interesting. It stirred your curiosity.[19]

Again, remembering sound does not happen through the sonic channel only—remembering the space in the interview, Scharnberg could sense more than acoustics; she remembered the specific light inside the station. All these sensual perceptions combined to loom as something larger, something uncanny, eerie, and unknown. She also mentions that these sounds were both threatening and interesting. Though there surely were other passengers, Scharnberg's sonic memories do not include human voices. By contrast, Claudia Armenious, a teacher from West Berlin, remembered East Berlin guards: "I will always remember the border guards asking you: 'Any weapons, ammunition, kids?' in this fierce tone you only knew from these guards."[20]

The section of the station open to West Berliners was sealed off from the terminal serving East Berlin trains. Only a few meters apart from each other—in contrast to the zone around the Wall—people from West and East changed trains, daily routines would rub against each other, and the material and corporeal proximity of divergent ideologies would intensify: the passengers from East and West could not see each other, neither their bodies and faces nor their movements, but they could *hear* each other. Exiting the confined space of the train and entering the space of Friedrichstraße station, one could encounter sounds from the other platforms, separated by walls. One of my interviewees, a woman from the former East, recalled that she could hear announcements like "long distance train to Munich, platform . . . please board now . . . please step back . . . the train to Hamburg is delayed five minutes." This was found to be horrifying. Cities existing on a map of West Germany, out of reach for East Berliners, were constantly announced. An East German could neither travel to Munich and Hamburg, nor participate in any of the other activities of the people on the other platforms; the only common experiences they shared were through sound: traveling air waves that intermingled and passed through the thin walls. Around 1984,[21] these *paroles of desire*, as I call them, were shut down. GDR authorities erected noise barriers in the form of huge walls of steel, blocking the sounds so the announcements and other sounds could not travel across anymore. The wall was then coated with a special antisound surface to correct the absurdity of the situation.[22] Two worlds with one sound became two worlds with two distinctive soundscapes that would no longer be shared.

Figure 6.2
The Berlin Wall, today part of the East Side Gallery, the world's largest outdoor art gallery.
Photograph by Frank Swenton, 2010.

THE BERLIN WALL: SILENCE AND PROTEST

Another example of the relationship of sound and structures in Berlin is its (in)famous Wall (1961–1989), which physically divided Berlin but not its two soundscapes (see Figure 6.2). Rather than the location of two sonic worlds clashing, however, the Wall is remembered as a space empty of sounds. Before 1989, the Berlin Wall, the taboo site of divergent ideologies, was one of the few geographical zones where sounds from East and West could mingle. The no man's land around the Wall, which was the geographical intermediate between East and West, resembles the condition of the medium, which is between transmitter and receiver. The characteristic thing about the soundscape of Berlin was not the difference between East and West, but the common ground of this intermediate territory: the Wall. Similarly, sound is the intermediate between its source and our ears, a "third space" with multiple meanings.

The following excerpts from interviews illustrate listening experiences and patterns of remembrance in conjunction with the Wall. When asked for sonic associations with the Wall, interviewees gave answers varying from bicycle brakes, pigeons, railways, and amphoric resonance, to hollow, threatening sounds. Yet silence was mentioned repeatedly as well, and the silence belonged to both sides, as historian at the Freie Universität Berlin and former GDR citizen Stefan Wolle recalled:

> The city was pulsating somewhere in the West, but it was so far away, that you couldn't hear that anymore. And in your back, another city was pulsating, too, but in between there was a

space of silence.... The Wall consisted of a huge area, whole blocks had been torn down, you couldn't directly get to it and you also saw very little of it. But there was a strange immobility and silence. Two guards were going up and down on foot or in a little car. They had these Trabi cars painted in green. But now that I try to remember, it was a threatening silence, an unnatural silence.[23]

Annette Scharnberg had described the silence at the Western side of the ghost train station Friedrichstraße as something uncanny, and here the silence perceived from the Eastern side of the Wall, the "strange immobility and silence," was also an eerie experience. The soundscapes were nothing unnatural, yet the interviewee could not put into words what she actually objected to.

Another historian, West German Andreas Ludwig, director of Dokumentationszentrum Alltagskultur der DDR (Center for the Documentation of Everyday Culture in the GDR) in Eisenhüttenstadt, tried to explain the silence:

It was quite spooky. You got there from the center of Berlin and you found yourself in this wasteland. There weren't many buildings, the tram tracks ended in the middle of nowhere, the streets all had cobblestones. At the Potsdamer Platz you could only see the streets that were directed at it, but not the square itself. The Wall was spray-painted all over. And then these bike routes had developed along the Wall: if you wanted to go from Kreuzberg to Wedding you would follow the Wall—there it was completely safe to cycle because there were no cars. And on the other side, it was also quiet, because there was the death strip before East Berlin started. So you couldn't hear East Berlin. And West Berlin you also didn't hear because of the lack of traffic. I always have the impression of complete silence at this Wall. You could hear squeaking bike brakes and pigeons, but mostly there was silence.[24]

Though Ludwig had rational explanations for the silence, he too found it spooky. There were visual cues for life on the other side of the Wall, but all streets and tracks were interrupted by it. Only a few meters above the Wall, one would imagine, would there be the common airspace heralded by sounds. Yet, again, most interviewees specifically remembered silence.

People who lived directly where the Wall separated East and West had different opinions, though. "People lived there," Walter Obermanns, an archive employee from East Berlin claimed, offended:

Silence? I wouldn't say so. You could sometimes wave to each other through your windows, so I wouldn't say it was an area of silence. In many ways, the two parts of the city were far apart from each other, but right by the Wall, on both sides, there was life. People lived there. It was actually a short distance between the two systems.[25]

Silence, the absence of sound, is taken here as the absence of life—a notion that the inhabitants of the border area vehemently rejected. Interestingly, Obermanns did not mention any sound but referred back to the visual: waving to people.

Claudia Armenious, who lived on the Western side of the Wall, was a bit more specific:

There were two worlds with this huge wall in between. And there was no contact to the East Berliners in everyday life. A memory as a West Berliner is riding your bicycle along this wall. You have the greatest bike path there, all quiet, no traffic, you cannot get lost, because you always have a means of orientation—it's almost embarrassing! But that's how it was. And, depending on where you were, you would maybe have some Turkish tunes, like in Kreuzberg. You could hear kids playing. Life did exist at the Wall, but in a reduced form, since there was nothing directly on the other side. It was pleasant.[26]

Armenious perceived silence as nothing threatening or uncanny, but as an agreeable state of mind. The Wall almost seemed like a blank canvas in front of which one was spared from the stimuli of the big city, an oasis with only a few quiet sounds to relax to and recharge. She also mentioned that she could use silence to acoustically orient herself; depending on where the sounds decreased, she would know her geographical position.

Yet the Western area around the Wall was not always an idyllic haven for bikers and playing children only. *Rock for Berlin*, a concert in West Berlin in June 1987, featuring David Bowie among others, was a rare moment of shared acoustic experience. Masses of people from East Berlin gathered at the boulevard Unter den Linden close to the concert on the other side. Uwe Bräuner, a lawyer from East Berlin recollected:

A big stage was put up on the Western side of the Reichstag. The interesting thing was that you could only hear. You couldn't see anything. The distance between the barrier in the East and the stage was at least one thousand meters. And then there was this one spot in front of the Soviet embassy where the sound could be caught especially well. Certainly, you could have heard it much better on the radio, but it was a sort of collective experience. . . . That was quite a ticklish situation for the East German authorities. At the Wall, there were a couple of thousand teenagers. What could the police have done if they had run wild and had started running towards the Wall? So they had widely blocked everything and then something happened that nobody had expected: the teenagers began to shout: "The Wall needs to go!"[27]

This the people in West Berlin could hear as well. Listening to the event on the radio would not have been the same as being there, as listening became synonymous for encouragement. The East Berliners were at all times aware of the West—they gathered to hear the sound waves traveling from West to East Berlin. They were facing the Wall, trying to imagine what was behind it, although they could only participate acoustically. The West Berliners, on the other hand, had gathered to see and hear the concert and had probably forgotten what was behind the stage and behind the Wall. When the East Berliners began to shout—their acoustic protest of the system—and were heard, they placed themselves back on the map. East Berlin existed behind the Wall—although none of the concertgoers and musicians could see it at this point in time, they could certainly hear it. Becoming aware of this, David Bowie asked for the speakers to be turned not to face the concertgoers, but to face the Wall. Now both Berlins participated in the concert, and the Western media broadcasted it into all households.

A project of sound cartography transforms the notion of the city space into something fluid. Like water, sounds and memories are soaked up, limits and borders cancelled—sound creates unity out of difference. By examining four urban landmarks, fountains, traffic sounds, a train station, and the Berlin Wall, it has become clear how the sounds associated with them define their geographical space, their political and social role, their utopian or dystopian character. Together with the other senses, these sounds create and trigger memory and lead to a feeling of belonging. Whereas the main concentration was on ambient sound in all other examples, the East Berliners' reaction to *Rock for Berlin* showed that sounds can overcome political and geographical barriers and that everyone who has a voice (literally and figuratively) has the ability to change history. Only two years after the concert, the masses shouting "Wir sind ein Volk!" ("We are one people!") had a sustained and group-constituting effect on their listeners; it was the power of these chants that led to the fall of the Wall and transformed the country.

With the unification of Germany, the GDR only exists in memories. The Wall has been deconstructed, and, although the renovated train station Friedrichstraße continues to be one of the main transfer stations in Berlin, it does not reveal its special past to the thousands of people rushing through each day. Soon the last Trabis will drive on the streets, and the fight for the public fountains might fall victim to budget cuts. The study of sound is paramount in the experience of the city, yet any kind of sound phenomenon—be it music, voice, or entire soundscapes—is closely linked to vanishing: the moment it is heard, it is already gone. Sonic testimonies are important. As with every sensual experience, sound phenomena represent experience, memory, and therefore history. They shape the notion of the city and its inhabitants: they represent the evasive part of history in their fluid as well as penetrating character.

NOTES

1. The research was conducted with Alex Arteaga from UNI.K/UdK Studio für Klangkunst und Klangforschung, Wolfgang Knapp from the Universität der Künste Berlin, and students of anthropology and the arts. All translations mine unless otherwise noted.
2. "Eine Straße in Berlin: Vogelzwitschern und Auspuffröhren, Graffitibunt und Asphaltgrau, Kopftuch und Lederjacke, Ost und West in Nebeneinanderschaft: die Adalbertstraße [in Berlin-Kreuzberg] ist Landschaft sinnlicher Gegensätze." Rolf Lindner et al., *Sensing the street*, www.sensingthestreet.de/swf/flash_7.html (accessed 7 Feb 2009).
3. Barry Truax, *Acoustic Communication* (Westport: Ablex Publishing, 2001), 18–19.
4. While this may often also hold true for noise, noise can be created intentionally. In its popular definition, noise is "unwanted sound" and carries the connotation of annoyance, disturbance; it provokes uneasiness. Noise is defined as such by the listener and the context. Ambient sound, on the other hand, must not necessarily annoy its listeners; on the contrary, it can be used as a tool to understand the city, as shown in this chapter.
5. Kodwo Ofori Eshun, *More Brilliant than the Sun: Adventures in Sonic Fiction* (London: Quartet Books, 1998).
6. Cage in conversation with Ev Grimes, in *Conversing with Cage,* ed. Richard Kostelanetz (New York: Limelight, 1984), 235.
7. For details on John Cage, see Brett Van Hoesen and Jean Paul-Perrotte's chapter in this book.
8. Compare to "Volumen" and "Lautstärke" in German.

9. The sound artist Sam Auinger complains about the lack of "sound characters" in the city; like in a symphonic orchestra, man needs order for well-being. Nicole Dietrich, interview with Sam Auinger, April 4, 2006, Berlin. See also Yaron Jean's chapter in this book, which shows that the accuracy of aural perception is also a question of training your ears, specifically under life-threatening circumstances like a technological war.

10. I argue that making a radio documentary needs good editing as a means of dramatization as well as a "feeling" for acoustic breaks and silence, just like filmmaking. Radio is the art of blind cinema. See also Jean-François Augoyard and Henry Torgue, eds., *Sonic Experience. A Guide to Everyday Sounds* (Montreal: McGill Queen's University Press, 2005).

11. For another perspective on the broad field of sound and definitions of identity, space and power, see Maria Stehle's chapter in this book.

12. Nicole Dietrich, interviews with anonymous former East Berliners, and Barbara Lauenburg, pub owner from East Berlin, Jannowitzbrücke, November 20, 2005, and January 1, 2006.

13. Nicole Dietrich, interview with Barbara Lauenburg, January 14, 2006.

14. Closely connected to this is the phenomenon called "ostalgia" (*Ostalgie*): nostalgic reminiscences of the GDR largely invented and fostered by the (Western) media as a source of commercialized compensation of lost prerogatives of interpretation as well as feelings of inferiority. For more detail see Christoph Dieckmann, *Rückwärts immer. Deutsches Erinnern* (Berlin: Schriftenreihe der Bundeszentrale für politische Bildung, 2005).

15. Much work has been published on the media of West and East Berlin, but one of the most recent is Jochen Staadt, Tobias Voigt, Stefan Wolle, *Operation Fernsehen. Die Stasi und die Medien in Ost und West* (Göttingen: Vandenhoeck & Ruprecht, 2008).

16. Nicole Dietrich, interview with Dirk Jacob, March 16, 2006.

17. Nicole Dietrich, interview with Karl Obermanns, Constanze König, Uwe Bräuner, March 1, 2006.

18. Truax, *Acoustic Communication*, 25.

19. Nicole Dietrich, interview with Annette Scharnberg, February 25, 2006.

20. Nicole Dietrich, interview with Claudia Armenious, May 2, 2006.

21. Although the year 1984 seems extraordinarily late to include sound in the calculation of barriers and borders, this capacity to control perception—and the passionate obstinacy with which it was done—should be taken into account. In this context, it is worth noting that the Staatssicherheit or Stasi (secret police of the GDR) became infamous not only for its collections of olfactory samples but also for analytic studies of idioms and voice layers as a means of secret identification and supervision. Stimmlagen- und Dialektforschung (dialect research) was based on recordings of wiretapped telephone conversations to identify alleged enemies of the state. These investigations were based on the assumption that certain sounds (in this case, ways of speaking) are specific to certain places. See Jens Gieseke, *Die DDR-Staatssicherheit: Schild und Schwert der Partei* (Bonn: Schriftenreihe der Bundeszentrale für Politische Bildung, 2000). 1984 is also the year the film *Das Leben der Anderen* (*The Lives of Others*, dir. Florian Henckel von Donnersmarck, 2006) is supposed to take place. For details see Christiane Lenk's chapter in this book.

22. Stefan Wolle, *Die heile Welt der Diktatur: Alltag und Herrschaft in der DDR 1971–1989* (Bonn: Bundeszentrale für politische Bildung, 1998), 72.

23. Nicole Dietrich, interview with Stefan Wolle, November 23, 2005.

24. Nicole Dietrich, interview with Andreas Ludwig, December 12, 2005.

25. Nicole Dietrich, interview with Walter Obermanns, January 1, 2006.

26. Nicole Dietrich, interview with Claudia Armenious, May 2, 2006.

27. Nicole Dietrich, interview with Uwe Bräuner, March 1, 2006.

The Politics of Sound
Walls with Ears

Just as seeing and viewing, hearing and listening can be actions influenced—or restrained—by (political) power structures. In his article "Open Ears," R. Murray Schafer notes that the Latin *audire* (to hear) forms the core of the English word *obey* (as its Latin root *obaudiere* literally translates as "hearing from below").[1] Similarly, the German words *hören* und *gehorchen* (hear and obey) are also linguistically connected. The chapters in Section III discussed how identity formation is connected to sound perception or memories of sounds in both Hilbig's novel *Das Provisorium* and in Dietrich's ear-witness reports. The chapters in Section IV examine ways in which producing and consuming sound were inextricably linked to East German politics during the Cold War era. Historically, East Germans went from acoustic irradiation by the Nazis to acoustic control and surveillance by the Stasi.[2] This acoustic manipulation, as both articles show, took place on multiple levels.

David Tompkins's chapter examines sound as a means of political control by investigating GDR musical culture from the immediate postwar years to the late 1950s. He concentrates on music festivals in both cities and rural areas, because the SED (Socialist Unity Party of Germany) saw festivals as a particularly effective means of propagating their ideas and values among the wider population. Tompkins studies festival advertising, official policies, and the music performed at these festivals to find out who participated in creating the socialist soundscape: in other words, did the sound of socialism come from above or was it a collective sound created from below? He also ultimately asks the question: what did socialist music sound like?

Christiane Lenk considers not which sounds were produced, but which sounds were heard in the GDR, because, as Bull and Back point out: "The history of surveillance is as much a sound history as it is a history of vision."[3] In her chapter, she points out the different functions of sound within the system of acoustic surveillance by the Stasi, as represented in Florian Henckel von Donnersmarck's award-winning film *The Lives of Others* (2006). Lenk views the writer Dreyman's wiretapped apartment as the sound equivalent of Bentham's panopticon, a nineteenth-century prison defined by visibility. By eavesdropping, Stasi officer Wiesler takes part in the lives of others, but he soon finds himself changing from the observer to the observed, as he becomes part of the aural panopticon himself. In the film, sound can be understood as a means of control but also as an avenue of rebellion to frustrate that control: to manipulate change and to deceive, and to eventually transgress boundaries. The model of the panopticon, however, poses the question of whether it is ever possible to escape from that acoustic surveillance.

NOTES

1. R. Murray Schafer, "Open Ears" in *Auditory Culture Reader*, eds. Michael Bull and Les Back (Oxford: Berg, 2003), 25–39, 30.
2. A fictional account of this can be found in Marcel Beyer's *Flughunde* (1995), translated as *The Karnau Tapes*. The protagonist of the novel is the lead sound engineer in the Nazis' Department of Propaganda in charge of broadcasting Hitler's voice into all corners of the Third Reich. For a detailed discussion of the role of sound in the novel and its ability to (re)construct memory see Leslie Morris, "The Sound of Memory," *The German Quarterly* 74:4 (2001): 368–78.
3. Bull and Back, eds., *Auditory Culture Reader*, 5.

CHAPTER 7

Sound and Socialist Identity

Negotiating the Musical Soundscape in the Stalinist GDR

DAVID TOMPKINS

Contrary to the common notion of the Stalinist era as uniformly gray and monotonous, surprisingly varied and rich musical offerings greeted the population of East Germany. Throughout the country, from the hallowed chambers of the Berlin Staatsoper to the crudest rural hall, music supported by state funds blanketed the landscape. To be sure, some of these works were ponderous, party-commissioned odes to Stalin himself, but such clearly ideological pieces mixed with other examples of socialist-realist compositions, like lively songs for the masses and engaging symphonies based on folk music. Workers, farmers, and the traditional urban concertgoers encountered Bach and Beethoven, but also contemporary cantatas describing workers, as well as catchy songs praising the party. At the same time as the aurally experienced 1954 World Cup (referenced in the introduction), this pre-television era was dominated by radio, the public loudspeaker, and mass events. The emerging East German musical soundscape was not only influenced by the party but also responsive to audiences.[1] This chapter will provide a fuller sense of this oft-evoked "music of the new socialist era" and add to the understanding of the German Democratic Republic through an investigation of sites of music such as festivals and concert halls. It explores the interaction around the creation of this new music in conjunction with a look at the complicated but fascinating question of how East Germans received and perceived this socialist music culture from the immediate postwar years to the late 1950s—the era of high Stalinism and the apogee of party control.

THE POLITICAL POWER OF MUSIC

In the wake of Nazism, music loomed particularly large as a tool for refashioning German identity. Music, like the arts more generally, was to shape a citizenry imbued with a socialist, progressively nationalist, and antifascist identity.[2] Contemporary socialist-realist works were melodic and accessible to the untutored ear, and were supposed to help shape the socialist utopia under construction. The Socialist Unity Party (Sozialistische Einheitspartei Deutschlands, or SED) worked closely with composers to create socialist-realist music, and then disseminated these politicized compositions through festivals, concerts in both the city and the countryside, and amateur musical group activity. Ordinary citizens of all social classes influenced musical production, as party officials, working with composers, made compromises to comply with audience taste. Maximal goals of a thoroughly Stalinized social-ist-realist concert life were not realized, but a politicized music was created and performed for and by the East German population. Cultural officials accorded music an exceptional power to shape its audience, and this belief motivated East German SED members who felt that "music is one of the few forces that, on a large scale and with nearly unlimited possibili-ties, seizes and influences all people," and considered "music an important factor in the formation of man's consciousness. Music can affect man's character in an ennobling, but also brutalizing manner."[3] A desire to harness this supposedly special power runs like a red thread through SED policy statements during the 1950s.

It comes as no surprise that party officials pushed for texted music like mass songs or large-scale choral works that could be sung by amateur choirs for audiences of workers and peasants according to socialist-realist ideology. Soon, mass songs occupied a prominent posi-tion in the soundscape of GDR citizens, and composers created these works for a variety of audiences and on myriad themes. Common elements across the variety of musical produc-tion were straightforward melodic lines, simple structure, and rhythm. Since music was sup-posed to "strengthen the ideological consciousness of people" and be used as "a means to move the masses and shape consciousness for the building of socialism,"[4] the lyrics were polit-ical in nature. They could be more serious, like "Dank an die Sowjetarmee" ("Thanks to the Soviet Army," 1950), with music by Ernst Hermann Meyer and text by Johannes R. Becher. More often, however, they were of a lighter cast, such as the popular "Lied von der Blauen Fahne" ("Song of the Blue Flag," 1950), with text again by Becher and music by Hanns Eisler (see Figure 7.1), a song about the Free German Youth (Freie Deutsche Jugend, or FDJ), which evoked a positive and vivid response decades later from an interviewee in the previous chapter. Another catchy and representative example was "Fritz der Traktorist" ("Fritz the Tractor Driver," 1952) by Eberhard Schmidt with text by Walter Stranka. The latter is a typi-cal and interesting example of the mass song, because it prominently features a folk-like accordion that carries an energetic melodic line. A mixed choir sings a text that praises Fritz for his agricultural skills, as well as for his studies and singing ability. A joyous-sounding refrain encourages the listener to emulate the well-rounded young hero. One particularly important subgenre of the mass song was that of songs for youth, such as "Tapfer lacht die junge Garde" ("The Young Guard Laughs Bravely," 1950), a collaboration between the writer Kuba (Kurt Bartel) and young composer André Asriel. Larger-scale works included accessi-ble instrumental pieces like Ottmar Gerster's second symphony, the *Thüringische Sinfonie* (*Thuringian Symphony*, 1949–1953), and Ernst Hermann Meyer's *Mansfelder Oratorium* (1950), based on the centuries-long history of a mining region.[5] Such cantatas were particu-larly favored due to their extensive, politicized texts and the setting of a large, often amateur, choir singing for a mass audience.

Figure 7.1
Composer Hanns Eisler and poet Johannes R. Becher, two East German cultural luminaries who collaborated on mass songs.
Bundesarchiv, Photo 183-S93325. Photographer unknown.

A wealth of music resulted from this interaction among communist ideology, cultural officials, composers, and society. Towering figures of twentieth-century music like Hanns Eisler and Paul Dessau, as well as hundreds of lesser known composers, created symphonies, cantatas, and politicized mass songs during this period. In addition to newly composed music, and more broadly with respect to concert and radio programming, cultural officials cast musical icons like Bach and Beethoven as progressives of their time: Bach for being close to the people, Beethoven for his sympathy for the French Revolution and occasional critiques of the aristocracy.[6] The result was the creation of an extensive musical infrastructure to perform accepted works; press articles and concert booklets formulated this interpretation for wider consumption.

Eastern Germany experienced a flowering of music-festival culture in the decade and a half after 1945 (see Figure 7.2). Hundreds of thousands of people took part through amateur choirs and musical ensembles, while millions came in contact with party-approved music by attending concerts. Cultural officials made great claims for these festivals, asserting that they

Figure 7.2
The German Festivals of Folk Art, a forum for the new socialist musical culture.
Bundesarchiv, Poster 103-039-026. Artist unknown.

would "develop people's consciousness in a progressive sense" and "affect the consciousness and feelings of millions of people and make a decisive contribution to the re-shaping of our world."[7] To this end, these officials sought to both include amateur groups and to bring in audience members from all population groups. Musicians and conductors appreciated the festivals, because they heightened audience interest and attracted attention to their activities. For contemporary composers, the festivals provided welcome and indeed essential opportunities to have their works performed before a live audience. Cultural officials deployed festivals as an incentive for composers to create socialist-realist music and then sought to bring the wider population into contact with this music in a festive context.

The GDR featured a wide range of festivals with music as the focal point, including those in smaller towns and rural areas, some devoted to amateur musical groups, and also high-profile festivals. Some festivals consisted of a handful of concerts extending over a long weekend, while others had hundreds of events and lasted weeks. Cultural officials and composers hotly debated the content of these festivals, as the former desired ideologically themed works and the latter wanted their latest pieces performed no matter the style and content. Controversy inevitably erupted as committees of composers suggested work sometimes denied by cultural officials. Programs generally included a mixture of politically acceptable pieces by past masters as well as socialist-realist works from contemporary composers. The audience included significant numbers of regular concertgoers, but the SED also made considerable efforts to attract and include workers and peasants.

Small-Town and Rural Festivals

Cultural officials recommended in particular that music festivals be mounted in small towns, because they cost less and garnered a relatively large amount of attention.[8] Such smaller-scale music festivals had taken place both intermittently and regularly throughout eastern Germany for many decades, in places like Schwerin, Markneukirchen, Eisenach, Rheinsberg, and Görlitz. The latter two are representative examples of party and mass involvement in festivals on this smaller scale, and thus of party ambitions to musically influence the population throughout the country.

The town of Rheinsberg had held an annual music festival since the late eighteenth century. The SED considered such smaller festivals an important opportunity to propagate its goals, and the local party organization "took control of the festival."[9] During the early 1950s, cultural officials organized the festival around the concept of cultivating past musical tradition, designed to demonstrate that the party held the true stewardship of a progressive national culture. The early festivals offered fairly traditional concerts of the classical greats; the main goal was to introduce workers to this music.[10] In 1951, a more ambitious final concert of the festival featured amateur groups made up of workers, playing pieces by Mozart and Schubert for their peers.[11] By 1953, under pressure from cultural officials in Berlin, the festival organizers added more contemporary and socialist-realist works to the program. While the vast majority of the twenty or so concerts included traditional classical music, two concerts featured contemporary pieces, for instance the opening-day performance of Ottmar Gerster's socialist-realist cantata about a huge, new steelworks, *Eisenhüttenkombinat Ost*. Several other concerts had contemporary GDR or Soviet composers as part of the program, such as the concert "German songs from six centuries," which included music by younger composers André Asriel and Siegfried Matthus.[12]

Görlitz, a town right on the Oder-Neisse border with Poland, had a tradition of festivals dating from the nineteenth century and organized an even more ambitious annual festival in the Stalinist era. Many of the ten to twenty concerts of these annual Görlitzer Musikwochen (Görlitz Music Weeks) consisted of traditional works by nineteenth-century German masters, but they also included a significant number of pieces by well-known composers from the Soviet Union and the other People's Democracies. Given its new postwar situation as a border town, the festival's programs unsurprisingly took on a highly political and ideological cast, as in 1951 and 1953, when the emphasis was on cementing good relations with neighboring Poland. Concerts in Görlitz included productions of nineteenth-century Polish composer Stanisław Moniuszko's nationalist operas *Halka* and *The Haunted Manor*, as well as many other works by Chopin and by contemporary Polish composers. This diverse mix also assured healthy audience numbers.[13] Festival organizers sought to attract a mass audience to the various concerts, and in fact counted thirty-eight thousand listeners in 1951, more than half of whom came from local factories.[14] As stated by Mayor Gleißberg on the occasion of the 1954 festival: "Our working people should receive new strength and zest for the peaceful reconstruction of our fatherland through the experience of the music of the great masters of the past and present."[15] In other words, local officials, too, invested considerable energy in such festivals.

The SED also made considerable efforts to bring music out to the countryside in order to extend politicized compositions to the farthest corners of the country. They, thus, organized a large number of rural music festivals, known as the Ländliche Musiktage. These rural festivals generally consisted of small-scale concerts, performed by local orchestras, chamber music groups, or soloists. The metropolitan area of Rostock organized the first of what would come to be known as Ländliche Musiktage from December 6–12, 1953. The cultural authorities' goal there was to mobilize and bring together professional and amateur musicians to play concerts for the greatest number of people possible. During that week, 354 concerts took place in nearly every village in Rostock's seven subdistricts (*Kreise*) and attracted the impressive number of forty thousand listeners. The organizers in Rostock praised themselves for bringing classical music to those who had never heard it before and made great claims about winning the ears of the rural population for this music.[16] Officials in the Ministry of Culture felt these festivals provided a method of creating the model socialist citizen and also helped to "overcome the cultural backwardness of the village."[17]

More and more music festivals in smaller towns across the GDR were organized as officials generally realized one of the party's main goals with respect to music: to present the finest works of approved past masters and the best of contemporary socialist-realist production to wider sections of society. The program booklet from the district of Grevesmühlen states: "The aims of the festival are to bring joy and gaiety to our people through music, and to acquaint them with the works of our present and past masters."[18] These rural music festivals were perhaps the best example of the ministry's goals for music festivals in general: "to introduce the broadest possible circles of the population to music, while at the same time introducing artists to the people."[19] Professional and amateur musicians from city and countryside came together to perform for rural audiences during these festivals. Cultural officials thereby hoped to promote solidarity among different sectors of the population and to realize the goals of collapsing the distinctions between high and low culture, between urban and rural citizens, and creating a party-influenced soundscape common to all.

Amateur Festivals

East German cultural officials organized a large number of festivals to involve amateur musical groups in activities under the aegis of the SED. Such festivals were generally linked to competitions among nonprofessional groups across the country; the best groups advanced to a series of concerts in a larger city for the final celebration. The festivals that perhaps best expressed the party's goal of mobilizing broad swaths of society to take part in party-sanctioned musical events were the German Festivals of Folk Art (Deutsche Festspiele der Volkskunst) held in 1952 and 1954. These festivals aimed to have amateur musical groups perform ideologically acceptable folk music as well as newer socialist-realist works like Eisler's "Neue deutsche Volkslieder" ("New German Folk Songs") or Meyer's "Mansfelder Oratorium." The inclusion and popularization of works by great German composers sought to demonstrate that the party was the true custodian of both the German cultural heritage and the new progressive culture. A series of contests in the provinces in which six to seven thousand amateur groups participated culminated in several days of concerts by the best groups.[20] The first festival of 1952 took place in Berlin and offered a handful of concerts over a long July weekend. It concluded with a massive performance in the center of the city, where "all of Berlin dance[d] on the Marx-Engels-Platz!"[21]

In the view of cultural authorities, these competitions "lead to political and professional qualifications [and] contribute to the development of our progressive culture, in that they strengthen the artistic work of the people, [and] increase the artistic achievements of the workers.... At the same time, our artists work more closely with the workers in the amateur groups and create works for them."[22] For the second German Festival of Folk Art in 1954, officials refined and expanded the competition among the various amateur groups, leading up to the actual Festspiele in Park Sanssouci in Potsdam. The juries judged the groups based on principles of Socialist Realism: tunefulness, or being pleasing to the ear; accessibility to musically unsophisticated audiences; and ideological appropriateness. These Festspiele in the GDR embodied a core ideal of Socialist Realism: professional artists working with ordinary people in a party-directed project designed to create a new, socialist musical culture.

Showpiece Socialist-Realist Festivals

Another festival took place in 1952 in conjunction with a meeting of the East German Composers' Union in Berlin.[23] This weeklong festival included one concert featuring contemporary mass songs and larger vocal works at the Bergmann-Borsig factory, where workers greeted the music eagerly. A delegation from the factory subsequently came to the Union Congress and expressed enthusiasm for the new, socialist-realist music, calling for more "good, lively light music, a useful music that will help working people to relax after fulfilling the plan."[24] The party combined this desire for music that entertained with the goal of promoting more ideological music in organizing festivals of all kinds throughout the country.

It is important to note that party officials, seeking greater concert attendance, were responsive to audience feedback. Just before the next major festival, linked to the 1954 Composers' Union conference, cultural officials stated: "The point is not to present our contemporary musical production in the form of interesting concerts that display today's 'sound,' but rather to prove how composers and musicologists are fulfilling their societal mission as 'engineers of the human soul.'"[25] The organizers of the Union-sponsored 1954 festival therefore made a great effort to invite workers to the various concerts and indeed encouraged composers to meet with ordinary audience members afterwards. At one such discussion, after a concert of contemporary works, female workers from a Leipzig factory were pleased with Ottmar Gerster's lyrical and accessible Symphony No. 2, considered one of the model socialist-realist works by officials and his fellow composers, but called the first two works: "Dreadful! Horrible!"[26] Most of the other audience members also seemed to enjoy the Gerster symphony, but the other works came under heavy criticism. One piece sounded to a female listener like "children pounding on the piano," and other audience members said "it gave me nothing" or "there was no heart and soul in it."[27] One official claimed that most audience members disliked the works and regretted buying tickets.[28] Another participant criticized all the works but Gerster's, saying they were technically good, but "not from the heart . . . they will never appeal to the workers, never!"[29] Another noted that a large portion of the audience left after the first half.[30] Audience members clearly had strong reactions to these contemporary works and made them known to composers and party officials.

When two men from the nearby Leuna factory attended a Union Congress session at the 1954 festival, they provided uniquely detailed feedback on general reception of the works. They had attended a different concert with a number of their colleagues; this program consisted of contemporary works by both younger and older GDR composers. Metalworker Otto Schnell expressed his disappointment with the concert in unvarnished and sarcastic terms, and called on composers to "introduce the workers to music" and "create music which the broad masses can tolerate."[31] He encouraged composers to write music that would be a moving experience upon first hearing, such as Tchaikovsky's Fifth Symphony. As in the case of a bar offering bad sausage, he said colorfully, he and his comrades would not return for a repeat of an unpleasant experience.[32] Schnell's colleague Horst Irrgang, choral director at the factory, reported on the lively and lengthy postconcert discussion he had organized among workers, musicians, and composers. Irrgang described the active musical life at the factory and urged the composers present to write for and make contact with the workers. He further called on composers to help explain their new works during a performance. Although Schnell and Irrgang had unusual access to a Composers' Union forum, they and other audience members alike reacted to the music offered to them and influenced future programs through their feedback. On these prominent central stages, composers, officials, and everyday workers worked to forge the East German musical landscape.

Concerts in City and Countryside

Outside of the festival context, many other concerts took place throughout East Germany—and these, too, exhibited significant signs of both party involvement and audience engagement. The leading institution for organizing these concerts in the GDR was a monopolistic state concert agency, known during most of its early existence as the German Agency for Concerts and Guest Performances, or DKGD (Deutsche Konzert- und Gastspieldirektion). The DKGD developed ideologically appropriate programs and worked with authors and composers, and its officials saw themselves as bringing culture to the masses.[33] As the official impresario of the state, the DKGD organized all manner of events, from special concerts given by major orchestras like Leipzig's Gewandhaus orchestra or the Dresden Philharmonic, to small dance productions or recitals, with audiences ranging in size from a handful to many thousands. Such concerts sometimes took place in formal concert halls, but far more often in factories or small venues out in the countryside. The more conventional of these concerts, as I will discuss, were only partially successful, prompting a search for a new kind of mixed concert that was politically appropriate and also appealed to broad audiences.

In general, programs contained "a positive approach to life and were optimistic and formative" and were also to "relate to societal problems."[34] Further, "cheerful programs and those entertaining on an elevated level are desired . . . joy in life should be encouraged and the productive energies of the workers should be further developed."[35] But these concerts were not just about entertainment: "The main aim of the programming of the DKGD must be to influence the developmental process of the masses."[36] The DKGD's aims resonated with the German understanding of *Bildung*. The agency's overarching goal was

> to organize events with educative and consciousness-forming character and to raise the cultural level of the population. The value of the DKGD's work . . . is taking culturally and educationally valuable artworks in an understandable form to the broadest reaches of the population in both cities and the countryside, and filling people with enthusiasm for great works of art.[37]

The DKGD aimed to fulfill the Enlightenment project of bringing art to the uncultivated in order to help fashion them into progressive human beings, which meant that these activities intended to mold the population into model GDR citizens. And indeed, the DKGD's principal objective for 1954 was "to win the workers for the 'New Course' of the party through the means of art" and to foster patriotism and loyalty to the state.[38] The party clearly attempted to determine how this development would take place, even as they worked on making it fun, too.

When the DKGD made a constant push for more serious, contemporary works, officials were met with conflicting responses from concertgoers. At the same time, lighter programs, like the *Volkslieder* and popular songs, received frequent and positive feedback from audiences.[39] Still, the concert agency's central authorities remained firm. In 1953, local cultural officials complained that people were less interested in contemporary works because they preferred lighter music and disliked works that were considered too difficult or demanding.[40] This hard line produced an unsurprising reaction from audiences—their response was to stay away from all events that were advertised as chamber or orchestral music.[41] In 1956, a Berlin newspaper article described the not untypical situation of a chamber music concert with an audience of ten.[42] The central administrators of the concert agency faced the intractable dilemma of balancing demanding and politicized programs with the musical taste of the people. Furthermore, the programming policy that had been developed in the agency's main offices proved to be at times quite divorced from concert reality out in the provinces. Local officials often did not follow the tough official line, and, in defiance of central control, organized less demanding or less politicized (but more entertaining) concerts to attract audiences.

Musical Revues: A Compromise

With the *Estradenkonzert*, one type of musical programming gradually emerged that was both entertaining and passed ideological muster: a sort of lightly politicized revue that combined song, instrumental music, and spoken word in a staged variety show. A narrator or emcee linked the songs and sketches together and played a crucial role in communicating the political message. The idea was to produce a party-approved, cabaret-like performance that would combine light entertainment with ideology in an attempt to attract, entertain, and educate large numbers of workers and peasants. Ideologically useful programs included concerts with music from the "progressive cultural patrimony," both national and foreign; contemporary compositions from the Soviet Union, the GDR, and from other People's Democracies; and dance and light programs, including cabaret, that had been approved by officials from the concert agency. These staged musical revues became increasingly popular to both officials and audiences alike and represented the zenith of the Stalinist concert, as an event that attempted to edify politically and also entertain. Audiences tolerated and even appreciated music with a political tinge, as long as it was melodic and preferably combined with a lighter tone.

CONCLUSION

In the early years of the GDR, the SED actively engaged its members and mobilized both cultural elites and the broader population to help create a master narrative that embodied a progressive, antifascist nationalism combined with socialism. Through music and sound, cultural officials encouraged composers to assist them in creating this paradigm, which, for music (as for all the arts), was embodied in the concept of Socialist Realism. All of the musical events presented here provided key tools in constructing and maintaining this political-cultural paradigm to which the party appealed in order to establish its legitimacy. The inclusion in the festivals of carefully screened works by great German composers of the past served to strengthen the party's claim to be the true heir of a national tradition, one it would carry into the socialist future. More concretely, the SED viewed music festivals and other concerts as a particularly effective means of propagating its ideas and values among the wider population, with the goal of influencing worldviews and beliefs through mass participation in the musical environment of the GDR.

During the Stalinist years, the majority of composers cooperated in the project to create a new music for the emerging socialist society. A vibrant and diverse musical soundscape emerged during this period, as concerts of politicized mass songs or ideologically themed cantatas competed with more traditional symphonic concerts and evenings of folk music or popular song. Workers and peasants were encouraged to attend concerts through the enticement of free or inexpensive tickets and even take part in some festivals through involvement in amateur musical groups. In this way, they not only came into contact with the ideas and aims of the parties, but in fact participated in their enactment. Audiences and amateur performers reacted to these musical offerings with a spectrum of emotions, including enthusiasm, interest, curiosity, and distaste. Even as they were influenced by it, they shaped the music produced for and at the festivals by directly giving their input and reactions during postconcert discussions and surveys, and also more generally through attendance—or lack thereof. Attendance was an abiding concern of cultural officials and festival organizers; tension always existed between fulfilling political goals through appropriate programming and performing popular, but ideologically worthless, works that would guarantee a full house. Over time and through a process of give and take, officials arrived at concert programs that both entertained and educated.

The music festivals and concerts described here were one element of a sonic universe that surrounded the composer, the factory worker, and the peasant, at leisure as well as at work. Though voices of dissent to the parties' aims were heard and negotiation of party goals did take place, during the Stalinist period the overwhelming majority of East German composers and much of the population willingly participated in the building of the socialist musical soundscape.

NOTES

1. I am employing the term "soundscape" in its basic dictionary definition of an environment created by sound and as elaborated in the introduction of this book. This chapter focuses on a particular kind of organized sound, music, in both its popular and "art" forms, which will be referred to as a "musical soundscape"—a concept quite different from the "soundsphere" or "ambient sound" described by Nicole Dietrich in the previous chapter.
2. See also Toby Thacker, *Music after Hitler, 1945–1955* (Aldershot: Ashgate, 2007); Daniel zur Weihen, *Komponieren in der DDR. Institutionen, Organisationen und die Erste Komponistengeneration bis 1961: Analysen* (Köln/Weimar: Stiftung Mitteldeutscher Kulturrat, 1999).
3. "Die Musik ist eine der wenigen Kräfte, die in einem großen Umfang und mit beinahe unbegrenzten Möglichkeiten alle Menschen erfasst und beeinflußt." Stiftung-Archiv der Parteien und Massenorganisationen der DDR im Bundesarchiv [SAPMO-BArch], DY-30, IV 2/9.06/284, ("Über die Entwicklung der Musikkultur der DDR," 76); "Musik ist ein wichtiger Faktor zur Bewußtseinsbildung des Menschen. Musik kann veredelnd aber auch verrohend auf den Charakter des Menschen einwirken." BArch, DR-1, 6203, "Aufgaben und Arbeitsrichtlinien der Fachkommission Musik," June 2, 1951.
4. "Das ideologische Bewußtsein der Menschen festigt." BArch, DR-1, 8, "Die Schwerpunktaufgaben der HA Musik," April 11, 1953; "als massenbewegenden und bewusstseinsfördernden Faktor im Sinne des Aufbaus des Sozialismus einzusetzen." BArch, DR-1, 6191, Quartalsplan III/53, May 16, 1953.
5. Music celebrating industrial production filled the ears of East Germans, and many embraced an optimistic interpretation of the ring of heavy industry, a sharp contrast to the negative sounds of the late 1980s in Curtis Swope's analysis of *Das Provisorium* in chapter 5 of this book.
6. For the former, see Thacker, *Music after Hitler*, especially chapter 5.
7. "Das Bewußtsein der Menschen in fortschrittlichen Sinn entwickelt werden kann." BArch, DR-1, 82; Schott, "Bericht zur Durchführung der Verordnung vom 10.12.53 auf dem Gebiete der Musik," July 6, 1954; "wirkt auf das Bewußtsein und die Gefühle von Millionen Menschen und hat deshalb entscheidenden Anteil an der Umgestaltung unseres Lebens." BArch, DR-1, 108; "Warum Woche der Musik in Potsdam?" no date.

8. SAPMO-BArch, DY-30/IV 2/9.06/283, 134–135.

9. SAPMO-BArch, DY-30/IV 2/9.06/288, letter from Stadtleitung, Stadtparteiorganisation Rheinsberg, SED, to ZK der SED, Abteilung Agitation/Kultur, April 25, 1952, 39.

10. Ibid., Program for the Rheinsberger Musiktage, 1950, 3–12.

11. Ibid., Program for the Rheinsberger Musiktage, 1951.

12. Ibid., Program for the Rheinsberger Musiktage, 1953, 47ff.

13. See programs in DR-1/104 and 108, also DY-30/IV 2/9.06/288.

14. Ibid., 15–18. Letter from the mayor of Görlitz to Ottmar Gerster, VDK, 10/8/51. The mayor was attempting to convince the Composers' Union to hold its 1952 festival in Görlitz.

15. "Unsere werktätigen Menschen sollen durch das Erlebnis der Musik der großen Meister der Vergangenheit und Gegenwart neue Kraft und Lebensfreude zum friedlichen Aufbauwerk in unserer Heimat erhalten." Ibid., Program for the Görlitzer Musikwochen, 1954, 30.

16. SAPMO-BArch, DY-30/IV 2/9.06/284, 94ff.

17. "Überwindung der kulturellen Rückständigkeit auf dem Dorfe." BArch, DR-1/138, "Erfahrungen aus den ländlichen Musiktagen," HA Musik, Schott, December 1, 1954.

18. "Die Aufgaben dieser Tage ist es, durch die Musik Freude und Frohsinn unseren Menschen zu bringen und sie mit den Werken unserer Meister aus Vergangenheit und Gegenwart zu machen." BArch, DR-1/103; Program for the Ländliche Musiktage, Kreis Grevesmühlen, December 4–11, 1955.

19. "Das Heranführen möglichst breiter Kreise der Bevölkerung an der Musik, aber andererseits auch das Heranführen der Künstler an das Volk." Stiftung-Archiv der Akademie der Künste [SAdK], Hans-Pischner-Archiv, 655.

20. BArch, DR-1/315, "Der Aufschwung der deutschen Kultur," 60.

21. SAPMO-BArch, DY-30/IV 2/9.06/287, Programm, Deutsche Festspiele der Volkskunst.

22. "Zur politischen und fachlichen Qualifizierung benutzt . . . zur Entwicklung unserer fortschrittlichen Kultur beitragen, indem sie das künstlerische Volksschaffen verstärken, die künstlerischen Leistungen unserer Werktätigen steigern . . . Gleichzeitig werden unsere Künstler enger mit den Werktätigen in den Volkskunstgruppen zusammenarbeiten und für sie Werke schaffen." SAPMO-BArch, DY-30/IV 2/9.06/16, "Betr. Wettbewerbe und Festspiele der Volkskunst 1954/54," Büro des Sekretariats, Schöne Literatur und Kunst, January 21, 1953.

23. This Verband der deutschen Komponisten und Musikwissenschaftler grouped together nearly all of the active composers and musicologists of the GDR, with a total membership of over three hundred in the mid-1950s.

24. " Protokolle I. Jahreskonferenz," Deutsches Musik-Archiv, Deutsche Musikbibliothek, Verband deutscher Komponisten [VDK], 155.

25. "Es geht nicht darum, irgendein klangliches Bild unseres zeitgenössischen Schaffens in der Form interessanter Konzerte zu vermitteln, sondern nachzuweisen, wie die Komponisten und Musikwissenschaftler ihren gesellschaftlichen Auftrag als 'Ingenieure der menschlichen Seele' erfüllten." SAPMO-BArch, DY-30, IV 2/9.06/281.

26. "Furchtbar! Entsetzlich!" SAPMO-BArch, DY-30, IV 2/9.06/281, 294. The concert included Günter Raphael's *Sinfonia breve* (1949), Rudolf Wagner-Régeny's Suite from the opera *Persische Episode* (1951), Helmut Riethmüller's *Divertimento* for Piano and Horns, and Ottmar Gerster's Symphony No.2 (*Thüringische*, 1953).

27. "Als wie wenn kleine Kinder auf dem Klavier herumhackten;" "das gibt mir nichts;" "Es ist kein Herz dabei, es ist keine Seele darin." Ibid, 297.

28. Ibid., 308–10.

29. "Das sind Werke, die bestimmt niemals die Werktätigen ansprechen werden, niemals!" Ibid., 301.

30. Ibid., 302.

31. "Die Werktätigen an die Musik heranzuführen . . . dass man sich ernsthaft damit befassen muss, Musik zu schaffen, die für die breite Masse erträglich ist." (Ibid., 336; Ibid., 339.) The concert

included Max Dehnert's *Heiteres Vorspiel für Orchester* (1949), Paul Kurzbach's *Divertimento für kleines Orchester* (1954), Dieter Nowka's *Konzert für Oboe und Orchester*, Jean Kurt Forest's "Three Arias" from the opera *Patrioten* (1951), and Max Butting's *Sixth Symphony* (1945).

32. Ibid., 338.
33. In 1952, the goal was to have 75 percent of the concerts out in the countryside. BArch, DR-1, 6200, "Protokoll über die Orchesterleitertagung," November 26, 1952; similarly in 1953, 80 percent of the DKGD's concerts with small orchestras were to take place in factories or rural areas. BArch, DR-1, 6191, Plan, March 28, 1953.
34. SAPMO-BArch, DY-30, IV 2/9.06–125, 127.
35. "Heitere, unterhaltende, auf hohem Niveau stehende Veranstaltungen sind anzustreben . . . die Lebensfreude zu steigern und die schöpferischen Kräfte der Werktätigen weiterzuentwickeln." BArch, DR-1, 278, "Entwurf des Arbeitsplanes der DKGD für das Jahr 1954."
36. "Den Erziehungsprozess der Massen zu beeinflußen, das muß die tragende Idee der Programmgestaltung der DKGD sein." BArch, DR-1, 281, "Plattform der SED-Betriebparteiorganisation zur Konferenz der DKGD mit den Künstlern und Kulturschaffenden," May 1956.
37. "Die Veranstaltungen sollen erzieherischen und bewußtseinsbildenden Charakter haben und das kulturelle Niveau der Bevölkerung steigern. Der Wert der Arbeit der DKGD bemisst sich danach, inwieweit es ihr gelingt, kulturell und erzieherisch wertvolle Werke der Kunst in verständlicher Weise an möglichst breite Schichten der Bevölkerung in Stadt und Land heranzuführen und sie für die großen Werke der Kunst zu begeistern." BArch, DR-1, 278; "Zur Verbesserung der Arbeit der DKGD," July 20, 1953, 1.
38. "Die Werktätigen für den neuen Kurs von Partei und Regierung zu gewinnen." BArch, DR-1, 278; "Entwurf des Arbeitsplanes der DKGD für das Jahr 1954."
39. SAPMO-BArch, DY-30, IV 2/9.06–125, 269–73.
40. BArch, DR-1, 279, letter from Rat des Bezirkes, Leipzig, January 31, 1953.
41. BArch, DR-1, 40, "Protokoll zur Musikreferenten-Konferenz," October 13, 1952, 9.
42. Eberhard Schmidt, "Künstler auf Reisen," *Berliner Zeitung* 29, February 3, 1956, in BArch, DR-1, 279.

CHAPTER 8

Audibility Is a Trap

Aural Panopticon in The Lives of Others (2006)

CHRISTIANE LENK

Florian Henckel von Donnersmarck's award-winning film *The Lives of Others (Das Leben der Anderen*, 2006) portrays the life of an artist couple in the German Democratic Republic (GDR) that is under surveillance by the state police (Stasi).[1] In the previous chapter, David Tompkins examined the role of music in the GDR as a tool of control for the socialist regime. He questioned whether this music came from the government or the people and what it actually sounded like. This chapter also examines sound as a tool of organized control in this regime; however, it focuses on the sounds of everyday life in the GDR as represented in Henckel von Donnersmarck's fictional account.[2] In *The Lives of Others*, sound serves as a means of oppression and at the same time as a vehicle to overcome it.

To start, the German verb "hören" translates as both "hear" and "overhear" as well as "listen." The first two translations imply passive acts: hearing is the perception of airwaves within the atmosphere. Ears do not come equipped with ear lids to block out sounds—in an awakened state, we experience our environment and it is hard not to overhear its sounds. Aural stimuli even continue to be perceived during sleep, although they are processed in a different manner. Listening, on the other hand, implies an active act. A listener's task is to intentionally extract aural information from the soundscape and interpret it. The different translations of "hören" manipulate the interpretation of the following line from the film: "I always have to think about what Lenin said about Beethoven's *Appassionata*: 'I can't listen to [or overhear] it, otherwise I can't finish the revolution,'" playwright Georg Dreyman says and continues: "Can someone who has listened to this music, really listened, still be a bad human being?"[3] These words either imply that Lenin actively listened to or simply could not help but overhear Beethoven's piano sonata. The latter translation would attest to the musical piece's power over Lenin: he is incapable of even overhearing the piece without being moved by it. Just as in this example, the sounds in *The Lives of Others* can be either actively listened to or be passively heard; they can assume power over those who hear them or even be used to subvert power. Similar to Tompkins' classification of sounds from above and below in the previous chapter, these sounds can be listened to from above (when the Stasi listens to its citizens—also in the case of interrogations) and from below (when Dreyman and his friends lie to their observers by manipulating their own soundscapes that are listened to or overheard by the Stasi).

From the founding of the Stasi in 1950 to the fall of the Berlin Wall in 1989, all GDR citizens were aware of the possibility that their conversations, their music, their everyday sounds could be and often were intentionally listened to. This continuous surveillance was a means to maintain power for the East German government; *Staatsfeinde* (enemies of the state) were sent to prison or excluded from many functions of life as a result of what was heard by the Stasi. Thoughts that potentially foreshadowed illegal actions, such as leaving the country or criticizing the government, were enough to earn one the title of *Staatsfeind*. As the French verb *surveiller* suggests, observation takes place through visual "overseeing." Yet, in the GDR, observation was primarily achieved through eavesdropping, which also forms the core of *The Lives of Others*. In the film, Stasi Hauptmann Gerd Wiesler listens to the lives of the potential *Staatsfeinde* Dreyman and his actress girlfriend Christa-Maria Sieland. Every step of their lives in their East Berlin apartment is listened to by Wiesler and his colleagues, who set up camp in the building's attic. They archive conversations by taping them and transcribing them as written reports. Wiesler's motive in the beginning is clear-cut: he listens in order to determine whether Dreyman is plotting against the state.

The conversations to which Wiesler listens serve three main functions in the film. First, these sounds serve as a tool of control and constant threat; the observer listens to the conversations to gain knowledge about the observed and their plans. The observed never know exactly when they are listened to, but have to assume that it can happen anytime. Hence, they have to "watch their tongues" at all times, both in public and in private spaces. A prime example of this is a scene in which Wiesler meets a little boy in the elevator, who conveys that his father had told him that the Stasi is evil and sends people to prison. The boy is too young to realize that his confession might implicate his father; he is too young to "watch his tongue." Second, sound also functions as a means of rebellion against the system of control and could, to a certain extent, serve as a vehicle to overcome it. The Stasi's assumption that what they hear and record is accurate and unmediated does not always hold true. As the film shows, this becomes a problem for the observers and the observed as the plot progresses. Not only can the observed (Dreyman, for example) manipulate their aural evidence, but even the relationship between observer and observed can be manipulated. Third, by listening to Dreyman's and Sieland's colorful and passionate lives, Wiesler realizes more and more that his own cold and sterile life lacks a deeper meaning. The sounds he hears lead him to question the infallibility of the East German government and to thus manipulate his sense of duty.

THE PANOPTICON

The first two dialectic functions of sound—control and rebellion—in *The Lives of Others* can be articulated through Foucault's theory of state control. Foucault describes the logic of the panopticon in *Discipline and Punish: The Birth of the Prison*. Using Jeremy Bentham's late eighteenth-century architecture of a prison that is defined by visibility, Foucault reveals the panopticon as a social construct of citizens' internalized obedience to their state.[4]

These prisons were circular in shape with cells on the outer edge of the buildings. Windows to the outside and to the interior courtyard allowed guards located in a central watchtower to observe the prisoners at all times. For Foucault, these cells were "like so many cages, so many small theatres, in which each actor is alone, perfectly individualized and constantly visible." The prisoners, on the other hand, could not see the guards, because Venetian blinds on the watchtower prevented the prisoners from seeing their observers. Foucault calls this power relation in the panopticon the "faceless gaze."[5]

Not knowing exactly when they are being observed, the prisoners must assume that it is a permanent condition. According to Foucault, the prisoners internalize this constant possible surveillance and threat to privacy. The mere thought of being observed leads to a kind of self-control, which Foucault calls "internalized obedience." He extends this system beyond prisons, namely to other institutions where masses of people need to be controlled, such as schools or hospitals. In such places, "One also sees the spread of disciplinary procedures, not in the form of enclosed institutions, but as centres of observation disseminated through society."[6] Foucault has larger issues in mind; he thinks that the logic of this architecture defines relationships between citizens and the state: "On the whole, therefore, one can speak of the formation of a disciplinary society in this movement that stretches from the enclosed disciplines . . . to an indefinitely generalizable 'panopticism.'"[7] Describing the internalization of the "Ausgeliefertsein" (state of being helpless and at somebody's mercy) of the prisoners as the panopticon's most important effect, Foucault argues its goal is "to induce in the inmate a state of conscious and permanent visibility."[8]

Yet Foucault's described internalization depends fully on vision: the guard watches the prisoner who in return cannot see him. Vision and the evidence gained visually provide power to the observer and serve to control the inmates. Foucault contrasts the architecture of the panopticon with prison dungeons, arguing that the darkness in dungeons creates security for the prisoners: "Full lighting and the eye of a supervisor capture better than darkness which ultimately protected."[9] What the guards did not see, they could neither punish nor use against the prisoners. In dungeons, the prisoners know that they are not constantly watched. When they are led out of the dark cells for interrogation purposes, they clearly know that observation begins at this point, and they can modify their behavior accordingly. While the truth might stay hidden in dungeons, the panopticon's constant visual accessibility leads one to suspect constant surveillance, regardless of whether this is the case.[10] This feeling is internalized and slowly breaks the inmate's will. He learns obedience because there is no room for a personal, disobedient life. "Visibility," Foucault states, "becomes a trap."[11]

SOUND IN THE PANOPTICON

Foucault's construction of the panopticon excludes the function of sound. Instead, he theorizes that the "faceless gaze" is the source of the observers' power. Foucault only mentions sound in relation to the panopticon when he describes the guards' tower. The tower's architecture creates a sound barrier that prevents the prisoners from locating the guards: "Zig-zag openings" instead of doors prevent the "slightest noise" from escaping the tower.[12] This would mean that, though unable to hear their guards, the prisoners could in fact hear each other within the architecture of the panopticon. However, this creates a problem in Foucault's argument, for his descriptions of sound seem rather vague. The prisoners are isolated in private cells that have windows to the inside and outside of the panopticon. Foucault does not specify the state of these windows. Nevertheless, one would assume that they have some kind of opening or even consist of bars. If this were the case, the prisoners could communicate with each other by whispering. Or does Foucault assume that the internal obedience created by the gaze prevents the prisoners from communicating with each other? If so, there would be no need at all to address sound in the logic of the panopticon. One must keep in mind that the reason for the omission of sound from Foucault's theory might simply have had to do with the less technically advanced stage of architecture in Bentham's times. This chapter, however, argues that sound must play a prominent role if the panopticon is connected to a societal construction that follows its logic, rather than its architecture. As *The Lives of Others* shows, even under the threat of surveillance, people continue to communicate with each other.

The film depicts Dreyman's apartment in East Berlin as a Foucauldian panopticon, yet adds the dimension of sound. The conversations, music, and sex noises to which Stasi agent Wiesler listens through his headphones from his "watchtower," the attic space occupied by the Stasi solely for surveillance purposes, provide knowledge for the Stasi just as vision provides knowledge in the architecture of the panopticon (see Figure 8.1).[13] Although the architecture of a panopticon was not originally applied to domestic spaces, its logic is nonetheless applicable to this panoptical state. The citizens in the GDR—as shown in the film—lived under permanent sound control, perhaps best described as a "panaural state." They internalized Stasi

Figure 8.1
Scene from *The Lives of Others*. Stasi Hauptmann Gerd Wiesler has taken position in the attic above playwright Georg Dreyman and his actress girlfriend Christa-Maria Sieland's apartment in East Berlin. From there, Wiesler and his colleagues monitor and record the couple's conversations and other sounds.
Photograph by Hagen Keller, Munich, www.hagen-keller.de

The Politics of Sound

control; the threat of acoustic surveillance inside their own four walls (made possible through sophisticated bugging and wiretapping technology) was a permanent condition. Even more than mere vision, sound reveals elaborate thoughts to the guards of the panopticon. Whereas visual evidence could only reveal the preparations of an escape to the West or the actual attempt, acoustic evidence could reveal much more: vocalized thoughts, ideas, and even names of people involved.

SOUND AS A TOOL OF CONTROL IN THE AURAL PANOPTICON IN *THE LIVES OF OTHERS*

Any sounds that we hear in the panopticon of *The Lives of Others*—such as the sounds of interrogations, the intimate *Bettgeflüster* (pillow talk) of the protagonists Dreyman and Sieland, or the *Einheitssprache*, the unified language of the Stasi—are a part of the film's soundscape. The term "soundscape" coined by R. Murray Schafer describes our sonic environments, in the way that the term "landscape" describes physical environments.[14] Emily Thompson uses Schafer's definition and extends it: a "soundscape is simultaneously a physical environment and a way of perceiving that environment; it is both a world and culture that is constructed to make sense of that world."[15] Not only does Thompson describe soundscapes as physical environments, she also further defines, "a soundscape's cultural aspects incorporate scientific and aesthetic ways of listening, a listener's relationship to their environment and the social circumstances that dictate who gets to hear what."[16] Thompson's description reflects what we see in the film.

The listener's relationship to what he hears and "who gets to hear what and where" are essential aspects of the sonic environment. In the film, the Stasi uses listening to observe the people of the GDR in two ways: directly through interrogations and indirectly through wiretapping homes and the use of undercover spies. In the GDR, this ever-present acoustic surveillance was made possible through hidden, state-of-the-art technology. Sound in contrast to vision can overcome spatial restrictions. Vision ends where a wall appears, but sound can overcome fences, bars, and (prison) walls. Within this panaural environment, walls grow ears. In *The Lives of Others*, visible walls are diminished; they are replaced by audible cells. The panaural cells are crueler than the panoptical ones; at first, they seem to provide shelter like the dungeons, but in the end only mock this sense of security.

The panaural state of observation in the GDR becomes apparent in the first scene of the film. Prisoner 227 is led through the hallways of the prison in Berlin-Hohenschönhausen. He enters a room in which he is being interrogated by Wiesler. The prisoner is asked to provide information on the recent escape of his friend Pirmasens to the West. Before he enters the room, 227 is given information on how to address Wiesler: "Anrede: Herr Hauptmann" (Salutation: Mr. Captain). Through the establishment of hierarchies between Stasi agent Wiesler and Prisoner 227, and by the seemingly endless interrogation, the Stasi's control is revealed early on. Even on his entering the room, Wiesler turns on the recording device to archive the conversation for later use as evidence. It is not hard to decipher the purpose of the following communication: the audience is informed that the Stasi can and will imprison 227 at will. "So you think that we imprison respectable citizens simply because we feel like it? . . . If you think our humanist state is capable of such a thing, then we would be right to arrest you, even if nothing else was up."[17] Being a potential *Staatsfeind* suffices in order to be treated as one. After this conversation, the hierarchies in the film are clear—and the audience expects to see more examples of the Stasi's power over its citizens.

In the beginning of the film's first scene, the audience catches a glimpse of the aural panopticon's structure, but it is not fully revealed until the setting changes to the Stasi College Potsdam-Eiche. Here, the audience first sees a tape recorder, then the rest of the room, including Wiesler operating the device (see Figure 8.2). It becomes apparent that Wiesler is the instructor of the new spy elite of the GDR: "In interrogations," he says, "you're working with enemies of socialism," adding, "never forget to hate them."[18] Here the film audience can see the different layers of panaural observation in the film. Not only does Wiesler interrogate 227 based on prior spying on others, but the students in the classroom listen to Wiesler and the prisoner on the interrogation tape. Though being trained as future observers, the students also find themselves in the position of being observed; when a student makes a remark critical of the regime, Wiesler takes note of his name. It is not likely that the student will make future progress in his Stasi training. While all of this is fairly obvious and might only confirm the audience's preconceived notions of the Stasi, suddenly, another layer of surveillance is added to the mix as the viewers and listeners of the film witnessing the scene become uncannily implicated in the film's system of surveillance: they become observers themselves and thereby a part of the panopticon. This raises the question as to who observes whom: Does the film audience function as guards observing the scene? Or are the viewers, like the students at the Stasi college, fellow prisoners hearing each other?

Figure 8.2
Scene from *The Lives of Others*. Stasi Hauptmann Wiesler practices interrogations with his students at Stasi College Postdam-Eiche. He plays a tape from his interrogation of a potential enemy of the state. The words on the board support his explanations: *Aufklärung* (elucidation), *Konspiration* (conspiracy), *OPK: Operative Personenkontrolle* (operational person control), *OV: Operativer Vorgang* (operative procedure). Photograph by Hagen Keller, Munich, www.hagen-keller.de

Once this environment of intensive and complex surveillance is established in the film, the viewer meets the film's other protagonists, who become the targets of the state's *Lauschapparat* (organized eavesdropping). Hempf, a Stasi official, has his eye on Dreyman's girlfriend, and, in an attempt to incriminate Dreyman and remove him from the picture, Hempf orders an *Operativer Vorgang* (operative procedure, abbreviated as OV) to spy on Dreyman. Though not necessarily an accurate representation of the 1980s in the GDR, Henckel von Donnersmarck's fictional account illustrates some of the Stasi's methods by sending a group of Stasi agents led by Wiesler into the couple's apartment to install cables behind the wallpaper and microphones in the bathroom, within a short period of time transforming the space into an aural panopticon. They also wiretap Dreyman's phone making it impossible to communicate with outsiders of the panopticon. No spot remains inaudible for the Stasi, who set up their "watchtower" in the attic. The extensive system of eavesdropping establishes the soundscape in which Dreyman and his girlfriend exist.

Wiesler in the watchtower can not only hear Sieland and Dreyman going about their day, but he also extends his panoptical endeavor by spying on their friends. In addition to the microphones and bugs that were placed in homes and phones, the Stasi used representatives, called *Inoffizielle Mitarbeiter* (unofficial collaborators, or IM), to spy on citizens, even including their family and friends. This system of surveillance was a constant threat within society, hence, the presence of the Stasi in whatever form was always expected, and the citizens internalized this surveillance. In *The Lives of Others*, IM "Max Reinhardt" poses as theater director Egon Schwalber and spies on citizens connected to the theater. Dreyman's friend and regime critic Jerska, who has already been banned from working in the theater, cannot withstand the pressure and eventually commits suicide. Toward the end of the film, Sieland is recruited to be an IM and spy on Dreyman—an unbearable burden that leads to her death as well.

SOUND AS A MEANS TO OVERCOME CONTROL

Sound in *The Lives of Others* has dialectic functions: it serves to control the citizens and, at the same time, helps them to overcome this control. Dreyman and his friends are aware that they live in a world of oppression, and they use sound control—the same method the Stasi utilizes to oppress—as a means to sabotage this surveillance. The artists (and other citizens of the GDR, as seen with Prisoner 227) acoustically manipulate the Stasi repeatedly throughout the film. Their sound resistance includes the use of other sounds, like playing loud music or running water to drown out their conversations; holding conversations in places outside that cannot be "bugged," i.e., outside of the aural panopticon; and voicing incorrect information in order to set the Stasi on the wrong track.

While numerous scenes throughout the film establish sound resistance, one scene in particular shows the different uses of sound as a means to overcome control. This scene appears about midway through the film; it involves Dreyman and his journalist friend Hauser and takes places in Hauser's apartment. After their friend Jerska's death, Dreyman decides to take action and plans to write an article about the unpublished suicide statistics in the GDR. He pays Hauser a visit to discuss the plan, and, after entering Hauser's apartment, Dreyman comes right to the point: "I have tried to obtain statistics that. . . ."[19] Hauser does not let him finish the sentence and quickly interjects, "that show how much more successful our

Staatssicherheit is than we generally believe."[20] Hauser walks over to the record player, and tells his friend Dreyman, but foremost the invisible ears, that he has become "very musical."[21] Pointing to the walls of the room where recording devices are hidden—a gesture not visible through headphones—Hauser pulls Dreyman to the middle of the room to converse and holds up a sign suggesting a meeting place at a lake later in the afternoon: "Three p.m. landing stage at Teufelssee."[22] As opposed to Bentham's panoptical prison, Hauser is able to lead the other "inmates" out of the aural panopticon to escape the hidden ears.

A few scenes later, Dreyman and his friends try to find out if Dreyman's apartment is part of the aural panopticon as well, or, in Hauser's words, whether it is the "last place in the GDR where I can say what I want without punishment."[23] In this scene, Dreyman and his friends find themselves in his apartment with Hauser's uncle from West Germany. To the invisible ears they pretend to plan to smuggle one of their friends over the border. Wiesler cannot believe his ears (Figure 8.3). Until now, Dreyman has not voiced any complaints or plots against the GDR, but now he gives a precise description of the uncle's escape. Wiesler hears the details: the exact day and time, the manner of transportation, and the border control station they will pass. As Wiesler is deeply committed to his job, Dreyman's comment on the Stasi ("who thought that they were such idiots?")[24] hits Wiesler hard and on a personal level. Though he believes what he just heard, Wiesler nevertheless decides not to turn them in to protect them from prison.

In this scene of alleged rebellion, the observed turned the table on Wiesler, the observer. More important, despite their sense of constant oppression, the lives of Dreyman and his

Figure 8.3
Scene from *The Lives of Others*. Dreyman and his friends pretend to smuggle one of their friends over the border. Stasi Hauptmann Wiesler cannot believe what he hears, yet decides not to turn them in—a momentous decision.
Photograph by Hagen Keller, Munich, www.hagen-keller.de

artist friends have become enviable; their conversations form a stark contrast to Wiesler's own sterile and lonely life. While their lives "sound" as being full of passion, love, and art, his own life is as gray and silent as his clothes and his apartment. Their vocabulary revolves around theater, literature, and music, which deeply fascinates Wiesler, who—after years and years with the Stasi—has succumbed to the unified Stasi language that is full of official abbreviations. Even during his theater visit, he does not look at the actors on the stage, but rather observes people in the audience. Listening to Dreyman and his friends, Wiesler acoustically—though initially only passively—becomes a part of their soundscape, which makes him feel as if he were participating in their lives. This leads him to ultimately question the GDR and thus manipulates his sense of duty. This influence of the observed on the observer is a significant change in the film and suggests that sound can be used to overcome control.

This chapter's emphasis so far has been mostly on the sounds of conversation, but, for Wiesler's final change from perpetrator to "good man," music, or organized sound, plays a significant role. Wiesler's final change takes place when he listens to "Die Sonate vom Guten Menschen" ("The Sonata of a Good Man"),[25] which Jerska gave Dreyman for his birthday. Dreyman plays the piece on the piano when he hears that Jerska has killed himself. Referring to Lenin's comment about Beethoven's *Appassionata*, he asks Sieland whether anyone who has really heard "Die Sonate vom Guten Menschen" could ever be a bad human being. The music pushes through the headphones to Wiesler, evoking an emotional response that the viewer has not seen before: despite maintaining his impassive facial expression, a tear runs down Wiesler's cheek.

During a visit to Dreyman's apartment while its inhabitants are out, Wiesler steals a Bertolt Brecht compilation. After reading Brecht and hearing the music that honors the death of Jerska, he can no longer resist his emotions—he has become a part of the Dreyman-Sieland-*OV*. Wiesler has actively entered the soundscape of the panopticon, the site of surveillance, and he has become enclosed in it. Until now he has functioned as the panopticon's guard. Now Wiesler can no longer maintain this position. Sound makes him reevaluate his relationship to the world as "sound makes us re-think our relational experiences, how we relate to others, ourselves . . . the space we inhabit . . . [and] our relationship to power."[26] The intrusion upon their soundscape and their sounds flowing into his soundscape are not necessarily voluntary acts for Wiesler either; just as Lenin's relationship with Beethoven's *Appassionata*, Wiesler cannot help but overhear Dreyman and Sieland's sounds and be moved by them—the sounds take on a life of their own as they force themselves into Wiesler's life. *The Lives of Others* therefore can be read as the story of a man undone when the soundscape of his life (that he has so carefully shored up) is flooded with sounds that he cannot control, stemming from areas unbeknownst to him: music, literature, and emotional intimacy. At this point in the film, Wiesler has listened to the couple's colorful lives, has gone into their apartment to finally see what he only knew from conversations, has seen the place of nightly activities, and even the back scratcher that Dreyman had received as a gift from a friend. In physically entering their apartment and touching some of their belongings, smelling the scents they left behind, and seeing for himself what he only knew through sound, Wiesler has not only intruded upon their soundscape but involved all his senses (with the exception of taste).

Wiesler's newly acquired knowledge and desire to help Dreyman and Sieland—instead of punishing them for not following the rules of the state—create problems for his position of power. As a result, once he has entered and modified the aural panopticon, he risks being observed himself. As articulated earlier, for the citizens who do not maintain a position of power in the panopticon, sound is used as a means of oppression. One can overcome this oppression through sound, yet this does not hold true without complication. In *The Lives of Others*, sound only *seems* to fulfill both of these roles: oppression and resistance. In fact, while it can serve to control, its effect in overcoming this control is rather limited. Since Thompson's definition of soundscapes includes "a listener's relationship to their environment and the social circumstances that dictate who gets to hear what,"[27] it becomes apparent that a soundscape must include the social surroundings. In *The Lives of Others*, the soundscape mirrors the structure of society as well, and since the structure of the society under the dictatorship of the GDR is not entirely visible to the citizens, the conditions of the soundscape are not entirely clear to them either. They are aware of the possibility of permanent observation, but they are also led to believe that they can overcome this control by staging conversations. This does not in fact hold true, as their deceit is only of a temporary nature—ultimately, there is no escape from the panopticon, not even if citizens decide or are forced to switch sides from observed to observer. Observers are also observed by higher powers in the hierarchy. Thus, the panopticon becomes limitless as its concentric rings enclose newer and higher watchtowers at the center of complex hierarchies. Former guards in the watchtower can find themselves among the inmates. As Stasi *Hauptmann* Wiesler loses his job and his privileges in the GDR, it becomes apparent that individual power is only a deceit; temporary power can be granted and withdrawn in a heartbeat.

AN INTERROGATION ON TWO LEVELS

In the last interrogation scene that involves Sieland, Grubitz, and Wiesler, the latter now tries to utilize both functions of sound. Wiesler tries to be simultaneously an unemotional interrogator and a merciful accomplice to Sieland. His position in the Stasi is already shaky; his boss Grubitz is suspicious about his *Parteitreue* (loyalty to the party). Furthermore, after Sieland ended the affair with *Minister* (secretary) Hempf, she lost his protection. Hempf has ordered Grubitz to arrest and interrogate Sieland. Wiesler is ordered to come to Hohenschönhausen, but it is not until his arrival that he finds out that he will interrogate Sieland himself.

The interrogation has two functions: first, on an obvious level, Wiesler is interrogating Sieland to find out whether Dreyman was the author of the suicide article published in the West German magazine *Der Spiegel*. But things have changed for Wiesler; in contrast with the interrogation scene at the beginning of the film, Wiesler now sits in a room with one-way mirrored glass, allowing Grubitz in the control room to observe the scene. Therefore, on a second level, Wiesler finds himself within the panopticon and is being tested. He has to fight for his position but tries to help Sieland as well. Wiesler attempts to walk a fine line: he needs to use sound as a means of control in order to keep up appearances in front of Grubitz, but also tries to overcome that control in incorporating help for Sieland in his questions.

At first, Sieland demonstrates that she is accustomed to life in the panopticon and knows how to play the game. Her attitude had been submissive since her arrival at

Hohenschönhausen. She has offered Grubitz sexual compliance to be let go in return. He refused, because his superior Hempf had an affair with her. When Sieland enters the interrogation room, she asks Wiesler to guide her: "So you're my leading officer."[28] Her ambiguous statement suggests she knows when and how to show a submissive attitude toward Stasi men. What we do see is that Wiesler tries to lead her to accept his help, but that Sieland does not understand his attempt. He explicitly reminds Sieland of her theater audience, a term that he used with her before when he followed her to a bar. Sieland had not known then that he was a Stasi member, and she now reacts with hurt rather than detecting his offer to help. She cannot make out "the multiple layers of meaning potentially embedded in the same sound."[29]

While in the interrogation room and visually observed, Wiesler has to rely on the sound of his voice and his own vocabulary—instead of Stasi vocabulary—to let Sieland know that he is trying to protect her. Once Sieland recognizes him as the man who helped her in the bar earlier, she ceases to believe him. She is disappointed in the man that she had described as "good"; she decides that resistance is pointless and that she cannot trust anyone. Thus, the intended meaning of Wiesler's words is lost. The guard in the panopticon cannot serve two functions at the same time—he can only be the guard and not the helper. Furthermore, the two functions of sound cannot coexist in this system of control. As an individual, Wiesler cannot escape; the panoptical and panaural structure controls his life and cannot be circumvented. In this last interrogation scene, the tension between the two functions of sound as a tool of control and as a means to overcome this control finds its climax. Earlier in the film, Dreyman's and his friends' rebellion seemed successful, not because they were not heard, but because Wiesler covered for them. But now it becomes clear that both Wiesler and Dreyman have only limited power to manipulate the panopticon and are both under the control of someone or something more powerful. Ultimately, sound cannot function as a means to overcome control in the panopticon, as the system has no space for individual resistance.

Audibility is a trap. In Henckel von Donnersmarck's *The Lives of Others*, the Foucauldian panoptical structure is established through aural cells. These cells created through constant eavesdropping isolate the prisoner and illustrate Foucault's logic of internalized obedience. In the film's aural panopticon, there is room to temporarily hide, if a guard protects one of the prisoners, from the aural gaze. One must be aware, however, that it is ultimately impossible to escape the aural panopticon. The hierarchy at its core promises false power, but the power relations become clear as the aural panopticon swallows individualized resistance. Dreyman's question of whether one can be a bad human being after listening to "Die Sonate vom Guten Menschen" is irrelevant. "Good" or "bad," everyone involved in the aural panopticon is observed, even if their job title suggests otherwise.

NOTES

1. *Das Leben der Anderen*, DVD, directed by Florian Henckel von Donnersmarck (Munich, Zurich, Vienna: Buena Vista Home Entertainment, 2006). Starring Dirk Hamm, Quirin Berg, Max Wiedemann, Martina Gedeck, Ulrich Mühe, Sebastian Koch, Ulrich Tukur, Thomas Thieme, Hans-Uwe Bauer, and Herbert Knaup. Anamorphic widescreen format (2.35:1). The film has won numerous awards, among others the Academy Award for Best Foreign Picture 2007, the German Film Award 2006, and the European Film Award 2006.

2. Critics point out that Henckel von Donnersmarck took considerable artistic license in his depiction of the Stasi. While acknowledging this issue, many prominent former East Germans agree with his treatment of the feeling of imprisonment and of constant surveillance in the GDR. Joachim Gauck, former East German and first federal commissioner for the Stasi Archives after Germany's reunification and former presidential candidate agreed: "Ja, so war es!" *Stern*, March 25, 2006, http://www.stern.de/kultur/film/das-leben-der-anderen-ja-so-war-es-558074.html (accessed January 26, 2011). See also Marianne Birthler, "Menschen, die ehrlich zu sich selbst sind, finde ich lebendig," interview with Thomas Leinkauf and Peter Pragal, *Berliner Zeitung*, June 17, 2006, http://www.berlinonline.de/berlinerzeitung/archiv/.bin/dump.fcgi/2006/0617/magazin/0001/index.html (accessed January 26, 2011); Wolf Biermann, "Die Gespenster treten aus dem Schatten. 'Das Leben der Anderen:' Warum der Stasi-Film eines jungen Westdeutschen mich staunen läßt," *Die Welt*, March 22, 2006, http://www.welt.de/print-welt/article205348/Die_Gespenster_treten_aus_dem_Schatten.html (accessed January 26, 2011).

3. "Ich muss immer daran denken, was Lenin von der Appassionata gesagt hat: Ich kann sie nicht hören, sonst bringe ich die Revolution nicht zu Ende. Kann jemand, der diese Musik gehört hat, noch ein schlechter Mensch sein?" (Minute 52). All translations in the text are mine. Henckel von Donnersmarck's stage directions from his film book (*Das Leben der Anderen*, Frankfurt am Main: Suhrkamp, 2006) have been consulted to make the translations as close to the original meaning as possible.

4. Jeremy Bentham, and John Bowring, *The Works of Jeremy Bentham* (Edinburgh; London: W. Tait; Simpkin, Marshall, 1843).

5. Michel Foucault, *Discipline and Punish: The Birth of the Prison*, 2nd ed. (New York: Vintage Books, 1995), 214.

6. Ibid., 212.

7. Ibid., 216.

8. Ibid., 200.

9. Ibid., 200.

10. According to Foucault the panopticon is designed to provide visibility and thus control, yet it is not clear how constant visibility could be achieved in Bentham's architecture. How was the constant visibility achieved at nighttime for example?

11. Foucault, *Discipline and Punish*, 200.

12. Ibid., 201.

13. Wiesler also had a few cameras installed that watched the couple's life, but all of them were located outside of the actual apartment in the hallway and outside of the building. Listening was the main tool of observation for him.

14. R. Murray Schafer, *The Soundscape: Our Sonic Environment and the Tuning of the World* (Rochester, VT: Destiny Books, 1994), 3.

15. Emily Thompson, *The Soundscape of Modernity: Architectural Acoustics and the Culture of Listening in America, 1900–1933* (Cambridge, MA: MIT Press, 2002), 1.

16. Ibid., 1.

17. "Sie glauben also, dass wir unbescholtene Bürger einfach so einsperren aus einer Laune heraus? . . . Wenn Sie unserem humanistischen Staat so etwas zutrauen, dann hätten wir ja schon recht, Sie zu verhaften, auch wenn sonst gar nichts wäre" (Minute 73).

18. "Bei Verhören arbeiten Sie mit Feinden des Sozialismus. Vergessen Sie nie, sie zu hassen." (Minute 16).

19. "Ich habe versucht, Statistiken zu bekommen, die . . ." (Minute 67).

20. ". . . die zeigen, wieviel erfolgreicher unsere Staatssicherheit arbeitet, als wir so allgemein glauben" (Minute 67).

21. " . . . bin ich sehr musikalisch geworden" (Minute 67).

22. "15:00 Bootssteg am Teufelssee" (Minute 67).

23. "Der letzte Ort in der DDR, wo ich ungestraft sagen kann, was ich will" (Minute 77).

24. "Wer hätte gedacht, dass das solche I-di-o-ten sind!!" (Minute 73).

25. "Die Sonate vom Guten Menschen" was composed for the film by Chilean film composer Gabriel Yared.

26. Michael Bull and Les Back, eds., *The Auditory Culture Reader* (Oxford: Berg, 2003), 4.

27. Thompson, *The Soundscape of Modernity*, 1.

28. "Sie sind also mein Führungsoffizier" (Minute 80).

29. Bull and Back, eds., *The Auditory Culture Reader*, 3.

Soundscapers of the Millennium
Sound Art and Music Sounds

M arshall McLuhan has suggested that the beginning of electronic culture could signal renewed interest in the acoustic, and the two concluding chapters of this book position sound artists as the pioneers of a new era. Both chapters also raise questions of borders between fields or disciplines: What is the difference between sound and music? Where is the line between music or performance and sound art? Indeed, the fluidity of the soundscape is central to its very definition, and it is this erasing of boundaries, this flexibility of definition, that is a fundamental quality of sound studies. As both chapters argue, the most avant-garde and forward-thinking sound artists are those who combine or transcend disciplinary restrictions.

As an art historian and a composer, respectively, Brett Van Hoesen and Jean-Paul Perrotte present their history of German sound art from two different yet intertwined perspectives. They use the term *sound art* as a means of challenging the separation of music and sound or noise, taking as examples artists who bring noise from the outside world into the concert hall. Their survey is not limited by restrictions of discipline, and they consider sound art to include electronic music, sound installations, and sound sculptures; and sound artists to include Dadaists to Fluxus performers to Karlheinz Stockhausen. Van Hoesen and Perrotte conclude with the contemporary artist Christina Kubisch, whose installations pay keen attention to the way in which sound and light function within certain spatial configurations and to the way in which sound can build or augment an architectural structure or an environment.

As another example of the avant-garde soundscaper, the hip-hop artist is the focus of Maria Stehle's chapter. Markedly different from the highly regulated (although collaborative) soundscapes of music festivals in the GDR that Tompkins discussed in chapter 7, Stehle makes a case for the liberating quality of soundscapes: seeing the world through auditory lenses, she argues, means giving more power to the marginalized, and she studies a variety of German hip-hop and rap songs to better understand the conflicting experiences of space and belonging in the German urban soundscape of the twenty-first century. She sees rap and hip-hop artists as soundscapers—sonic cartographers of their neighborhoods, who inscribe their presence and their identifications onto urban environments with a combination of sound, speech, and imagery. More than a soundtrack, these sounds claim, define, and gender (public) space; they (re)claim power over spaces and create new meanings; and they negotiate identity politics between rich and poor, German and "other," insider and outsider, and agent and victim.

CHAPTER 9

Sound Art—New Only in Name

A Selected History of German Sound Works
from the Last Century

BRETT M. VAN HOESEN AND JEAN-PAUL PERROTTE

O ver the last decade or so, sound art has emerged as a seemingly new genre in the art world. Digital technology has certainly played an integral role in this development, significantly aiding the creation and presentation of soundscapes, sound installations, sound sculpture, etc.[1] While this trend has undeniably and rightly started to challenge the dominance of visual culture and visual theories, the label of *sound art* dangerously delimits and potentially denies the long, rich history of sound projects that span the twentieth century.[2] This chapter begins with deconstructing the term *sound art* by examining it from the perspective of art history and music composition, the respective fields of the co-authors. Collectively, we seek to create a dialogue between these two disciplines and to create a more expansive notion of what constitutes sound works. The second, larger aim of this chapter is to examine the long historical trajectory of German-based sound projects, which in many cases avoided the contemporary disciplinary divide discussed in the first section. While seminal publications such as Douglas Kahn's *Noise, Water, Meat: A History of Sound in the Arts* (1999) includes reference to German projects, and Nora M. Alter and Lutz Koepnick's edited volume, *Sound Matters* (2004), charts the role of acoustics in constructing a concept of modern German culture, no studies to date focus solely on the history of German sound works and their important legacy. In an attempt to fill this void, this chapter provides a selective history of seminal projects of many sorts, ranging from early twentieth-century avant-garde experiments to contemporary sound works recently exhibited at venues such as the Berlin Biennale für Zeitgenössische Kunst and Documenta in Kassel.

Modernist projects such as Kurt Schwitters' *Ursonate*, from 1922, and László Moholy-Nagy's written theories about sound from the 1920s illustrate that sound was not taken for granted by avant-garde communities affiliated with Dada and the Bauhaus. This attention to privileging the expressive possibilities of sound gained greater momentum by the 1950s, when centers of German electronic music such as the WDR (Westdeutscher Rundfunk) in Cologne sponsored some of the earliest examples of *elektronische Musik* by Karlheinz Stockhausen, Robert Beyer, and Herbert Eimert.[3] Summer lectures by Beyer and Werner Meyer-Eppler in Darmstadt in 1950 also generated considerable excitement about the possibilities of generating new worlds through electronic sound. In the early 1960s, Fluxus projects expanded Dada-esque notions of alternative instruments and compositions with Benjamin Patterson's performance "Solo for Double Bass" (the double bass turned upside down) in Wuppertal in 1962; and George Maciunas' rendition of George Brecht's "Drip Music" (water poured from the top of a ladder), presented in Düsseldorf in 1963. The work of Christina Kubisch from the 1970s to the present has likely set the stage for the range of sound projects dating to the last decade, many of which have played a prominent role in recent large-scale exhibitions. Collectively, the stylistic and historical range of these works reinforces the idea that sound has not always been ignored. In fact, for many individuals and movements based in Germany over the past century, sound was a ripe arena in which to know and explore the world.

I. SOUND ART: DEBATING ITS BEGINNINGS, CONNOTATIONS, AND RAMIFICATIONS

The Beginnings of Sound Art

In a general sense, the invocation of the term *sound art* could be considered a means of challenging the parameters of what constitutes the line between music and sound and/or noise. This development is marked in part by the appropriation of noise from the outside world and its introduction into the concert hall. In addition, sound art could be linked to the incorporation of organized sounds in a variety of performance scenarios and venues. In this sense, music as a practice is not the only disciplinary boundary that has been opened up by the invention of the term. Indeed this concept has been adopted by a number of fine arts disciplines, which find this acoustic realm attractive for its innate ability to transgress. This said, exactly what *sound art* is and when it started is certainly up for debate. A number of recent publications have attended to this term and its chronology, forging a variety of historiographies, which operate with a myriad of agendas. What becomes clear from these histories is that sound art has emerged as a serious concept and at the same time one that remains under contention.

Douglas Kahn's seminal book *Noise, Water, Meat*, first published in 1999, notably does not use the term *sound art* in his history of sound in the arts. His chronology begins with noise experiments of the avant-garde including the work of the Italian Futurist composer Luigi Russolo, who is best known for the invention of *intonarumori*, or noise machines, as well as a new form of notation.[4] Kahn makes the contention that the environment for avant-garde noise experiments was shaped and foregrounded by the predominance of phonographs and records, which contributed to the *democratization* of all types of sound. In other words, what was traditionally perceived to be "noise" could now exist in the same realm as what was considered to be "music." In addition, for avant-garde experimentations, the culture of phonography enabled the storage and dissemination of sound, which served as an inspiration to individuals like Russolo. Kahn additionally notes the avant-garde experiments of Dada—specifically the usage of the voice and sound poetry as a means of making an alternative form of music. These two movements in particular share a like-minded history; as Kahn notes, "the Futurists had been involved in the trafficking of noise since 1913 and proved to be an inspiration for Dada noise as Richard Huelsenbeck wrote in 1920."[5] These early avant-garde activities in their own right bridged the concert hall, cabaret, café, salon, and private space. By their very nature, they transgressed the disciplinary boundaries of music, performance, theater, and visual arts. Perhaps for this very reason, Kahn found the usage of the term *sound art* in this context unnecessary. Despite this omission of terminology, his history of what might be considered integral to the trajectory of sound art begins with popular inventions at the end of the nineteenth century and avant-garde movements dating to the early twentieth century.[6]

In direct contrast to Kahn's work, Alan Licht's 2007 publication *Sound Art: Beyond Music, Between Categories* self-consciously identifies and analyzes the concept of sound art as a thing unto itself. In fact, the first chapter of Licht's book is titled "What is Sound Art?" It begins with a bold declaration that "sound art is a term that has been used with increasing frequency since the late 1990s."[7] He further states that "the term sound art was coined by Canadian composer/audio artist Dan Lander in the mid-1980s."[8] Licht's emphasis on the 1980s is then tempered by his historical revisions, which seek to resituate sound art within an earlier tradition, dating to the work and influence of John Cage from the 1960s. If Licht's trajectory and agenda contrast distinctly with Kahn's, then Brandon LaBelle's recent book sets out a slightly different path. LaBelle's 2006 publication, *Background Noise: Perspectives on Sound Art*, notes that, "since the early 1950s, sound as an aesthetic category has continually gained prominence."[9] Like Licht, LaBelle's analysis is concerned with the division between music and sound; the two see Cage as the initial propagator of the notion that sound works can function as a legitimate form of experimental music. Furthermore, they both note that *musique concrète* as a genre helped to solidify sound works as a serious mode of composition. While Licht and LaBelle do not outright deny the longer history of sound art or at least sound works that date closer to the start of Kahn's time line, there does seem to be a prevailing emphasis on the 1960s and the mid-1980s as the seminal moments when sound art emerged. Privileging these decades, while legitimate to the history of sound works, sets up a bias that precludes a whole host of significant precursors and, for that matter, simultaneous developments that exceed the work and influence of John Cage.

From a self-consciously authored interdisciplinary perspective, one drafted from the fields of music composition and art history, we advocate for a lengthier history more along the lines of Kahn's time frame. Additionally, however, we would like to build a history that encompasses significant developments in both the realms of music composition and art history, which could structure a cross-communication and dialogue that has long been denied as a result of historiographies and shifting emphases within each discipline.

The Connotations of Sound Art

Undeniably, the term *sound art* has become especially popular over the past decade or so, particularly and rightly thanks to the help of the publications just cited. The moment of *sound art's* exact inception as a term is of less interest to us; we are more concerned with the implications and related popularity of the term, which seem to ignore the implicit baggage attached to its components: *sound* and *art*. By its designation as *art* does *sound art* no longer function as music composition? For that matter does the modifier "sound" denote a special category of art, seen in contrast to visual art, or positioned more along the lines of labels such "theater arts"? While certainly the tradition of modifying the word "art" has been linked to a plethora of alternative terminologies, the term *sound art* is vague and suggests a realm that exists neither in music composition nor in the visual arts.

While this might be seen as empowering, by embodying sound art's intrinsic capabilities to transgress disciplinary boundaries, the term does establish a canon or set of standards in its own right. In other words, it would be wrong to assume that the term implies complete openness or freedom of expression. Sound art, as it has emerged as a specific terminology, seems to be viewed as a mode of production that performs a particular redemptive service to the arts. According to Licht: "Music like drama sets up a series of conflicts and resolutions either on a large or small scale."[10] In contrast, he suggests that sound art "rescues music from this fate by aligning this kind of sound work with the aims of non-time-based plastic arts rather than the aims of music." Sound art, he further contends, "belongs in an exhibition situation rather than a performance situation."[11] These statements prompt a worrisome presumption concerning the context of sound art—one that might, at least according to Licht, be better suited to the museum or gallery than the concert hall. If sound art warrants an exhibition space rather than a performance space, we run the risk of committing acoustic works to a rarified realm, one that discounts the larger popular interest in acoustics.

Another problematic connotation with the label *sound art* is that the methods of evaluation used to assess the merits of a work are unclear. How should the musical aspect of a sound art piece be judged? Should traditional standards of rhythm, pitch, dynamics, and timbre be scrutinized or are music theories no longer relevant to sound art? Conversely, should performance elements, the uniqueness of the transmission of sounds, and the general presentation of the work outweigh the rigorousness of the acoustic component? Is sound art an "art practice" more than it is an "exercise in sound"? What role does sound play in this genre? These questions are not easily answered and are integrally linked to the ambiguous nature of sound art as a practice that blends disciplines. Again, however, the label itself and the theories as touted by Licht, for instance, do suggest that there are standards by which sound art is expected to function. These rules, however, seem to have little in common with systems of contemporary music composition. Considering this breach, we contend that something is lost when contemporary electronic music composition is perceived to occupy a territory completely removed from the realm of sound art. If for instance, we were to employ a less belabored term such as *sound works* in the place of *sound art*, we propose that a change in terminology would at least provisionally provide a more inclusive environment, one that truly embraces an interdisciplinary exchange between composers and artists, the museum and concert hall. This said, is changing the terminology enough? Has sound art truly emerged as a new field that indeed has liberated itself from the historical trajectory of *sound in the arts* as established by historians such as Kahn? While we are certainly not advocating for a rigid canonization of what constitutes sound art, we would like to assuage its exclusionary tendency by employing a more general term such as sound works, which would encompass a wider range of projects.

The Ramifications of Sound Art

The current characterization of sound art, as a concept that originated with composers such as John Cage, establishes a problematic paradigm. On the one hand, we come back to a historical problem. Cage, while certainly influential, was not the first to suggest that all sound is music, or for that matter that the acoustic realm is worth probing. On the other hand, the privileging of Cage and his disciples implies that methods such as improvisation and chance temper the character of sound art, a denotation that has significant ramifications. Once you have cast sound art in this light, it precludes the legitimization of a whole range of methods, attitudes, technologies, and aesthetics. For example, given the emphasis on the nature of the Cagean school, individuals such as Stockhausen or Christina Kubisch might be removed from the discussion. Furthermore, seen as part of the trajectory of Cage's influence, these sound art projects bear an "Art" status, conferred by sheer inference to Cage and Marcel Duchamp. This appellation flows into the market appeal for sound art as a "sexy trend" that situates it apart from other acoustic-based works. This special attention denotes a separation between "sound artists" and "composers," again a divide we feel is unnecessary and perhaps in some ways simply market-driven.

So what is the future of sound art? Is it more than just a trend? Given the technologies available, it is almost certain that soundscapes, sound sculptures, and other acoustic-based works will contribute to an increasingly growing field. In light of this, perhaps it is time to do away with fixed labels such as sound art, and for the time being allow the flow of creativity from a variety of fields to enter into the same discursive space. Eventually, as with all major movements, boundaries, definitions, substyles, and labels will likely be applied. At the moment, however, we would advocate for a wider scope, one that does not subscribe to a historical or stylistic bias rooted in the 1960s, in the work of Cage, or for that matter the more recent innovations dating to the 1980s and 1990s.[12] It is too soon to narrow the field of sound works as it is finally gaining the historiographic recognition that it deserves, one that chronicles over a century of developments. Today, discussions and debates between sound artists and composers are greatly needed before the divide between "museum" and "concert hall" or "art" and "music" forges a barrier that is insurmountable and marked by silence instead of dialogue.

II. A SELECTED HISTORY OF GERMAN SOUND WORKS FROM THE LAST CENTURY

While German composers, artists, and inventors have certainly played a contributing role in the recent publications devoted to the history of sound in the arts, and for that matter, sound art, they have not been discussed to the extent that is warranted. In fact, no studies to date evaluate a comprehensive history of German sound works from the early twentieth century to the present. This task is admittedly beyond the realm of this chapter; however, we would like to present a selected history of German sound works, which embody a wide range of historical and stylistic arenas to stress that, for many individuals and movements based in Germany over the past century, sound has not been ignored. Furthermore, the examples that we will discuss here embody a rich combination of technologies from spoken word to early electronic music, from installation to sound sculptures.

Early Twentieth-Century German Avant-Garde Experiments

The avant-garde has been credited with a host of achievements. According to Peter Bürger, one of the prerequisite traits of the historical avant-garde is that it embraced new technologies.[13] While Bürger focuses on practices such as collage and photomontage, an equally worthy endeavor worth historicizing would be the avant-garde's exploration of the acoustic arts—particularly those generated through sound poetry, both written and performed, as well as experimentations with human-produced sounds and sound machines as a means of creating new sensory experiences. As mentioned, one of the fathers of avant-garde sound experiments, Luigi Russolo, helped to establish a body of works that impacted movements beyond the realm of the Italian Futurists. For Dadaists based in Zurich, Berlin, and Hannover, the ideas underlying *bruitism* were applied to a range of scenarios.[14]

While Kurt Schwitters was certainly inspired by Futurist sound innovations, the evolution of his own *Ursonate (Primal Sonata)*, 1922–1932, which drew upon an "ur-language," a so-called early or even prelinguistic form of communication, began with the phonetic poetry of fellow Dadaist Raoul Hausmann. Believing in the transformative power of the performance, Schwitters was inspired by the recital of one of Hausmann's early poems from 1918, which he witnessed during a performance in Prague in September of 1921.[15] As an homage to Hausmann, the prelude of the *Ursonate* mimics the first line of Hausmann's 1918 poem; Schwitters transformed and extended Hausmann's line, "fmsbwtäzäu," into "Fümms bö wö tää zää Uu."[16] The performed and eventually recorded final version of Schwitters' work, scored with typographical assistance from Jan Tschichold, totaled forty minutes in length.

While Schwitters' sonata has been historicized within the genre of sound or phonetic poetry, his work certainly functions as an early fusion of music composition, sound art, and performance art. Schwitters seems to have made a concerted effort to embrace this *Gesamtkunstwerk* (total art work) mentality in that he wanted the score to look like a "composition" and believed that its true essence could only be realized in its recitation, its performance. The compositional character of the work is emphasized by the organization of the score—which includes a prelude, as well as multiple movements, themes, transitions, developments, and finales.[17] A sonata is a piece of music for a solo instrument generally composed of three or four movements. While Schwitters took some creative liberties by incorporating forms that normally exceed the language of a sonata, the overall structure of this multimovement piece is indeed loosely based on a piano sonata capped with a cadenza-like element from a concerto.

Schwitters was extremely interested in the reception of his piece, particularly the reaction from and eventual transformation of the audience as they endured the forty-minute-long performance. He noted the way in which their initial shock morphed into nervous laughter and eventually turned into awe, admiration, even gratitude, as they were forced to digest acoustic sensations they had never before experienced.[18] Hans Richter, who was in the audience at the first public reading of *Ursonate*, also noted the emotive power of the work as well as the interaction between Schwitters and members of his audience.

> I remember the first public reading of the *Ursonate* at the house of Frau Kiepenhauer in Potsdam, about 1924 or 1925. Those invited were the "better sort" of people—and in Potsdam, the military citadel of the old Prussian monarchy, this meant a crowd of retired

generals and other people of rank.... At first they were completely baffled, but after a couple of minutes the shock began to wear off.... And then they lost control.... The dignified old ladies, the stiff generals, shrieked with laughter, gasped for breadth, slapped their thighs, choked themselves. Kurtchen [Schwitters] was not in the least put out by this. He turned up the volume of his enormous voice to Force Ten and simply swamped the storm of laughter in the audience, so that the latter almost seemed to be an accompaniment to the *Ursonate*.[19]

In this sense, Schwitters' composition is akin to many midcentury and contemporary electronic sound works, as the focus was not only on the form and execution of the work, but on the desired effect, the way in which the audience experienced and reacted to the piece. The lasting impact and legacy of Schwitters' *Ursonate* is partially attributed to his keen interest in preserving and documenting its performance, which he recorded in 1932. Later made as a record and then a CD, the work now lives on through various Web venues.[20] Regardless of the means or technology of its transmission, Schwitters' voice remains impressively intact; undeniably the documentation of his performance style greatly enhances the written score.

Other German-based avant-gardists were probing the potential of sound as a new medium, including the Hungarian-born artist László Moholy-Nagy. Based at the Bauhaus in Weimar starting in 1923, Moholy-Nagy had an insatiable appetite for a variety of media; he not only experimented with and mastered painting, sculpture, photography, photomontage, and film, but he theorized these practices as well. Sound was not exempt from his theoretical writings. Concerned with the sensual possibilities associated with sonic experiments, Moholy-Nagy focused on the influx of sound films dating to the later 1920s. In essays such as "Problems of the Modern Film," written in 1928–1930 and first published in 1932 in *Cahiers d'Art*, Moholy-Nagy discussed the need to "diligently expand our acoustic receptivity."[21] He legitimately believed that "the sound film ought to enrich our aural experience sphere by giving us entirely unknown sound values, just as the silent film has already begun to enrich our vision." Furthermore, Moholy-Nagy argued that sound films should not employ acoustics merely as a means of amplifying the visual. Instead, he advocated that the fusion of these two realms should augment each sensation to the extent that a new sensory experience would be created.

In order to realize this climactic moment, Moholy-Nagy recommended that sonic experiments independent of film be executed in order to further investigate the creative possibilities associated with sound. These included a number of steps, the first of which involved experiments with "acoustic realism," including natural sounds, the human voice, or musical instruments. Another involved the use of "sound units." According to the artist, "Every mark on the sound track is translated into some note of noise in projection. My experiments with drawn profiles, letter sequences, fingerprints, geometrical signs printed on the track also produce surprising acoustic effects."[22] Additional experiments involved manipulating sounds to generate "different sound angles, just as there are different angles of sight."[23] These modes could be generated by a variety of techniques including "sound contraction, distortion, duplication and other methods of sound montage." Ultimately, Moholy-Nagy was committed to probing sound with the same level of curiosity he devoted to a roster of visual media. Sound was just another arena worth exploring, one that could hypothetically prompt an expansion of human sensory capabilities.

If ever there is a case to be made for an institution having an impact on the history of German sound works, it would be for the construction of the electronic music studio at the Westdeutscher Rundfunk (WDR) in Cologne in 1951–1952.[24] From the studio's official opening in 1953, Karlheinz Stockhausen found a home where he could experiment with electric tone generators to create new synthesized sounds, recording these ideas on tape. The prominence of the WDR in promoting new music and providing a workspace for an innovative crop of composers interested in the possibilities of sound creation and timbre manipulation is integral to the development of electronic music in Germany and the world. It was the exuberance of summer lectures by Robert Beyer and Werner Meyer-Eppler in Darmstadt in 1950, as well as the 1951 lectures by Herbert Eimert, that prompted considerable excitement about the possibilities of creating new worlds through electronic sound. Present at these lectures were composers such as Pierre Boulez, Karel Goeyvaerts, and Stockhausen, who were invited to come to the studio to work. Stockhausen's compositions *Studie I* and *Studie II*, completed in 1953 and 1954 respectively, were a direct extension of his work with serialist technique and his studies in Paris with Olivier Messiaen. These compositions, whose sounds were produced by sine-wave tone generators at the WDR, were rooted in the quest for a total serialization of sound.[25] This method involved carefully controlling the timbre of each individual sound. While pitch, dynamics, and rhythm were elements that could be controlled with other compositional methods, the manipulation of timbre was a product unique to electronic music.

Stockhausen continued to work out of the WDR, experimenting with a wide range of techniques and approaches. Compositions such as *Gesang der Jünglinge* (1955–1956) and *Hymnen* (1966–1967) incorporated concrète recordings that were not solely based on his work with sound generators. What is significant about this change in technique is that concrète recordings were skillfully modulated or seamlessly morphed between disparate concrète and electronic sounds.[26] *Hymnen*, for instance, incorporated recordings of national anthems of roughly forty different countries from around the world. This work not only crossed national borders, but it successfully merged the fixed boundaries between 1950s German *elektronische Musik* and French *musique concrète*. Stockhausen's experiments at the WDR also involved new methods of delivering sound to the listener. His work with quadraphonic sound and with rotating speakers came to life in his composition *Kontakte* (1958–1960), a piece for percussion, piano, and tape, as well as four rotating speakers. The rotating speakers, each with its own audio track, were placed in a square surrounding the audience. This method presented sound as we truly hear it; unlike the standard mode of presenting music, which emits sound from one spatial perspective, the surround-sound technique employed by Stockhausen engulfed listeners in a total acoustic environment.

In 1954 Stockhausen met John Cage for the first time. This meeting introduced the German composer to American discourses involving new music composition. At the time, Cage was touring Europe to promote his music performed by David Tudor. Both Stockhausen and Boulez, young leaders of the European serialism, supported Cage's music at first. While Stockhausen remained an ardent supporter of Cage, Boulez eventually took a critical stance toward Cage's use of chance in his compositions. Boulez called Cage's methods, "a philosophy tinged with Orientalism that masks a basic weakness in compositional techniques."[27]

This can be seen as a sign of the inevitable clash between the traditional European school and the emerging American school of Cage and Morton Feldman.

Fluxus: Alternative Instruments-Alternative Means

If Stockhausen and the experimental environment of the WDR created a basis for German electronic music, then the international Fluxus movement, based in Germany as well as in New York, proved to be a rich testing ground for alternative instruments and methods of performance. The group was composed of members including Joseph Beuys, George Brecht, John Cage, Dick Higgins, Alison Knowles, George Maciunas, Nam June Paik, Yoko Ono, Wolf Vostell, La Monte Young, and others. Fluxus artists, adopting a term coined by Maciunas, embraced a wide variety of activities from writing manifestos to performing theatrical works and ephemeral events, designing anthologies and other publications, creating games and Fluxkits, as well as exploring the creative possibilities of correspondence or mail art. The group equally valued sonic experiments and embraced what could be considered a range of "acoustic events," often self-consciously staged shock tactics that ranged from Maciunas pounding a piano with a hammer to seemingly ridiculous ensembles of performers featuring noisemakers made out of unlikely materials such as paper, as in the case with Ben Patterson's *Paper Music* piece from 1962. During the early 1960s, Fluxconcerts took place in a host of cities—including Wiesbaden, Düsseldorf, Wuppertal, Paris, Copenhagen, Amsterdam, Nice, Stockholm, and Oslo—as a means to widely disseminate the group's experimental mentality. Patterson's work, "Solo for Double Bass," performed in Wuppertal in 1962, challenged audience members' expectations for how the upright bass should be played. Turning the instrument upside down and manipulating the strings with objects other than a bow, Patterson's piece reimagined a traditional instrument as an alternative sounding device. Following the legacy of earlier avant-garde movements, George Brecht, on the other hand, did away with traditional instruments. His work titled "Drip Music," performed by Maciunas in Düsseldorf in 1963, embraced the tonal surprises associated with quotidian acts such as pouring water. The execution of the piece required that the performer climb a tall ladder with a jug of water in hand. The water was then poured at various speeds down to a collection container below. Depending on the performer's choice, the process could be repeated. Embracing the sounds of the everyday interlaced with chance elements, Brecht's "Drip Music" to a certain extent reinforced the aesthetic of musique concrète without the use of recording technology. The simplicity and at times ridiculousness of Fluxconcerts contributed to the history of German sound works by making improvisation and quick, live performances real "events" removed from the strictures and formality of traditional music composition or official performances.

German Sound Projects Starting in the 1970s

Born in Bremen in 1948, Christina Kubisch received her initial education in painting at the Akademie der Bildenden Künste, Stuttgart (1967–1968) and music at the Staatliche Hochschule für Musik und Bildende Kunst, Hamburg as well as the Hochschule für Musik,

Graz (1969–1972). She continued her study of music at the Musikhochschule Zurich and the Freie Kunstschule, Zurich (1972–1974) and then trained specifically in composition and electronic music in Italy at the Conservatory of Milan from 1974 to 1976. From 1974 until 1980, Kubisch performed concerts in Europe and the United States with the video artist Fabrizio Plessi. These early shows featured musical works like *Teil der Performance: "Two and Two"* (1976) for cello, vibrator, flute, and contact microphone. Others like *Tempo Liquido* (1976–1977) were collaborative video performance pieces for panes of glass, water, water filter, metal thimbles, audiotape, and video. In 1980, Kubisch turned her attention to creating sound installations and sound sculptures. While still exploring acoustic worlds, this was a departure from her previous work as a "composer." To reduce the baggage attached to her previous labels, Kubisch from this point on considered herself to be a "craftsman," a term that allowed her to remain concerned with the way in which sound was portrayed in her works, without functioning under the limited connotation of the terms "composer" or "artist."[28] Thanks to this freedom, Kubisch's "musical activity" involved and continues to entail "collecting sounds, processing them, putting them together and imagining their later effect in the room," filling the room with sound.[29] This simple utilitarian approach to her work is apparent throughout her projects from the 1980s to the present.

Like Schwitters and Stockhausen, Kubisch is interested in the response to her work. This is reflected in the format of her sound installations. So-called electrical walks, such as *Il respiro del mare* (1981), and *Der Vogelbaum* (1987), involved wireless headphones that received audio signals from labyrinth-like drawings made of wire fixed to the gallery's walls. These wire figures sent different sounds to the headphones as the visitor walked around the room. This allowed the visitor to assume an active role in mixing the sounds sent to them by choosing their own path through the installation. This unimposing, even democratic, element is still evident in more current works, such as her collaboration with Berhard Leitner titled *Zeitversetzt: Ettersburger Klangbildräume* from 2004.

Another element of her work involves creating sound sculptures that engage with preexisting objects, structures, or environments. Her *Clocktower Project* from 1996 resuscitates the clock tower of a closed factory in North Adams, Massachusetts, abandoned after ten years of inactivity. Solar panels adhered to the site read the intensity of the sun. This information is used to trigger acoustic samples of the long-inactive clock tower bells. The result is that loud, distinct, metallic tones resonate from the tower on sunny days while softer, more melancholic tones ring out on days that are overcast. Kubisch also enhances the structure with the symbolism of light: the tower is illuminated with cool blue and white lights in the evening when no sound is produced. In this work, Kubisch brings back to life what was once the center of activity and the heartbeat of North Adams.

Her latest piece, *Licht Himmel* (2006), also involves a fusion of light and sound elements (see Figure 9.1). The work was installed in a former 100-meter-high gas tank in Oberhausen, Germany. Involving 212 special light bulbs and a fourteen-channel sound environment, this project draws much of its character from the space that Kubisch selected to host this work. The visually stunning Parthenon-like interior of this former gas tank produces a long reverb time that is aurally wondrous. Kubisch's use of sparse lighting and ethereal sounding instruments such as the Trautonium, glass harmonica, Tibetan metal bowls, double bass, field recordings, synthesizer, voice, tuning forks, glass gong, and a glass cornet functions well with the acoustic environment inherent to the space.

Figure 9.1
Christina Kubisch, *Licht Himmel*, Gasometer Oberhausen, 2006.
Photograph by Wolfgang Volz.

Like Stockhausen, Kubisch is devoted to tireless experimentation with new ways of presenting her ideas. Both view composition as much more than merely assigning notes to instruments in an orchestra or presenting music and/or sounds to an audience seated in a concert hall. As evidence of the legacy of Stockhausen, Kubisch is concerned with controlling timbre as well as the delivery of sound in her works. While embracing Stockhausen's legacy, she also moves beyond it by paying even keener attention to the way in which sounds (and light) function within certain spatial configurations, and the way in which sound can build or augment an interior, architectural structure, or environment.

Sound Works in the German Contemporary Art World

One might argue that the fascination for sound works has never completely left the German contemporary art scene—from the 1970s to today. As testament to this continuum are the range of examples of sound works featured in permanent museum collections, special exhibitions, and art fairs. The rationale for this presence is likely in line with the fact that there is a strong appetite for electro-acoustic and electronic music in Germany. In the summer of 2001, Berlin featured an amazing array of venues both publicized and underground that hosted concerts of electro-acoustic music compositions and improvisational sound works. The first, perhaps most memorable of these early experiences in Berlin was thanks to a festival called *Format 5*, which featured an elaborate sound and video piece titled *Symphony #2 for Dot Matrix Printers*. The work was created by the Canadian artist collective The User, co-founded by architect Thomas McIntosh and composer Emmanuel Madan. The *Symphony* was realized with the additional assistance of Thaddeus Thomas, a freelance software architect; Dave Ozsvari, a hardware and technical consultant; and Jean-Pierre Côté, a sound consultant. The work employed a roster of twelve different kinds of dot-matrix printers, numbering roughly twenty in total, which were each connected to microphones as well as mini-digital cameras, the latter attached to the print carriages. Some of the printers were prepared in advance to encumber paper jams and other malfunctions that were acoustically captured by the microphones. The sounds generated by each printer were collectively combined through a mixer and broadcast in surround to the audience. Projected onto two large video screens, the images recorded by the mini-digital cameras were also run through a video mixer. While the sounds and images did not directly correlate with one another, they worked in tandem, thanks to the shared aesthetic effect of sampling. According to the description of the work provided by The User's Web site:

> The Symphony for Dot Matrix Printers is a work that transforms obsolete office technology into an instrument for musical performance. The Symphony focuses the listener's attention on a nearly forgotten technology. . . . Dot matrix printers are thus turned into musical "instruments," while a computer network system, typical of a contemporary office, is employed as the "orchestra" used to play them. The orchestra is "conducted" by a network server, which reads from a composed "score."[30]

Embodying the mentality of John Cage that "all sound is music," the creators of this work push numerous boundaries through the adaptation of old technologies that work in unison with the implementation of new ones, resulting in an impressive event.

Similar to smaller festivals, such as Format 5, larger international contemporary art shows in Germany in the 2000s have also hosted a number of acoustic-oriented works. These entities include Documenta, an international art fair held every five years in Kassel, and the Berlin Biennale für Zeitgenössische Kunst, which in 2008 celebrated its fifth exhibition. While not all of the sound artists or composers included in these shows are German, these German-based venues serve as a forum for exploring sound as a viable medium. In 2002, at Documenta XI, the American artist team Steve Badgett and Matthew Lynch, the founders of Simparch, presented a collaborative work with Chicago-based experimental musician and electro-acoustic composer Kevin Drumm. Their work titled Spec consisted of a 72-foot-long barrel vault structure that provided a conducive and alluring environment in which to experience Drumm's electronically generated soundscape (see Figure 9.2). Incorporating granulated sound alongside longer bits of concrète recordings, Drumm also added white noise and a low-frequency hum to result in a multitextured composition. The arched structure, which held up to eighty people, morphed the divide between "installation art" and "alternative concert hall." With a wide bench running the length of the vault, people were offered the option of sitting and experiencing Drumm's sonicscape or walking the length of the vault listening to the sounds as they entered the space through speaker panels. Characteristic of sound sculpture or installation art, this piece was not simply about the performance of Drumm's composition, but it engendered a "total experience" that was based on an engagement with the environment as a whole.

Simparch contributed another work to Documenta XI entitled Free Basin. Unlike Spec, which was referenced as a soundscape, Free Basin, which consisted of a kidney-shaped skate

Figure 9.2
Simparch, *Spec*, 2002 (Kassel, Documenta XI), 72-foot-long barrel vault.

bowl made of plywood, was termed a *noisescape*. This differentiation might have to do with the type of sound that comprised the work. The installation was activated by skateboarders who took turns skating the basin, or in some cases skating in unison, all of whom were observed by visitors to the site. While the act of skating constituted the main noise element of the piece, the audience also had the potential to contribute in the form of reactive cheers and applause. While the sound of skateboard wheels on the wooden basin generated a meditative rhythm, these patterns were regularly interrupted by skater's disengagement with the space for a momentary rest as well as the occasional instance of audience interjection. Whether called a soundscape or a noisescape, the collaborative installations of Simparch contribute to the positive reception of acoustic-oriented works within a contemporary German art world.

While the previous examples featured non-German composers, artists, and collectives, there has been a strong showing of German sound works in recent international art fairs including the Berlin Biennale. The third biennial held during the spring of 2004 and collectively hosted by three institutions, the KW Institute for Contemporary Art, Martin-Gropius-Bau, and the Kino Arsenal, was divided into five major themes, one of which was titled "Sonic Scapes."[31] According to the show's artistic director, Uta Meta Bauer, the scope of the exhibition was meant to reinforce Berlin's heterogeneity, celebrating the "broad international spectrum of fine art, architectural, cinematic, performative, sonic, and urban stagings that enter into dialogue with Berlin-specific discourses." Sound art works were included in the show as well as featured electronic music events, such as Florian Hecker's *Performance Jam*, hosted twice at the KW Institute for Contemporary Art, April 16–17, 2004. Hecker, who considers himself part of the first generation of laptop musicians, prefers a minimalist aesthetic. His works are improvisatory in nature as they eschew order and orientation, allowing his rhythms to avoid any obvious structure. Furthermore, Hecker denies a connection to established genres of electronica such as Clicks'n'Cuts or electro-acoustic music. Hecker is a classic example of an acoustic practitioner who strives to avoid categorization; this enables him and his works to exceed labels. The fact that the Berlin Biennale 2004 hosted Hecker's performances, in conjunction with other programs associated with the "Sonic Scapes" section, denotes a keen interest in having sound represented at one of the premiere biennial contemporary art fairs.

CONCLUSION: THERE IS HOPE

There is hope for what we are advocating both in terms of historicizing the "long history" of sound works as well as in acknowledging the strong presence of German contributions over the past century. From our disciplinary backgrounds of music composition and art history, there are many indications that there is hope for a mutual openness and cross-dialogue concerning sound works. Upon the recent death of Stockhausen, *Artforum*, the preeminent journal devoted to contemporary art, featured a lengthy, multiauthored tribute to the German composer. Never considered a sound artist during his lifetime, he has been recognized and now perhaps remembered within the context of a growing interdisciplinary interest in sound works and acoustics in general. The fact that such attention was paid to a composer in a contemporary art journal implies a changing mentality. Not only does sound matter, but composers appear to be increasingly relevant to the contemporary art scene. In short, it is time that pioneers of sound art and electro-acoustic composition, particularly those who contributed to a collective German presence in the field, be considered in relationship to one another in order to celebrate this rich history. If the rising number of recent publications on the topic of acoustic culture is any indication, sound studies is a burgeoning field—one that has the capacity and responsibility to embrace a broad spectrum of practitioners, histories, contexts, methods, and technologies. [32] The increasingly noted acknowledgment that sound plays an integral role in our comprehension of the world suggests that acoustic culture, in all of its dimensions, is finally receiving overdue attention and acceptance in modern discourse.

1. Digital technologies have dramatically changed the production and exhibition of sound works. From a production side, digital editing programs such as Pro Tools, Logic, Digital Performer, and even Garage Band have made processing and editing sound increasingly quick and inexpensive in comparison to older technologies such as tape machines. From an exhibition standpoint, these technologies enabled the machinery required to run the installation to be less intrusive. Simply put, these technologies provide a much easier setup for audio works. One computer can run multiple outputs as opposed to multiple devices that would have to be synched to run simultaneously.

2. Recent studies based in the field of neurology have also helped to privilege an increased interest in sound reception, which has, at least in terms of the layman's literature, been overshadowed by studies of optics and visual perception. See for example Daniel J. Levitin, *This Is Your Brain on Music* (New York: Plume/Penguin Group, 2006).

3. The term *elektronische Musik* refers to a specific movement in the development of electronic music composition promoted by Robert Beyer, Herbert Eimert, and Werner Meyer-Eppler in the late 1940s through the early 1950s.

4. Douglas Kahn, *Noise, Water, Meat: A History of Sound in the Arts* (Cambridge, MA: MIT Press, 1999), 45–67.

5. Ibid., 45–46.

6. The phonograph was invented by Thomas Alva Edison in 1877 and was patented in 1878.

7. Alan Licht, *Sound Art: Beyond Music, Between Categories* (New York: Rizzoli, 2007), 9.

8. Ibid., 11.

9. Brandon LaBelle, *Background Noise: Perspectives on Sound Art* (New York and London: Continuum, 2006), xii.

10. Licht, *Sound Art: Beyond Music, Between Categories*, 13.

11. Ibid., 14.

12. We do not want to imply that Cage's work in the 1960s is his most important nor do we want to suggest that Cage came from a musically deficient background. That is certainly not the case. He studied with both Arnold Schönberg and Henry Cowell. In addition, Cage's important collaboration with Merce Cunningham as well as his prepared piano pieces began in the 1940s. We would simply like to stress that Cage saw the era of the sixties as a point when American music could wrestle its way out from under the history of European dominance.

13. Peter Bürger, *Theory of the Avant-Garde* (Minneapolis: University of Minnesota Press, 1984), 73–82.

14. It is interesting to consider that these avant-garde sound experiments were taking place in the years after World War I. For a consideration of the sonic experience of the First World War, see Yaron Jean's chapter in this book.

15. Schwitters and his wife accompanied Hausmann and Hannah Höch to Prague in the fall of 1921 as part of their "Anti-Dada-Merz" tour. According to John Elderfield, this event not only inspired Schwitters' abstract poems, but likely prompted the beginnings of his *Ursonate*. See Elderfield, *Kurt Schwitters* (London: Thames and Hudson, 1985), 175.

16. This was originally the start of a smaller work titled *Portrait of Raoul Hausmann*, which was eventually expanded to become the *Ursonate* (Elderfield, *Kurt Schwitters*, 176).

17. For reproduction of the full written score of *Ursonate* with English translations of Schwitters' directions for the performance of the piece, see Jerome Rothenberg and Pierre Joris, eds., *Kurt Schwitters PPPPPP: Poems, Performances, Pieces, Proses, Plays, Poetics* (Philadelphia: Temple University, 1993), 52–80; 233–237.

18. Dorothea Dietrich, "Hannover Dada," in *DADA: Zurich, Berlin, Hannover, New York, Paris*, ed. Leah Dickerman (Washington, D.C.: National Gallery of Art in association with

D.A.P./Distributed Art Publishers, 2005), 173. Although Dietrich relays Schwitters' philosophies concerning audience reception to his work, her account is supported by citations of Hans Richter's first-hand experiences with performances of the *Ursonate*.

19. Hans Richter, *Dada Art and Anti-Art* (London: Thames and Hudson, 1965), 142–143.

20. A variety of performances by Schwitters and others can for example be found on YouTube. com.

21. László Moholy-Nagy, "Problems in the Modern Film," in *Moholy-Nagy: An Anthology*, ed. Richard Kostelanetz (New York: Da Capo Press, 1970), 135.

22. Moholy-Nagy, "Problems in the Modern Film," 136.

23. Ibid.

24. The creation of the electronic music studio at the Westdeutscher Rundfunk is contemporaneous with the performance of Günter Eich's radio play *Träume*, discussed in Robert Ryder's chapter. Both projects share an interest in creating new worlds through sound.

25. Karl H. Wörner, *Stockhausen: Life and Work* (Berkeley and Los Angeles: University of California Press, 1973), 130.

26. Traditionally *musique concrète* is a style of music that comprises exclusively real-life sounds in contrast to *elektronische Musik*, which traditionally comprises synthesized sounds.

27. Quoted in Glenn Watkins, *Soundings: Music in the Twentieth Century* (New York: Schirmer Books, 1975), 561.

28. Kubisch in an interview by Christoph Metzger, in *Christina Kubisch: Klangraumlichtzeit, Works from 1980 to 2000* (Heidelberg: Kehrer Verlag in association with Kultur Arts der Stadt Rüsselsheim, 2000), 89.

29. Ibid., 89.

30. See www.theuser.org/dotmatrix/en/intro.html.

31. The additional four themes of the 2004 biennial were *Migration, Urban Conditions, Fashions and Scenes,* and *Other Cinemas.*

32. Recent publications on acoustic culture include: Garret Keizer, *The Unwanted Sound of Everything We Want: A Book About Noise* (New York: Perseus, 2010); Brandon LaBelle, *Acoustic Territories: Sound Culture and Everyday Life* (New York and London: Continuum, 2010); Salomé Voegelin, *Listening to Noise and Silence: Towards a Philosophy of Sound Art* (New York and London: Continuum, 2010); Louis Niebur, *Special Sound: The Creation and Legacy of the BBC Radiophonic Workshop* (Oxford: Oxford University Press, 2010).

CHAPTER 10

Ghettos, Hoods, Blocks

The Sounds of German Space in Rap and Hip-Hop

MARIA STEHLE

Eko Fresh, ghetto boss, guys, because it has to happen.
Cologne, Kalk, Hartz 4, come to my hood!
Come and see what it means to live in this neighborhood,
where one has to live from drugs and prostitution.
— Eko Fresh, featuring Bushido, "Gheddo"[1]

S ound can serve as a means of claiming or disavowing an identity. It is through sound that rap and hip-hop artists inscribe their presence onto German space, even when that space is marginal and that identity is marginalized.[2] In the song "Gheddo" (2006), German rapper Eko Fresh asks the listener to join him on a tour through his "Hood," so that he can demonstrate what it means to live in an environment dominated by drugs, prostitution, and social welfare.[3] To set the mood, the song starts with the noise of thunder, which merges with a slow and melodic drum beat. Bushido, one of the best known rappers in Germany, joins Eko Fresh in the second verse as a tour guide. They rap about wanting to get out of the ghetto and becoming rich and famous; at the same time they emphasize their identification with this poor and marginal urban space. Their "tour" features Eko's neighborhoods in the vicinity of Cologne (Kalk, Gremberg, Mönchengladbach) and Bushido's neighborhood, Tempelhof in Berlin; in the video, these descriptions are accompanied by black-and-white images of concrete landscapes, graffiti art, and other generic snapshots of life on the margins of the postmodern urban jungle.[4]

The tour offered in this rap song depicts the negotiations over identity and belonging in the German "Gheddo" at the beginning of the twenty-first century. Eko Fresh and Bushido create boundaries in an urban space that is both recognizable and nonspecific; they negotiate space and power by creating a tension between the insiders who understand and know their specific neighborhoods and life in the "Gheddo" and an audience in need of guidance, protection, and interpretation. The representation fluctuates between romanticizing poverty and ghetto life and a call for change. The visual and textual references range from recognizable German cityscapes to film scenes and allusions to U.S. inner-city life. Repeatedly, the rappers accuse the listener of failing to recognize a certain reality: "you all have rich parents and claim that there are no ghettos in Germany."[5]

HIP-HOP SOUNDSCAPES

These depictions of city spaces in German rap and hip-hop productions[6] describe the conflicting experiences of space and belonging in German urban spaces in the twenty-first century. Rap and hip-hop artists act as "soundscapers," who inscribe their presence and their identifications onto the urban environments with a combination of music, speech, and imagery. Nora Alter and Lutz Koepnick argue that sound is "a primary medium through which the boundaries of shared meanings, ethnic differences, political representation, codes of gender identity, and the organization of private and public spaces are constituted."[7] They summarize their exploration of the importance of sound by quoting Jaques Attali, who understands sound as representing "the social organization of noise, a source of political control as much as of subversion."[8] Sound mirrors cultural anxieties over definitions of space, power, and identity[9] and uncovers tensions among order, chaos, the status quo, change, and utopia.[10] Ulrich Werner contends that soundscapers come from various contexts, disciplines, and cultures and that "their subjective knowledge and social positions, that incorporate all areas of life, are of central importance for knowledge production." Werner understands the soundscaper as a source of disruption of social convention.[11] Similar to landscapers, soundscapers aim to transform and resignify spatial orders. Judith Butler argues that "the resigni-fication [sic] of speech requires opening new contexts, speaking in ways that have never yet been legitimated, and hence producing legitimation in new and future forms."[12] The different soundscapes depicted in rap and hip-hop music, their speech, voices, noises, and music, combined with imagery, open new contexts that make the tensions and anxieties that exist in German urban spaces visible and audible. The following discussion exemplifies this process of renegotiation and change by analyzing different aural and visual depictions of the German capital city Berlin as caught between its (self-)representation as a global city and a provincial "Hood": how do the songs and the performances resignify, interpret, and script the city? Where are the boundaries and borders and who can transform them?[13]

Rap and hip-hop rely heavily on the techniques of collage, sampling, montage, and quotation by using imagery, sound bites, and beats from other rap songs and videos.[14] These references, however, serve different functions in the different songs. Some artists celebrate the city as a rough space, and others describe the segregated features of urban landscapes; some songs present us with a small section of the city that they own, and others suggest movement through the city in order to transgress these spatial boundaries. These rap and hip-hop productions are intended to create more than a soundtrack for the city; they claim, define, and gender (public) space; they (re)claim the power over spaces and their meanings; they negotiate identity politics between rich and poor, Germany and "other," insider and outsider, and boss and victim. The artists function as soundscapers by recombining aural and visual elements in order to create maps of their neighborhoods and of their perception of "the city" in general. In the tension between the different songs, their images, music, representations, and depictions of social agency, rap and hip-hop present different and often conflicting kinds of irritations and disruptions that produce urban maps in motion.

This struggle—or battle—between different interpretations of urban spaces is mirrored in one of the most common tropes in mainstream German rap songs: when describing a city-scape, German rap and hip-hop music uses the term "ghetto," sometimes also referred to as *Gheddo, Hood, Block,* or *Viertel* (Quarter). Until the end of the Nazi regime, the German "ghetto" described the forced confinement of European Jews to a particular part of the city. By the midtwentieth century, most German speakers also understood "the ghetto" as refer-ring to poor, mostly African American neighborhoods in metropolitan areas in the United States. In the 1970s, West German news media used images of poor, crime-ridden, and non-white neighborhoods in U.S. cities to conjure up horrible visions of what could happen in German cities, if the foreigners that had arrived during the 1950s and 1960s "guest worker programs" were to bring their extended families to Germany and settle in urban centers. Since the 1990s, debates over the ghettoization of neighborhoods, ghetto schools, honor killings, headscarves, and "Eurabia" have increased in reports about supposed failed integra-tion and multiculturalism in Germany and Europe.[15] In both decades, news media depictions of "ghettos" present contradictory definitions of German and European spaces that nonethe-less function as powerful tools of exclusion. Rap and hip-hop songs feature "voices from the ghetto" that reflect the tensions in the history of the "ghetto" concept between its usage to describe and reflect specific, local, and national conditions on the one hand and being a transnational concept on the other.

Scholars have struggled with the problematic connotations of the term "ghetto." Ayse Caglar asserts that "a narrative which reduces immigrants' spaces in Berlin to ethnic neigh-bourhoods centred around the stigmatised ghetto image is bound to miss the complex trans-national networks that orient, for instance, German Turks' lives and the strategies they employ in their struggle over access to full participation in German society."[16] But in many cases, the "complex transnational networks"[17] that constitute urban centers in the twenty-first century exist within the tension between confinement, exclusion, and essentialist notions of belonging and globalized cityscapes. Caglar confirms this when she acknowledges that "Turkish immigrants have adopted the ghetto metaphor as an important component in the repertoire used to define their situation and their relationships to Turkey and Germany. From this perspective, the way German-Turkish rappers play on the notion of ghetto is noteworthy."[18] The urban ghettos that the performers sing about and feature in video and YouTube clips are clearly marked as "German," in this case, identified as a particular neigh-borhood of the capital city Berlin. The larger frame of reference, visually and musically, how-ever, is often global, or "translocal."[19] The ghetto trope has multiple agendas, i.e., the "ghetto" can be a nightmare, a fantasy, or a lifestyle; it can serve as a tool of ethnic identification; it can be revealed as a tool of racist exclusion. The "ghetto" signifies a site of transnational identifica-tion and at the same time a space of national, racialized, and class-based exclusion.

While popular adaptation of hip-hop in Germany produced pop-rap,[20] some musicians in Germany emphasized the political origins of the rap genre by exploring the mechanisms of racialized exclusions and by using "rap to critique the construction of immigrants as foreigners."[21] The political tradition of U.S. hip-hop and rap offered a foil through which issues like marginalization and racism could be thematized. As opposed to collective efforts initiated by different citizen groups in Germany who rallied against xenophobia and for an "integrative" and "multicultural" Germany, the emphasis in hip-hop was on claiming space, voice, and agency; on difference; and on creating a counterdiscourse to neo-Nazi, neoconservative, and nationalistic politics. This became particularly pertinent in the wake of the increasingly violent racist and xenophobic attacks on immigrants and nonwhite Germans in the early 1990s.[22] The 1993 song "Fremd im eigenen Land" ("A Foreigner in Your Own Country") by the group Advanced Chemistry, performed by three rappers who are German citizens with Haitian, Ghanaian, and Italian backgrounds, confronted this issue.[23] The song asserts that Germany is their country and that the public's refusal to see and accept that is a manifestation of racism. Cultural studies scholar Andy Bennett speculates that this kind of "cultural work"[24] triggered a set of reactions that led to productions of nationalist hip-hop by immigrant or minority groups, especially Turkish rap, as a "defiant message of Turks against white Germans."[25] This wave of rap songs reasserting fixed national identities, however, is not limited to productions by minority or immigrant artists. The so-called subgenres of gangster rap or battle rap and popular rap songs by white Germans also use the transnational references, but in order to produce a national—and in some cases nationalistic—message. At the same time, other artists continue the "cultural work" of Advanced Chemistry by deconstructing confining and essentialist understandings of national identity and by proposing postnational and translocal forms of identification.

THE AUTHENTIC AND THE LOCAL

Sido—next to Bushido, probably the best known and most notorious German rapper—locates himself within the tension between these two strategies (Figure 10.1). Similar to Eko

Figure 10.1
Posters for Sido's new album Ich & meine Maske, Berlin.
Photograph by Maria Stehle, 2008.

Fresh, he starts his song "Mein Block" ("My Block," 2004) with an invitation to take a tour, first in the car, then on a stroll, through the "ghetto"—his Block—with the insider:

Get in the car! / I want to show you something. / The space where my people hang: / tall buildings, thick air, a few trees, people on drugs. / Dreams die here. / We, in the hood, are OK with this life. . . . / Don't be afraid of this guy with the brass knuckles. / He is a bit screwed up, but I like him. / I can understand that you don't feel so comfortable here, that you would rather be at home in your pool. / You would rather sit at a well-set table. / Then you realize quickly that Berlin is not for you. / Get in! / Here I can get everything. / I don't ever have to leave. / Here I have drugs, friends, and sex.[26]

While considered battle rap or sometimes even gangster rap in Germany, the musical composition of Sido's popular song has little in common with U.S. gangster rap. The music is not overtly aggressive or noisy, and the beats and samples are neither complicated nor multilayered. The different versions of this song all feature a fairly simple, almost minimalist electronic beat combined with conventional melodies.[27] The rapping itself is also melodic, contrary to the convention of U.S. gangster rap, which usually features fast, complicated rhythms combined with disturbing and disruptive sound bites and scenes from media and documentary films of police brutality and urban warfare. The sound and the lyrics suggest that, for Sido, his Block is a comfortable environment that he never has to leave. It contains everything he needs.

The video clip also shows that Sido moves through his Block with great ease: his attitude, his music, and his voice are almost playful; he is and feels at home. The clip begins with Sido getting into an expensive BMW with a friend. He is wearing his signature (death) mask.[28] The car drives down the street lined by large concrete apartment buildings; the images consist of concrete structures, asphalt, and a few leafless trees. Sido gets out of the car, and the city is shown at dusk. The beat is fast. When the actual song starts, the beat slows down significantly, and we see Sido walking up and down the street, in front of his Block in public spaces, on the rooftop, and sometimes glancing out the window or on a balcony. The chorus reiterates his ownership of this fairly small and confined urban section: "My city, my section, my quarter, my neighborhood, my street, my home, my block; my thoughts, my heart, my life, my world extends from the first to the sixteenth floor."[29] The rhythm of the refrain underscores Sido's ownership of this Block.

The identification with the Block, as this chorus suggests, is physical; in the lyrics, Sido zooms in from the whole city to a single block, which is the location of his heart and his life. Most of the subsequent lyrics describe his Block. They introduce the inhabitants of the different apartments: drug dealers, addicts, prostitutes, and other social outcasts. The doors to their "private" spaces seem to be open to the protagonist himself; if he chooses to enter, he can. In the video, we only get a few very quick glances of the insides of apartments, intercut with Sido walking—and owning—the streets. The rather tame images and the fairly soft beat stand in contrast with the crass and sexually explicit lyrics. This beat is only interrupted once, for a few seconds, in order to resemble Jennifer Lopez's commercially successful pop song "Jenny from the Block," when Sido proclaims that in spite of his success, "I am still Sido from the Block." He equates himself with Jennifer Lopez, who claims that in spite of all her fame and money, she is still "Jenny," the girl who grew up in the South Bronx. Similar to Lopez's claim, Sido then asserts, "no matter where you go, it all depends on where you come from." The song concludes with the cryptic and somehow out-of-context statement that superimposes his experiences onto the world: "And the whole world is on fire." This sets up tensions in the song between movement and stagnation, between the whole world as a battle-field and the comfort of this clearly laid out and familiar kind of confinement in the Block.

As Gabriele Klein and Malte Friedrich argue, the reception and self-representation of rap-pers is often caught in a tension between a claim for the "authentic" voice as the native informer and a strong sense of theatricality, performance, and exaggeration.[30] On the one hand, "Rappers in Europe are seen and heard as 'voices from the ethnic ghetto,' speaking out on behalf of new generations of postmigrant 'communities.'"[31] On the other hand, the "voices" as well as the attitudes, the clothing, and the imagery are highly mediated forms of collage and mimicry. The claim for authenticity is often combined with "the complex process and politics of mixing, fusion, syncretism of contemporary youth culture."[32] Frequently, the meaning of the "authentic" in hip-hop culture refers to the assumption that the authentic does not result directly from your social status, but can be measured by the degree of inter-nalization of the hip-hop lifestyle.[33] Sido's Block could be anywhere and stands in for "the world," but at the same time it signifies an internalized, specific, and familiar space. Sido has escaped the poverty of his Block, only in that, within his Block, he has everything he needs. He never has to leave—and "Sido" never really can, since his identity is closely tied to this space. The song does not present a model for "breaking out" or "breaking free" of the con-fines of its ghetto. The ghetto is Sido's cherished "home." But the representation of Sido's Block draws on images and codes that universalize this German, suburban Block, most of them familiar from popular U.S. rap culture and its use of ghetto clichés:[34] the male rap star, often with his homies, cruising down the street of the neighborhood he owns or rules. He is powerful, sexually assertive, and connected; he drives, walks, explores, and controls the streets of a very small section of the city. The repetitive lyrics and catchy musical composition reinscribe Sido's ownership over his Block again and again. His representations, however, are stripped of any direct reference to racism, discrimination, or police brutality.

GERMAN SPACE AND MEDIATION

At least as successful as Sido in terms of record sales and visibility, German gangster-rap star Bushido, son of a white German mother and a North African father, and formerly Sido's col-league at the label Aggro Berlin, offers a similar collection of images and a similarly contradic-tory sense of spatial ownership in his songs. His Block, however, is less clearly defined; he seems to claim a larger territory, and he presents himself as tougher, less approachable, and elusive. The music is melodic and melancholic and completely lacks hard beats or noisiness. As opposed to Sido's gritty depictions of the social underclass filmed with a shaky handheld camera, Bushido's representations have a digital, clean, and aestheticized look and sound, which seems to stand in sharp contrast to his claim of authenticity and realness.

Bushido's most popular song "Von der Skyline zum Bordstein" ("From the Skyline to the Curb" from his 2003 album with the same title) relies on stereotypical rap tropes, which emphasize masculinity, violence, and toughness:

It goes from the skyline back to the curb, / do you see our world how it never stands still? Yeah. / I looked from the horizon to the asphalt, / this is our life in a city that never sleeps, yeah. . . . I am hard like my cock, come out of the closet at night. / I am untouchable, the rapper who was in the can, / you and your friends are the guys who were never tough . . . / and from the horizon back to the street, / Yeah, Sonny Black, back on the block, Mission Complete.[35]

The video shows Bushido walking down the aisle of an Asian grocery store while a group of people is involved in an armed robbery. Bushido moves throughout the whole video, and the few other people populating the city are shown as blurry stills. With the start of the chorus, the camera cuts to the outside and we see Bushido rapping in front of abandoned ruins. Contrasted with the soft, melancholy music, the other images in the song include the inside of what looks like an Arab coffee shop and Bushido in front of a fence and in prison, while he proclaims that this depicts "our world how it never stands still." The obligatory scene in the expensive car follows the prison scene: Bushido drives down a street lined with prostitutes; he seems to venture out of "his" neighborhood to downtown Berlin. As opposed to Sido in "Mein Block," however, Bushido's song transgresses the borders of his Block; he claims ownership and power in districts outside of his 'hood. The imagery and the lyrics reference the style and language of U.S. hip-hop culture: for example, the street scenes in the video clip are reminiscent of the popular video game "Grand Theft Auto,"[36] and the interiors featured in the video show a globalized Berlin. In combination with the rather clichéd lyrics and the clean, electronic sound, Bushido's soundscape resembles a slick, digitized video game that features a generic global city "owned" by the bad boy from the "ghetto."

Bushido's lyrics refrain from making any direct reference to Berlin, and the video only shows the famous Berlin TV tower for a brief moment, which locates him close to the center of the city. Shortly after, the video cuts to what looks like the inside of an expensive shopping center. As Bushido rides up on an escalator, we see a quick shot of a jackknife and other weapons while he proclaims that he is "hart," tough. In fast cuts, the last third of the video repeatedly shows previous sets and scenes and the song fades out with the soft music that it started with. The brief images of recognizable Berlin landmarks, the generic and often static impressions of big city scenes, and the soft music stand in contrast to Bushido's claim that the world never stands still. The melancholy tone challenges the self-representation of the rapper as detached video-game character or tough U.S.-style gangster.[37] The song does not contain any direct political or historical references.

The reception and appropriation of U.S. hip-hop in Germany was, from the very beginning, a reception not just of music, but also of the images and modes of identification that are expressed through music, street art, dance, language, attitude, and fashion. This process of "transculturation"[38] is messy; the chronology remains somewhat unclear and the political identifications are often vague.[39] Lothar Mikos summarizes the three factors that play into the cultural memory of hip-hop in Germany: first, the allusion to an Afro-American cultural identity; second, aspects of local cultural identities; and third, the concept of a global "Hip-Hop Nation."[40]

As the examples I have analyzed so far show, in spite of the fact that German hip-hop has developed its own modes of expression, with local differences within Germany, the reference to U.S. cultures and global hip-hop communities dominate the representations and influence the creations of urban soundscapes in German rap and hip-hop. Both popular mainstream artists, Sido in "Mein Block" and Bushido in "Von der Skyline zum Bordstein," construct ownership of their respective ghettos in the German city in part by casting themselves as ghetto-gangsters in the tradition of U.S. rap cultures. Whereas U.S. gangster-rap compositions usually use fast beats and dissonance, in Bushido's and Sido's music the construction of a tough ghetto-gangster identity stands in contrast to the soft melodies and rather slow beats of their songs. In Bushido's case, the transcultural references are generic, vague, and highly mediated, and Sido remains tied and confined to his rather provincial Block in Berlin. In both songs, poverty and social marginalization are depicted in an almost romantic light and explicit political references are absent. Both set up a tension between a transnational movement and an allusion to change and a sense of local belonging, ownership, stagnation, and (comfortable) confinement at "home." While these tensions are rather interesting and their techniques of transculturation and quotation are unique, these two popular artists refrain from composing soundscapes that offer challenging resignifications of city space. Their modifications and reinterpretations avoid political interventions, remain confined to very small sections, and do not challenge any clichés of traditional rap and hip-hop representations.

THE SOUND OF GERMAN NATIONAL SPACES

In some of Bushido's less popular songs of the early twenty-first century, he deliberately plays with the tension between transnational and transcultural frames of reference and national identifications. While Bushido's "Von der Skyline zum Bordstein" emphasizes his macho identity, his own commercial success, and his identification with mostly black, successful, and rich U.S. rap stars, his self-representation since the release of "Electro Ghetto" in 2004 plays with German national history and identification. Michael Putnam and John Littlejohn discuss Bushido's famously ambivalent line:

"Salute, stand at attention, I'm the leader like A." The offensive line is the potential analogy with Adolf Hitler, the "leader like A." Though Bushido claims the reference is to rapper Azad, who indeed does rap a similar line in an earlier song, there is very little doubt that Bushido is at least partially referring to Hitler.[41]

The imagery of the video that accompanies the song is laden with historical references. Not only do we see shots of ruins that resemble the aesthetics of German expressionist cinema, but the buildings in the clip echo the destruction of cities after the World War II: bombed ruins, bare walls, and abandoned cityscapes. Read in the national context of Germany's involvement in World War II, this music video supports the interpretation of "A" as "Adolf Hitler." In aligning himself with Hitler, is Bushido making an aggressive, nationalistic statement? Or, as Putnam and Littlejohn suggest, is this reference to Hitler simply "pop," with Hitler coming to represent the "Übergangsta"?[42] Bushido composes a contradictory and provocative collage in a calculating move that guarantees media attention; in the interaction with cultural, historical, and social contexts, however, Bushido's song plays with the tensions between national and transnational frames of reference. Similar to the way in which he creates a friction between his soft, melodic music and his self-representation as a tough guy, his claim for movement and his depiction of a static society, he creates a tension between the image of the victim and of the perpetrator that remains unresolved.

While these references are ambivalent in Bushido's song, later productions by the label Aggro Berlin feature a plethora of national and National Socialist imagery that leave less room for ambivalence. This is particularly prevalent in Fler's music and his 2005 album *Neue Deutsche Welle* (*New German Wave*): "The release of Fler's album Neue Deutsche Welle . . . in May 2005 precipitated a wave of articles in German newspapers and magazines highly critical of the nationalistic phrases and imagery present in Fler's music."[43] In the music video for "Neue Deutsche Welle," Fler's rap is slow and he performs in a monotone voice: "Here comes the new German wave, German wave" as he drives through the center of Berlin—mostly around the newly reconstructed Potsdam Square—in a shiny Mercedes, picks up prostitutes, fights in a basement (similar to the movie *Fight Club*), has a confrontation with the police, and presents himself with a giant eagle landing on his arm. The lyrics are very repetitive and the chorus, sung by a group of low, male voices, sounds threatening and is easy to "rap" along to. The ominous atmosphere is fostered by an underlying static or machine-like noise and hard, but slow, beats. The video shows images of the German flag, aggressive-looking pit bulls, motorcycles, and empty old warehouses. Fler asserts his own Germanness by pointing to his German blood: "That is black-red-gold, hard and proud, one can't see it in my face, but believe me, my *mom* is German."[44] He casts himself as part of a German minority that grew up mostly among immigrants and other "outsiders" in the poor, working-class neighborhoods of Berlin: "That's normal, this is multi-cultural, my *homies* come from everywhere, you call the cops. We are outsiders, we are Aggro Berlin. Black, white, no matter, everybody here is aggro and Berlin, I told you."[45] He further emphasizes that his rapping in German makes him a target of censorship: "Go ahead, play Ami-rap, because nobody understands a word, and I am censored mercilessly because everyone understands."[46] He casts himself as a victim of the German cultural scene and "Americanization." His claim for Germanness and his ownership over the newly constructed center of the German capital is intended as provocation. In his song "Ich bin Deutscha" from the album *Fremd im Eigenen Land* (*A Foreigner in Your Own Country*, 2008) Fler makes his identity claim even clearer: "I am a German. Even when nobody understands it, I am a German because I have an identity; I am proud of what I am, because I have an identity."[47]

Elizabeth Loentz argues that "Fler's use of National Socialist symbols and nationalist rhetoric have tested the limits of what is socially acceptable in twenty-first century Germany"[48] and points out that his "logo consists of a slightly altered *Reichsadler* [Reich's Eagle, a National Socialist emblem] that blends into his name written in lower case *Fraktur* script [the old Gothic print commonly used by the Nazis]."[49] Some critics suggest that, considering

> Fler's insistence that he is a supporter of the SPD (Social Democratic Party of Germany) because 'it's cooler, more social and just and all that,' and his long-standing cooperation with minority and immigrant Hip-hoppers . . . his Nazi allusions cannot be taken all too seriously. They are merely part of an attempt to create a tough image or street credibility, or even part of a clever marketing ploy.[50]

Putnam and Littlejohn, on the other hand, read "these references to National Socialism . . . as an articulation of a new German identity constructed through a complex engagement with American popular culture and its own [i.e., German] past."[51] The question of whether Nazi imagery serves to gain "street credibility," to engage with German identity in a complex and messy net of cultural references to U.S. pop culture and Germany's past, to fuel a dangerous kind of nationalism, or simply to make money, remains unanswered; but Fler's song once again creates a different soundscape of the German capital as he moves through the newly reconstructed center of Berlin, rapping and imitating the gestures of black U.S. rap stars. Fler positions himself as a member of a marginalized group and aims to provoke by claiming ownership of the center of the German capital city.

When Fler released the album with the same title as Advanced Chemistry's song "Fremd im eigenen Land" ("A Foreigner in Your Own Country") in 2008, he referred to feeling foreign as a white German in certain German neighborhoods that are dominated by immigrant culture(s), i.e., "ghettos." While the song's title was initially used to challenge a racialized understanding of Germany and Germans as exclusively white, Fler's claim for Germanness as a white underclass macho is equally provocative; but the question is, who is being provoked? By referencing Nazi imagery, Fler reproduces an essentialized notion of race, blood, nationality, and sexual identity. This twisted, but nonetheless dangerous German nationalism corresponds with, responds to, and competes with Turkish national symbols and Turkish nationalisms in Turkish-German and Turkish hip-hop, sold in Germany and Turkey. Fler's self-identification as part of a white, proud, German minority in Germany—however strange that might seem—is a form of self-racialization. By claiming his whiteness, Fler manages to cast himself as a minority of particularly tough macho-gangsters. His voice is often electronically altered, and the musical compositions are less harmonious and more dissonant and jarring than Sido or Bushido's, but they also rely on conventional beats, a simple structure, and unoriginal melodic parts. Fler's music and imagery transform the tension between a claim for a transnational space and the insistence on owning a particular "Block" of the German "ghetto"; he uses these references to reclaim a space and an identity that is explicitly "German."

B-Tight's album *Neger Neger* (*Nigger, Nigger*) released in 2007, presents another facet in this messy negotiation over space, ownership, and identity. Particularly the song "Der Neger"[52] and its marketing campaign featuring the words "Neger Neger" printed in white on a black background triggered discussions over racism, appropriation, self-identification, commercialization, and transcultural reception. In an online version of the song, the artist added what sounds like a disclaimer: "Everybody has to make it, Turks, Arabs, Germans, and the rest of the world, so don't bullshit . . . this is not a nigger-thing, I am a ghetto kid, and I don't make any distinction, because all cool guys are ghetto."[53] The lyrics continue with a list of racist clichés and are a hymn to the pot-smoking, unreliable, hypermasculine, and sexualized "Neger" that B-Tight himself, son of an African American father and a white German mother, performs. B-Tight's texts are generally laden with offensive language against gays and women and he tends to cast himself as the hypermasculine fighter who "fucks" everyone. The videos show familiar scenes: tall apartment buildings, overgrown urban parks, abandoned playgrounds, and extensive concrete landscapes. Not only does B-Tight redefine the position of the marginalized "other" in German culture as a source of power, he attempts, in reference to U.S. urban cultures, to reappropriate racist language and racist clichés to assert this power. Placed explicitly within the German cultural context, this attempt for a cultural reappropriation is certainly provocative, but the song itself fails to address the issue of racism and propose "alternative maps." Aside from the attempt to present the cliché as a positive form of identification, B-Tight's song does not convey a sense of movement or transgression;

his composition remains within the traditional, confining, and stagnant imagery of ghetto clichés. In *Excitable Speech,* Judith Butler argues

> that the citationality of discourse can work to enhance and intensify our sense of responsibility for it. The one who utters such [injurious] speech is responsible for the manner in which such speech is repeated, for reinvigorating such speech, for reestablishing contexts of hate and injury.[54]

The reception of his song mostly by white, male, middle-class adolescents does not foster a shift in the meaning of the term "Neger" or its political or historical contexts. Similar to Fler's "Neue deutsche Welle," the chorus is composed as a sing-along: B-Tight asks rhetorical questions to which the answer is always the same: "Der Neger!" The manner in which hateful speech is repeated in the song does little to question the contexts of hate and injury.

This offensive repetition of hate speech in the song, however, did trigger a series of responses and discussions about racism and the effects of racist language in Germany. These discussions addressed pressing questions about German identity and the "new" Germany's relation to its past(s): What has changed in Germany? How and where do the legacies of National Socialism still produce something specifically German? In response to B-Tight's album *Neger Neger* and the accompanying advertisement campaigns, the hip-hop collaborative Brothers Keepers organized a panel discussion at the pop convention PopComm to address the issue of racism in rap songs.[55]

TRANSLOCAL CHALLENGES

In their own productions the members of the collaborative Brothers Keepers offer different versions of "taking back the streets," of adaptation, transculturation, and memory. They explicitly use their art and their performances to fight against spatial confinement, "ghettoization," ghetto clichés, and exclusions (Figure 10.2). Their most popular song, "Adriano: Letzte Warnung" ("Adriano: Last Warning"), for example, responds directly to an act of political violence: Afro-German Alberto Adriano was murdered by a gang of neo-Nazis in 2000 in the German town of Dessau.[56] In the song and the accompanying video clip from 2001 a group of mostly, but not exclusively, male artists join forces as they walk through the city streets, subway tunnels, and empty lots to confront neo-Nazi violence. Neither the "ghetto" nor the violence within the marginalized space of the "ghetto" poses a threat, but the racism and xenophobia that lurk in every dark corner of the German cityscape do. The rather generic cityscapes, as shown in the video and described in the lyrics, convey a feeling of narrowness: not because they depict ethnic ghettos, but because Germany is experienced as provincial, "white" ghetto.[57] As the group walks through the streets, train stations, and subway tunnels, and across parking lots and backyards, more people join them. The chorus consists of a clear "warning" with the implication that German city streets are not safe for people of color:

> This is something like a last warning / our retaliation has long been planned / we appear (attack) where you stand out / and finally stop your Nazi bullshit / what you are looking for

Figure 10.2
"Hip-Hop speaks," Berlin 2008.
Photograph by Maria Stehle, 2008.

is your own demise / and we don't offer you a handshake but our fists / your downfall for good / and what we will hear is your crying and sobbing.[58]

The song takes the murder of Adriano as a starting point for a call to action against a specific situation in Germany in which the government reacted to racist violence—or what government officials and mainstream media called "xenophobia"—by tightening immigration laws in the second half of the 1990s. A common strategy in U.S. rap performances, Brothers Keepers stage "authenticity" in the video and pair it with references to authentic, historic documents. The video shows contemporary and historical documentary footage to highlight the history of racist violence on German streets and in a global context. The lyrics also reference national histories and politics, the increasingly alarmist discourse over the security of the European borders, and global histories of racist oppression and slavery.

Ayhan Kaya argues that rap songs and hip-hop productions often signal the wish of young people to get out of the narrow borders of their "ghetto" lives and "wander across the city in search for the peripheries of urban life, spray graffiti and tag. . . . [S]uch groups can also point to the attempt to build informal networks of solidarity that lead to heterogeneous forms of individuality."[59] Brothers Keepers' performance makes "claims to the 'non-ethnic' spaces of the city from which they had been excluded. They are struggling to inscribe their presence in the urban space beyond the given terms (namely ethnic) and conditions of visibility available to them."[60] The composition combines the contributions of various rap and hip-hop artists. They rap in different speeds to a driving, electronic beat that occasionally halts or slows down, and the lyrics switch between German and English. By producing an eclectic song that includes various national and global, historical and political references, different musical influences, languages, and artists, the group transgresses the borders of the "ghetto," and redefines the sound of the "ghetto" and the politics of urban space. They use "insurrectionary speech"[61] in their lyrics as a "necessary response to injurious language,"[62] and at the end of the multivocal and multilingual song, the different voices gradually merge into shared lines and one call for action and solidarity. Together, they call for a transformation of the racist German cityscape to a translocal, heterogeneous, and inclusive platform for antiracist activism. The artists in the collaborative Brothers Keepers apply the transnational foils of rap and hip-hop to collapse the boundaries of "a priori spatialized cultures"[63] and show that the sound of the German city is "increasingly multilocal."[64]

Even though most mainstream German rap is conventional and often politically questionable and problematic, rappers' soundscapes and claims for space, identity, and belonging never remain unchallenged. The "battles" that take place within each song and among the different soundscapers in the German rap and hip-hop scenes constantly question fixed notions of spatial belonging: by producing conflicting soundscapes, artists engage in the process of repetition, resignification, and contestation of space and territory. When read in dialogue with one other, the conflicting soundscapes uncover anxieties over spatial belonging and change, and ask us to confront the shifting politics of belonging within urban space.

At the same time that Brothers Keepers promote such new and future spatio-political practices, other artists create rap and hip-hop soundscapes to (re)claim essentialized notions of national identity, Germanness and whiteness as German; and/or to appropriate racialized concepts of the "ghetto" and the racist term "Neger" as positive forms of (German) identifications. In 2008, Fler and B-Tight produced city-soundscapes that responded to assertive gestures by Advanced Chemistry and Brothers Keepers. By offering offensive, provocative, racist, and/or fascist representations of the tough, marginalized macho from the ghetto— as a white "Deutscha Bad Boy" (also from the 2008 album *Fremd im eigenen Land*) or as "Der Neger"—Fler and B-Tight take back the streets of the ghettos and claim space in German city centers. All the while Sido raps about—and romanticizes—his poor, lower-class Block and, accompanied by melancholy music, Bushido ventures out into the postmodern, digital-looking shopping malls and prisons to showcase his masculinity and power.[65]

As demonstrated by the examples just discussed, the competing soundscapes of German rap and hip-hop highlight the "changing notion[s] of urbanity in a globalized and mediated world."[66] They reveal the tensions and intersections between transnational cultural connections and identifications and a frame of reference that is confining, provincial, and nationalistic and often based on racist and sexist identifications. Soundscapers compose opposing auditory maps of Berlin and Germany in the twenty-first century that reflect the social fabric of the *Hoods*, *Blocks*, *Gheddos*, and urban centers where different kinds of nationalisms and postnational identifications battle, overlap, and clash.

NOTES

1. All translations in German are my own unless otherwise noted. I apologize for the clumsy translations of rap lyrics. "Eko Fresh Ghetto Chef Junge denn es muss sein / Köln Kalk Hartz 4 komm in meine Hood rein. / Komm und guck was es heißt im Block hier zu wohnen / Wo man Leben muss von Drogen oder Prostitution." Hartz IV is the name of the German social welfare program.

2. In chapter 7, Tompkins argues that sound was a means of participating in creating a (socialist) East German identity, and the interviews in chapter 6 also attest to the sonic proof of belonging, that is, members of a group attaching meaning to certain sounds. In chapter 5, Swope points out that the main character of Hilbig's novel has feelings of revulsion or affinity for certain sounds, and these feelings speak to his affiliation with different political regimes (East or West Germany). These affiliations need not be only national, however. As chapter 1 pointed to the different relationships to sound that were evident in different classes in turn-of-the-century Germany, so, too, does this chapter look at sound across socioeconomic lines.

3. For a discussion of the "tour" motif in French hip-hop see Susanne Stemmler, "Bienvenu Dans la Zonarisk: Soundtrack des Aufstands in Frankreichs Vorstädten, " in *Sound and the City*, eds. Dietrich Helms and Thomas Phleps (Bielefeld: Transkript, 2007), 97–111, 99.

4. The importance of the music video to create meaning in rap and hip-hop illustrates the interplay between the visual and the oral in the process of meaning making. See Feiereisen and Hill in the introduction to this book.

5. "Ihr habt alle reiche Eltern und sagt in Deutschland gibt's kein Ghetto."

6. I am aware of the need to distinguish between hip-hop as a cultural form and identification, and rap as a musical art form that is often associated with hip-hop culture. In this article, I continue to use both terms without engaging in these discussions in order to offer an inclusive analysis that relies on an intentionally broad definition.

7. Nora Alter and Lutz Koepnick, eds. *Sound Matters: Essays on the Acoustics of Modern German Culture* (New York: Berghahn Books, 2004), 4.

8. Ibid. 5.

9. See, for example, Uta Poiger's discussions about jazz and rock and roll in postwar East and West Germany in *Jazz, Rock, and Rebels: Cold War Politics and American Culture in a Divided Germany* (Berkeley: University of California Press, 2000).

10. Michael Bull and Les Back, eds., *The Auditory Culture Reader* (Oxford: Berg, 2003), 1.

11. Ulrich Werner. *Soundscape-Dialog—Landschaften und Methoden des Hörens* (Göttingen: Vandenhoeck & Ruprech, 2006), 197: "Soundscaper entstammen vielen Kontexten, Disziplinen und Kulturen. Ihr subjektives Wissen und gesellschaftliches Sein, das alle Bereiche des Lebens umfasst, ist als Erkenntnisweg und Katalysator unverzichtbar. Es ist keinesfalls auszublendender Störfaktor akademischen Designs."

12. Judith Butler, *Excitable Speech: A Politics of the Performative* (New York: Routledge, 1997), 41.

13. Cultural studies scholars in the United States and in Europe have controversially discussed the cultural and political contributions of rap and hip-hop cultures over the course of the last decade (for example Russel A. Potter, Tricia Rose, George Lipsitz, Tony Mitchell, Gabriele Klein and Malte Friedrich, Hannes Loh und Murat Güngor, Ayhan Kaya, Fatima El-Tayeb). My argument is based on this research and claims that by employing the concept of *soundscapes* we can further investigate the tensions in this discourse as they manifest themselves in Germany.

14. Rap and hip-hop shares this characteristic with electronic club music.

15. In previous research I compared print media reports from the 1970s and the twenty-first century that discuss the ghettoization of German and European urban spaces. See Maria Stehle, "Narrating the Ghetto, Narrating Europe: From Berlin, Kreuzberg to the Banlieues of Paris," in *Westminster Papers in Communication and Culture*, Special Topic Issue: Narrations of Europe—Narrators of Europe, 3:3 (2006): 48–70.

16. Ayse S. Caglar, "Constraining Metaphors and the Transnationalisation of Spaces in Berlin," *Journal of Ethnic and Migration Studies* 27:4 (October 2001): 601–13, 607; also see Levent Soysal, "Rap, Hiphop. Kreuzberg: Scripts of/for Migrant Youth Culture in the WorldCity Berlin," *New German Critique* 92 (2004): 62–81, 65.

17. Caglar, "Constraining metaphors and the transnationalisation of spaces in Berlin," 607.

18. Ibid., 605. Also see discussion on Web forums and discussion boards about the term, its usage, and the questions of whether there are ghettos in Germany, where they are, and who is able to represent them (see for example http://www.rap.de).

19. Fatima El-Tayeb, "Urban Diasporas: Race, Identity, and Popular Culture in Post-Ethnic Europe," *JCAS Symposium Series* 22 (2005): 133–55, 155.

20. Dietmar Elflein, "From Krauts with Attitudes to Turks with Attitudes: Some Aspects of Hip-Hop History in Germany," *Popular Music*, 17:3 (October 1998): 255–65, 259.

21. Ibid., 259. This is not meant to be a comprehensive study of German rap. I will not analyze "Deutschrap" in this article. For a discussion of it, see Gabriele Klein and Malte Friedrich, *Is This Real? Die Kultur des HipHop* (Frankfurt: Suhrkamp, 2003), 76; or Elizabeth Loentz, "Yiddish, *Kanak Sprak*, Klezmer, and HipHop: Ethnolect, Minority Culture, Multiculturalism, and Stereotype in Germany," *Shofar: An Interdisciplinary Journal of Jewish Studies* 25, no. 1 (2006): 33–62, 56.

22. For a more detailed exploration of the reception of U.S.-American hip-hop among second-generation immigrant youth in Germany, see Elflein "From Krauts with Attitudes."

23. Andy Bennett, "HipHop and Main: Die Lokalisierung von Rap-Musik und HipHop Kultur," in *HipHop: Globale Kultur—Lokale Praktiken*, ed. Jannis Androutsopoulos (Bielefeld: Transcript, 2003), 26–42, 34.

24. Ibid., 35.

25. Ibid., 35.

26. "Steig ein! / Ich will dir was zeigen. / Der Platz an dem sich meine Leute rumtreiben: / Hohe Häuser - dicke Luft - ein paar Bäume - Menschen auf Drogen. / Hier platzen Träume. / Wir hier im Viertel kommen klar mit diesem Leben . . . / Hab doch keine Angst vor dem Typen mit dem Schlagring. / Er ist zwar 'n bisschen verrückt, doch ich mag ihn. / Ich kann versteh'n, dass du dich hier nicht so wohl fühlst, dass du viel lieber zu Hause im Pool wühlst. / Du sitzt lieber am gutgedeckten Tisch. / Dann merkst du schnell, Berlin ist nix für dich. / Steig ein! / Hier kriege ich alles. / Ich muss hier nicht mal weg. / Hier hab' ich Drogen, Freunde und Sex."

27. Since this song was very successful, a plethora of different versions exist; some are melodic and soft, others electronic, fast, and driven, but they all share the basic characteristics described. My analyses refer to a later version of the song. Compared to the first release on the 2004 album *Maske*, this remix contains an introduction, a few vocal interludes, and the Jennifer Lopez reference, none of which are in the original version.

28. Sido used to wear a metallic mask that covered the top half of his face. The mask had the features of a skull and Sido refused to take it off until 2005. The wearing of the mask contributed to the speculations about Sido's ethnicity and his "real" identity—a major part of his marketing campaign during the beginning of his career.

29. "Meine Stadt, mein Bezirk, mein Viertel, meine Gegend, meine Straße, mein Zuhause, mein Block, meine Gedanken, mein Herz, mein Leben, meine Welt reicht vom ersten bis zum 16. Stock."

30. See Klein and Friedrich, *Is This Real?*

31. Tom Cheeseman, "Polyglot Politics: Hip Hop in Germany," in *Debatte*, 6, no. 2 (1998): 191–214, 191.

32. Sanjay Sharma, "The Sounds of Alterity," in *The Auditory Culture Reader*, eds. Bull and Back, 409–418, 409.

33. Klein and Friedrich, *Is This Real?* 55.

34. For a detailed history of hip-hop reception in Germany see Andy Bennett in *HipHop*, ed., Androutsopoulos, 26–42; or Hannes Loh and Murat Güngör, *Fear of a Kanak Planet. HipHop zwischen Weltkultur und Nazi-Rap* (Hofen: Hannibal, 2002).

35. "Es geht, von der Skyline zum Bordstein zurück, / Siehst du uns're Welt wie sie niemals still steht? Yeah. / Ich hab vom Horizont zum Asphalt geblickt, / Es ist unser Leben in 'ner Stadt die

niemals schläft, yeah . . . Ich bin hart wie mein Schwanz, komme nachts aus dem Schrank. / Ich bin, unantastbar, der Rapper der im Knast war, / du und deine Freunde sind die Typen die nie krass war'n . . . / Und vom Horizont zurück auf die Street, / Yeah, Sonny Black, back am Block, Mission Complete."

36. Similar to the "hero" of "Grand Theft Auto," Bushido moves through an empty cityscape as a "bad boy" on a quest. The depictions of the different spaces suggest that danger might lurk behind every corner and at any moment, and Bushido might have to assert himself.

37. See Levent Soysal, "Rap, Hiphop. Kreuzberg: Scripts of/for Migrant Youth Culture in the WorldCity Berlin" for a detailed discussion of the global imaginary of Kreuzberg rap and hip-hop.

38. James Lull, *Media, Communication, Culture: A Global Approach*, 2nd ed. (New York: Columbia University Press, 2000), 242.

39. Russell A. Potter, *Spectacular Vernaculars: Hip-Hop and the Politics of Postmodernism* (Albany, NY: SUNY Press, 1995), 29 and 48–51.

40. Lothar Mikos, "'Interpolation and sampling': Kulturelles Gedächtnis und Intertextualität im HipHop," in *HipHop*, ed. Androutsopoulos, 64–84, 70–71.

41. Michael T. Putnam and John T. Littlejohn, "National Socialism with Fler? German Hip Hop from the Right," *Popular Music and Society* 30, no. 4 (October 2007): 453–68, 454.

42. Ibid., 463.

43. Ibid., 454. For an ironic commentary see "Schwarz, rot, böse," *Jungle World*, January 10, 2008, http://jungle-world.com/artikel/2008/02/20978.html (accessed April 5, 2008). The title of the album and the song is also a reference to the music and culture of the "Neue Deutsche Welle" from 1980, represented through artists like Nena or Falco.

44. "Das ist schwarz-rot-gold, hart und stolz, man sieht's mir nicht an doch glaub mir meine Mom ist deutsch."

45. "Das ist normal, das hier ist multi-kulti, meine Homies komm' von überall, ihr holt die Bullen. Wir sind die Außenseiter, wir sind aggroberlin. Schwarz, weiss, egal jeder ist hier aggro und Berlin ich hab's gesagt."

46. "Spielt nur Ami Rap, weil man da kein Wort versteht und ich werd gnadenlos zensiert, weil man's sofort versteht."

47. "Ich bin Deutscha. Auch wenn es niemand versteht, ich bin Deutscha, denn ich hab' Identität; ich bin stolz auf was ich bin, denn ich hab' Identität."

48. Loentz, "Yiddish, *Kanak Sprak*, Klezmer, and HipHop: Ethnolect, Minority Culture, Multiculturalism, and Stereotype in Germany," 61.

49. Ibid., 61.

50. Ibid., 61–62.

51. Putnam and Littlejohn, "National Socialism with Fler? German Hip Hop from the Right," 453.

52. B-Tight had already released a song with the title "Der Neger (in mir)" in 2002.

53. "Jeder muss es schaffen, Türken, Araber, Deutsche, und der Rest der Welt, also labert keine Scheiße . . . das ist kein Neger Ding, ich bin ein Ghetto Kind, ich mach kein' Unterschied weil alle coolen Ghetto sind."

54 Butler, *Excitable Speech: A Politics of the Performative*, 27.

55. See http://vimeo.com/335137/ (accessed April 5, 2008). Also, see various mock-videos published on YouTube.

56. Klein and Friedrich also emphasize the claim for the "authentic" in this song and its video clip. For a detailed analysis also see Klein and Friedrich, *Is This Real?* 119–21. For background information on the recording of the song and the production of the video, also see the documentary film *Yes I Am* (Brothers Keepers, 2007).

57. For a sarcastic take on this issue see the short film "Weisses Ghetto," produced by the antiracist collaborative Kanak TV and described on their Web site at http://www.kanak-attak.de/ka/kanaktv/volume1.html (accessed August 6, 2008).

58. "Dies ist so was wie eine letzte Warnung / Denn unser Rückschlag ist längst in Planung / Wir fall'n dort ein, wo ihr auffallt / Gebieten eurer braunen Scheiße endlich Aufhalt / Denn was ihr sucht ist das Ende / Und was wir reichen sind geballte Fäuste und keine Hände / Euer Niedergang für immer. / Und was wir hören werden, ist euer Weinen und euer Gewimmer."

59. Ayan Kaya, "'Scribo Ergo Sum': Islamic Force und Berlin Türken," in *HipHop*, ed. Androutsopoulos, 246–72, 251.

60. Caglar, "Constraining Metaphors and the Transnationalisation of Spaces in Berlin," 609.

61. Butler, *Excitable Speech: A Politics of the Performative*, 163.

62. Ibid., 163.

63. Caglar, "Constraining Metaphors and the Transnationalisation of Spaces in Berlin," 607.

64. Ibid., 607.

65. Female rap and hip-hop artists challenge these masculine representations and offer yet another range of perspectives on urban space, power, and identity in the twenty-first century. Unfortunately, I won't be able to analyze the gender politics of rap and hip-hop and the contributions of female hip-hop artists in this chapter. It is important to note, however, that female artists have offered different forms of critique and interventions; see, for example, Lady Bitch Ray, CoraA, Aziz-A, Sahira, and many others.

66. Klein and Friedrich, *Is This Real?* 97.

SELECT BIBLIOGRAPHY AND
FURTHER READINGS

Alter, Nora, and Lutz Koepnick, eds. *Sound Matters*. New York: Berghahn Books, 2004.

Attali, Jacques. *Noise: The Political Economy of Music*. Brian Massumi, trans. Minneapolis: University of Minnesota Press, 1985.

Augoyard, Jean-François, and Henry Torgue, eds. *Sonic Experience. A Guide to Everyday Sounds*. Montreal: McGill Queen's University Press, 2005.

Bijsterveld, Karin. *Mechanical Sound: Technology, Culture, and Public Problems of Noise in the Twentieth Century*. Cambridge, MA: MIT Press, 2008.

——, and José van Dijck, eds. *Sound Souvenirs: Audio Technologies, Memory, and Cultural Practices*. Amsterdam: Amsterdam University Press, 2009.

Birsall, Carolyn, and Anthony Enns, eds. *Sonic Mediations: Body, Sond, Technology*. Newcastle: Cambridge Scholars Press, 2008.

Blesser, Barry, and Linda-Ruth Salter. *Spaces Speak, Are You Listening? Experiencing Aural Architecture*. Cambridge, MA: MIT Press, 2006.

Bosseur, Jean-Yves, ed. *Sound and the Visual Arts*. Brian Holmes and Peter Carrier, trans. Paris: Dis Voir, 1993.

Bull, Michael. *Sounding Out the City: Personal Stereos and the Management of Everyday Life*. Oxford: Berg Publishers, 2000.

——, and Les Back, eds. *The Auditory Culture Reader*. Oxford: Berg Publishers, 2003.

Burnett, Charles, Michael Fend, and Penelope Gouk, eds. *The Second Sense: Studies in Hearing and Musical Judgment from Antiquity to the Seventeenth Century*. London: Warburg Institute, 1991.

Cage, John. *Silence*. Middletown, CT: Wesleyan University Press, 1961.

Carter, Paul. *The Sound In-Between: Voice, Space, Performance*. Sydney: New South Wales University Press and Endeavour Press, 1992.

Chion, Michel. *Audio-Vision: Sound on Screen*. Claudia Gorbman, trans. New York: Columbia University Press, 1994.

Classen, Constance. *World of Sense: Exploring the Senses in History and across Cultures*. London: Routledge, 1993.

Coleman, Mark. *Playback: From the Victrola to Mp3: 100 Years of Music, Machines, and Money*. New York: Da Capo Press, 2004.

Corbin, Alain. *Time, Desire and Horror: Towards a History of the Senses*. Jean Birrell, trans. Cambridge, UK: Polity Press, 1995.

——. *Village Bells: Sound and Meaning in the 19th-Century French Countryside*. New York: Columbia University Press, 1998.

Cox, Christopher, and Daniel Warner, eds. *Audio Culture: Readings in Modern Music*. New York: Continuum International, 2004.

Douglas, Susan. *Listening In: Radio and the American Imagination*. New York: Times Books, 1999.

Doyle, Peter. *Echo and Reverb: Fabricating Space in Popular Music, 1900–1960*. Middletown, CT: Wesleyan University Press, 2005.

Drobnick, Jim, ed. *Aural Cultures*. Toronto: YYZ Books, 2004.

Erlmann, Viet, ed. *Hearing Cultures: Essays on Sound, Listening and Modernity*. Oxford: Berg, 2004.

Eshun, Kodwo Ofori. *More Brilliant than the Sun: Adventures in Sonic Fiction*. London: Quartet Books, 1998.

Feld, Steven. *Sound and Sentiment: Birds, Weeping, Poetics, and Song in Kalui Expression*. Philadelphia: University of Philadelphia Press, 1982.

Gomery, Douglas. *The Coming of Sound: A History*. New York: Routledge, 2004.

Goody, Jack. *The Interface between the Written and the Oral*. Cambridge: Cambridge University Press, 1987.

Grueneisen, Peter, ed. *Soundspace: Architecture for Sound and Vision*. Basel: Birkhäuser, 2003.

Howes, David, ed. *The Varieties of Sensory Experience: A Sourcebook in the Anthropology of the Senses*. Toronto: University of Toronto Press, 1991.

Ihde, Don. *Listening and Voice: The Phenomenology of Sound*. Athens: Ohio University Press, 1976.

Johnson, James H. *Listening in Paris: A Cultural History*, Studies on the History of Society and Culture, 21. Berkeley: University of California Press, 1995.

Jütte, Robert. *A History of the Senses: From Antiquity to Cyberspace*. Cambridge, MA: Polity Press, 2004.

Kahn, Douglas. *Noise, Water, Meat: A History of Sound in the Arts*. Cambridge, MA: MIT Press, 1999.

———, and Gregory Whitehead, eds. *Wireless Imagination: Sound, Radio, and the Avant-Garde*. Cambridge, MA: MIT Press, 1994.

Kang, Jian. *Urban Sound Environment*. London; New York: Taylor & Francis, 2007.

Kittler, Friedrich A. *Gramophone, Film, Typewriter*. Geoffrey Winthrop-Young and Michael Wutz, trans. Stanford, CA: Stanford University Press, 1999.

Kruth, Patricia, and Henry Stobart, eds. *Sound*. Cambridge: Cambridge University Press, 2000.

LaBelle, Brandon. *Background Noise: Perspectives on Sound Art*. New York and London: Continuum, 2006.

———, and Steve Roden. *Site of Sound: Of Architecture and the Ear*. Los Angeles: Errant Bodies Press, 1999.

Leitner, Bernhard. *Sound: Space*. Ostfildern, Germany: Cantz Verlag, 1998.

Levin, David Michael, ed. *Modernity and the Hegemony of Vision*. Berkeley: University of California Press, 1993.

Licht, Alan. *Sound Art: Beyond Music, Between Categories*. New York: Rizzoli, 2007.

Marvin, Carolyn. *When Old Technologies Were New: Thinking About Electric Communication in the Late Nineteenth Century*. New York: Oxford University Press, 1998.

McLuhan, Marshall. *The Gutenberg Galaxy: The Making of Typographic Man*. Toronto: University of Toronto Press, 1962.

Morris, Adalaide Kirby, ed. *Sound States: Innovative Poetics and Acoustical Technologies*. Chapel Hill: University of North Carolina Press, 1998.

Morton, David L., Jr. *Sound Recording: The Life Story of a Technology*. Baltimore, MD: Johns Hopkins University Press, 2006.

Ong, Walter. *Orality and Literacy: The Technologizing of the World*. New York: Routledge, 1988.

Picker, John. *Victorian Soundscapes*. New York: Oxford University Press, 2003.

Schafer, R. Murray. *The Tuning of the World: Toward a Theory of Soundscape Design*. Philadelphia: University of Pennsylvania Press, 1980.

———. *The Soundscape: Our Sonic Environment and the Tuning of the World*. Rochester, VT: Destiny Books, 1994.

Smith, Bruce R. *The Acoustic World of Early Modern England: Attending to the O-factor*. Chicago: University of Chicago Press, 1999.

Smith, Mark, ed. *Hearing History. A Reader*. Athens: University of Georgia Press, 2004.

———. *Listening to Nineteenth-Century America*. Chapel Hill: University of North Carolina Press, 2001.

———. *Sensing the Past: Seeing, Hearing, Smelling, Tasting, and Touching in History*. Berkeley, Los Angeles: University of California Press, 2007.

Sterne, Jonathan. *The Audible Past. Cultural Origins of Sound Reproduction*. Durham, London: Duke University Press, 2003.

Suisman, David, and Susan Strasser, eds. *Sound in the Age of Mechanical Reproduction*. Philadelphia: University of Pennsylvania Press, 2010.

Thompson, Emily. *The Soundscape of Modernity: Architectural Acoustics and the Culture of Listening in America, 1900–1933*. Cambridge, MA: MIT Press, 2002.

Truax, Barry, ed. *The Wold Soundscape Project's Handbook for Acoustic Ecology*. Vancouver: ARC Publications, 1978.

Truax, Barry. *Acoustic Communication*. Westport: Ablex Publishing, 2001.

Werner, Ulrich. *Soundscape-Dialog: Landschaften und Methoden des Hörens*. Göttingen: Vandenhoeck & Ruprech, 2006.

Wishart, Trevor. *On Sonic Art*. Amsterdam: Harwood Academic Publishers, 1998.

INDEX

An italicized number indicates a figure in the text.